PERSONAL SAFETY

Are You Ready?

Personal Safety
Are You Ready?
A book by D. Q. Phan
2026

All inquiries, please contact:
DQ.Phan.author@gmail.com
ISBN: 978-1-966182-05-4

To my beloved wife and daughters, whose unwavering support and steadfast love have been my anchor through every storm, I dedicate this book with all my heart.

Foreword

Important Disclaimer: Before we proceed, I want to be clear: I am not a financial advisor, a licensed investment professional, or a retirement planner. Nor do I claim to be a preeminent academic expert in personal safety or tactical defense. I am an ordinary person—a father, a husband, and a veteran of nearly three decades in law enforcement—sharing my personal perspectives and the hard-earned life experiences I've gathered from the field. The insights and strategies shared here are for informational and educational purposes based on my own observations. It is incumbent upon you to seek professional advice from qualified financial, legal, or security experts before making any significant decisions or life changes. Your safety and your future are your responsibility; I am simply here to offer a roadmap based on where I have been.

The case studies and scenarios referenced in this book are adapted from public court records, official federal indictments, and verified forensic reports. These real-world examples are utilized for illustrative and educational purposes, providing a stark look at the catastrophic consequences of unmanaged internal threats. While the details remain rooted in factual integrity to serve as cautionary tales, I have made a conscious decision to omit specific names. I have chosen not to mention the victims' names, as they have already suffered enough, nor the defendants' names, as they are currently serving time for their crimes; there is simply no need to drag their names through public forums again.

Ultimately, this book explores the reality that personal safety isn't just about "stranger danger," but also about the internal choices we make every day and our commitment to independent verification. I encourage you to use the keywords provided throughout these chapters—such as "deed fraud alerts," "romance scam indictments," or "use of force legal standards"—to conduct your own research and stay informed on the evolving nature of these threats.

From my personal experience, I have come to believe that nearly all of us rank our life priorities in remarkably similar ways at the very top—only to diverge sharply afterward. For many, family and personal happiness stand highest. For others, it is career advancement and financial success. For countless more, religious faith or spiritual growth holds the greatest importance. Qualities such as patriotism, generosity, kindness, good health, and educational achievement also frequently appear near the top of people's lists. Yet one priority stands out for how rarely it cracks the top three: personal safety.

We tend to take our safety for granted. It remains almost invisible in our daily decision-making because we instinctively believe the odds of becoming a victim—of crime, violence, accident, or disaster—are overwhelmingly in our favor. We move through life with the quiet assumption that "it will not happen to me," comforted by statistics that suggest victimization is rare and far removed from our own lives.

This sense of security is both understandable and, in many ways, healthy. Constant fear would paralyze us and rob life of its joy. However, this very complacency can leave us—and those who depend on us—unprepared when threats do arise. Recent surveys show that while violent victimization rates have declined in some areas, public fear remains elevated, with forty percent of Americans now afraid to walk alone at night near their homes—the highest level in three decades. Many also worry frequently about identity theft, burglary, or car theft. These concerns remind us that risks, though not constant, are real and can strike without warning.

Personal safety reaches far beyond protecting only ourselves. It also encompasses the safety of everyone we hold dear—our families, the loved ones we have sworn to protect, our colleagues, and even strangers who may need help in a moment of crisis. True personal safety means developing the awareness, skills, and readiness to safeguard not just our own well-being, but the well-being of others when it matters most. It is an act of profound responsibility and love.

After nearly three decades as a law enforcement officer, I have witnessed the worst of humanity, and those experiences have profoundly shaped my views on personal safety. I have responded to scenes of sudden violence, comforted families shattered by preventable tragedies, and seen how quickly complacency can turn an ordinary day into a nightmare. Time and again, I watched capable, good-hearted people caught off guard—not because they were reckless, but because they never imagined it could happen to them or to someone they loved. These hard-earned lessons taught me that personal safety is not paranoia, but a vital act of responsibility and love. It equips us to protect what matters most instead of merely hoping danger stays away.

I have often encouraged my daughters and those around me to take personal safety seriously. By building awareness and practical skills, we can move from passive hope to confident readiness. Improving personal safety requires time and dedication, yet it is never too late to begin. Small, consistent steps—such as practicing situational awareness, learning basic self-defense principles, securing our homes and vehicles, and creating family emergency plans—compound over time into powerful protection.

From my experience, true peace of mind does not come from ignoring risks. It comes from quietly and diligently preparing for them so that when challenges arise, we are not caught entirely off guard. Safety, when thoughtfully integrated into our lives, does not diminish our freedom or joy. On the contrary, it becomes the quiet, steady foundation that allows us to fully and confidently pursue the things we value most: our families, our goals, our happiness, and our purpose.

People who actively cultivate awareness and take proactive steps are far less likely to be selected as victims. They spot potential threats earlier, make better decisions under pressure, and respond with calm effectiveness rather than panic. This preparation brings tangible benefits: greater confidence in daily life, reduced anxiety about the unknown, stronger family bonds forged through shared safety plans, and the empowering knowledge that you are doing everything within your power to protect those you love.

By strengthening our personal safety, we empower ourselves to live more boldly, protect those we love, and face each day with greater confidence and serenity. Drawing from my years of experience as a law enforcement officer, I share my personal perspectives and practical insights on the subject. I do not claim to be the ultimate expert; rather, I offer ideas based on what I have seen and learned in the field. My goal is to provide clear, actionable steps that everyday people can understand and implement to enhance their own safety and the safety of those around them.

Of course, no single measure can ever be foolproof. Even the mightiest defenses have their limits. Thousands of years ago, China constructed the Great Wall—an extraordinary feat of engineering meant to stop invaders. Yet despite its immense scale and strength, it could not fully prevent determined forces from eventually entering China.

In the same way, the suggestions in this book are not guarantees of absolute safety. They are simply starting points—practical ideas meant to spark awareness, encourage thoughtful planning, and inspire you to identify and adopt measures that fit your unique circumstances. What works well for one person may need to be adapted for another.

Ultimately, my hope is that together we can shift personal safety from an overlooked afterthought into one of the strongest pillars supporting the fulfilling lives and safer society we all deserve to build.

D. Q. Phan

Table of Contents

Chapter 1

Personal Safety Begins With You

Safety is, first and foremost, a personal responsibility—as the word itself suggests. While communities, law enforcement, and technology can provide support, no one else can fully protect you from the wide range of threats that exist today. In a world where emergency response times are measured in minutes but life-altering events happen in seconds, the individual is always the first responder. True safety extends far beyond physical security. It encompasses intellectual safety, financial safety, emotional safety, digital safety, and more. It is a comprehensive shield that must be maintained daily through deliberate action.

In the chapters ahead, I will explore each of these areas in greater depth, sharing practical insights drawn from real-world experience, hard-learned lessons, and careful observation. My goal is not to provide a rigid rulebook, but to equip you with the awareness, principles, and tools you need to thoughtfully assess your own unique situation and build a personalized safety framework that truly works for you—one that respects your individual strengths, lifestyle, vulnerabilities, and goals. By taking ownership of your safety across all these dimensions, you empower yourself to live with greater freedom, confidence, and peace of mind in both the physical and digital worlds.

In our increasingly blended physical-digital world, where artificial intelligence continues to blur the lines between real and virtual interactions, this personal responsibility has never been more important—or more challenging. Scammers, predators, and opportunists thrive when individuals relinquish control and assume someone else will look out for them. They look for the "seams" in our lives—the moments when we are distracted by our devices or complacent in our routines. The reality is that lasting safety cannot be outsourced to a security guard, a software update, or a government agency. It must be actively built and maintained by each of us through consistent awareness, smart habits, and deliberate choices.

What makes the human race truly beautiful is our profound individuality. Each person is uniquely different from the next—in appearance, personality, strengths, talents, life experiences, and circumstances. This rich diversity is precisely what makes human interactions so endlessly fascinating, dynamic, and rewarding. While some individuals are blessed with remarkable physical strength, athletic prowess, or Herculean endurance, others possess extraordinary intellectual depth, sharp analytical minds, or boundless creativity that can reshape society, spark innovation, and solve complex problems. Some excel at building deep emotional connections and offering profound empathy, while others shine through quiet determination, strategic thinking, or artistic vision.

No two people are wired the same way. One person may light up a room with natural charisma and leadership, while another transforms ideas into reality through meticulous focus and quiet genius. Some thrive in high-energy, fast-paced environments; others bring calm wisdom and thoughtful reflection. These differences are not weaknesses—they are complementary gifts that enrich our families, workplaces, communities, and the world at large. When we recognize and celebrate this beautiful diversity instead of comparing ourselves to others, we unlock greater appreciation for both our own unique strengths and those of the people around us.

By the same token, the need to enhance our own personal safety is vastly different for each individual. What constitutes effective protection for one person may be insufficient or even impractical for another, depending on their physical capabilities, daily routines, living environment, personality, occupation, and unique vulnerabilities. For example, individuals blessed with a massive body frame—such as someone who stands 6'4" and weighs 275 pounds—are statistically less likely to be targeted for certain street crimes like muggings, as perpetrators often prefer easier, less intimidating victims. In contrast, smaller-statured individuals may appear as softer targets in the eyes of opportunists.

However, size alone is never a guarantee of safety. No matter how physically imposing someone is, they can still be overwhelmed by determined, persistent perpetrators who use weapons, numbers, or surprise. Conversely, no matter how small or seemingly vulnerable a person may be, they can significantly harden themselves—both physically and mentally—through consistent training, heightened situational awareness, and smart habits that make them far less attractive as targets. This individualized reality means that situational awareness and personal safety strategies should never be approached with a rigid, one-size-fits-all mentality. True safety begins when we honestly assess our own strengths, limitations, lifestyle, and specific risk factors, then deliberately build tailored habits that align with who we genuinely are.

Everything truly starts with us, individually. When we accept ownership of our own safety across all its dimensions and tailor our defenses to our unique strengths and circumstances, we not only reduce our personal risk but also contribute to safer families, stronger communities, and a more resilient society. When most people think about personal safety, the first thing that comes to mind is physical safety—and for good reason. It is the most visible, tangible, and immediate aspect of personal protection. We instinctively worry about our ability to defend ourselves, deter threats, or escape danger when confronted in the real world.

Like many others, I have often wished I had been blessed with an imposing physical presence. Growing up, I dreamed of becoming a high school teacher, sharing my passion for computer programming with the next generation. However, during my senior year at a local university, I was unexpectedly recruited into law enforcement. As luck would have it, this tiny 5'5", 150-pound kid—soaking wet—somehow passed all the demanding physical agility exams and was accepted into a regional police academy. Only a decade or so before my time, many police departments maintained unofficial height preferences, often favoring candidates who were at least six feet tall. The rest became my personal history: a rewarding yet demanding 28-year career in law enforcement—a path I never originally planned but one that profoundly shaped my understanding of safety, risk, and human vulnerability.

That experience taught me a powerful and humbling truth: physical size is only one small piece of the puzzle. While a larger, stronger build can offer certain advantages and may deter some opportunistic predators, it is far from a guarantee of safety. Even the biggest and strongest individuals can be overwhelmed by surprise, weapons, determination, or sheer numbers. Conversely, those of us with smaller or average frames are not helpless. We can dramatically improve our odds through sharp situational awareness, strategic habits, consistent training, and mental resilience. In many cases, a smaller person who is alert, confident, and prepared can be far harder to victimize than a larger person who is complacent or unaware.

This personal realization became one of the most important lessons in my own safety journey. True physical safety is not primarily determined by the body you were born with, but by the habits, skills, and mindset you deliberately develop. Your starting point—whether tall or short, strong or slight—matters far less than what you choose to do with it.

Over my 28 years on the job, I witnessed this truth time and again: safety is far more about preparation, awareness, and adaptability than raw physical size. One of the most effective strategies for preserving safety—both on the street and in daily life—is to avoid physical confrontations whenever possible. De-escalation, situational awareness, and smart decision-making can prevent the vast majority of potential conflicts from ever turning violent.

However, during my law enforcement career, this principle didn't always hold. When California's Three Strikes and You're Out law took effect in 1994, I noticed a noticeable shift in how many suspects behaved during arrests. It seemed that repeat offenders, now facing the very real possibility of a lengthy prison sentence or even life behind bars for a third felony, became far more willing to fight their way out rather than submit peacefully. Whether it was my own unlucky streak at the time or a broader pattern, I distinctly remember encountering more frequent and intense physical confrontations after the law passed. Some individuals appeared to have little to lose—knowing that compliance could mean decades in prison pushed a few to resist aggressively, sometimes with surprising ferocity.

That experience reinforced a key lesson: while avoidance remains the gold standard for personal safety, real-world encounters don't always allow that luxury. When confrontation becomes unavoidable, mental preparedness, tactical skills, and the ability to stay calm under pressure become critical. Size, strength, or prior assumptions about "easy" targets matter far less than training, awareness, and the willingness to adapt in the moment. When you find yourself backed into a corner where words can no longer bridge the gap and a physical confrontation is imminent, you are essentially left with three primal choices: run, hide, or fight.

If you are alone, fleeing is often the most pragmatic solution, yet it demands a brutally honest self-assessment of your own physical limits. You must ask yourself whether you truly possess the explosive speed and sustained stamina required to outpace an aggressor who may be younger, faster, or fueled by adrenaline. The logic of "flight" relies entirely on your ability to create distance, and if your physical condition doesn't match the demands of the moment, running could inadvertently leave you exhausted and even more vulnerable. The complexity of this decision-making process intensifies exponentially when you are responsible for the safety of others. If you are accompanied by loved ones—perhaps children, elderly parents, or those with limited mobility—running and hiding may quickly transition from viable strategies to impossible luxuries.

In such high-stakes scenarios, your tactical focus must shift toward immediate mitigation. This includes calling emergency services immediately while simultaneously guiding your group toward areas of safety, such as well-lit, crowded areas where the presence of witnesses might act as a natural deterrent to a perpetrator. Moving toward the light and the crowd leverages the environment to your advantage, potentially forcing an aggressor to reconsider their intent. However, when every exit is blocked and all other options have been exhausted, you are left with the daunting reality of physical defense. It is vital to ask yourself now—not later—if you actually know how to protect yourself and those you love.

For those with the resources and the inclination, enrolling in professional self-defense or martial arts courses is a significant blessing, offering structured environments and expert feedback. Yet, formal training is not the only path to preparedness. For the rest of us, a modest investment in a used punching bag and a disciplined commitment to studying reputable fighting and defense lessons on YouTube or other social media platforms are viable alternatives. Through consistent practice, you can learn the mechanics of repelling an attacker and, in extreme cases, managing multiple threats simultaneously. While throwing a punch or a kick may seem like a primal human instinct, there is a vast gulf between raw movement and tactical effectiveness.

Most people assume they can naturally defend themselves, but without refined mechanics, it is incredibly difficult to generate the kinetic energy required to stop a determined perpetrator. Although I do not claim to be a trained fighter capable of teaching the physics of maximum force, I have spent decades developing a practical, lived understanding of the struggle. My training has been a solitary, disciplined pursuit, utilizing old, reliable punching bags and instructional videos to adapt professional techniques to my own physical capabilities. This self-guided preparation proved vital during my career when facing aggressive individuals who attempted to fight their way out of an arrest.

While I was strictly bound to the specific techniques authorized by my department, my supplemental home training provided the edge that manuals cannot teach: the confidence to stand my ground, the breath control to keep my heart rate from spiking, and the mental clarity to remain calm, not panicked. These internal elements were just as essential to my safety as any physical maneuver. In the field, I was frequently outmatched by suspects with biceps the size of my head, a reality that forced me to prioritize tactical strategy over brute strength. In those high-stakes moments, I learned that effective self-defense is built on the principle of fighting "smart"—managing a crisis rather than merely reacting to it.

This is a mindset anyone can adopt: you fight to buy precious seconds for backup to arrive, you fight to maintain the distance necessary to avoid injury, and you fight to identify the fleeting opportunities to disable a threat or facilitate an escape. To execute this under the crushing pressure of a real-world confrontation, one must train with such diligence that the movements transition from conscious effort to pure intuition. The ultimate goal is to move beyond the need for thought entirely, allowing the body to act and react with fluid muscle memory when the stakes are highest and there is no room for hesitation. The bottom line is that readiness is not a matter of chance; it is a matter of preparation. These heavy questions must be answered with total candor in the quiet safety of your home, rather than in the heat of a life-threatening crisis.

Because there is no "one size fits all" manual for survival, what works for a trained athlete will not work for someone with different physical constraints. Ultimately, we must all embrace the responsibility of learning to fight both smartly and effectively when all other options have been exhausted. This requires more than just a general knowledge of self-defense; it demands the cultivation of a personalized strategy that honestly accounts for our specific physical strengths and inherent weaknesses. By tailoring a defensive plan to our unique capabilities, we ensure that we aren't merely guessing in a moment of crisis, but rather executing a practiced, deliberate response that was forged long before the threat appeared.

The reality of personal safety is that the worst-case scenario does not offer time for a rehearsal. Therefore, it is essential to conduct a candid self-assessment of your current state of readiness. Ask yourself: what concrete steps have you taken to prepare your body and mind for a violent encounter? If you were faced with an aggressive perpetrator today and de-escalation had failed, would you have the conditioned reflexes and the mental fortitude to defend yourself, or would you be left paralyzed by indecision? Preparation is the only bridge between victimhood and survival. While mastering fighting skills and self-defense techniques is an essential pillar of survival, possessing technical knowledge alone is often insufficient.

In a high-stakes physical encounter, your body is the engine that drives those techniques; if that engine stalls, even the most sophisticated maneuvers will fail. To be truly prepared for the unpredictable nature of violence, one must cultivate a foundation of physical readiness that balances aerobic endurance, raw strength, functional flexibility, and aquatic proficiency. A robust regimen of aerobic exercise is the first line of defense, building the cardiovascular stamina necessary to sustain a struggle that lasts longer than a few frantic seconds. In a real-world confrontation, exhaustion is a silent enemy that clouds judgment and weakens execution, but a conditioned heart and lungs allow you to maintain a high level of intensity until the threat is neutralized or help arrives.

Complementing this endurance is weightlifting, which provides the explosive power and structural integrity needed to exert force and resist an opponent's mass. Building functional strength ensures that when you land a strike or attempt a clinch, the impact is meaningful and your body remains resilient against injury. Furthermore, one must not overlook the importance of flexibility and mobility training; incorporating stretching ensures your muscles can achieve the necessary range of motion to kick, pivot, or escape a hold without the risk of debilitating tears or strains. However, survival scenarios are rarely confined to dry land, and a comprehensive defense strategy must account for the environment. Knowing how to swim and, more importantly, how to control your breath and maintain composure when submerged, is a life-saving skill set.

Should a perpetrator successfully push you into a lake, a pool, or any body of water, the nature of the fight shifts instantly from a trial of strength to a battle against panic and suffocation. Mastery over your breathing under water prevents the instinctive gasp that leads to drowning, allowing you to stay calm, regain your bearings, and fight your way back to the surface. By integrating these four pillars—stamina, strength, suppleness, and aquatic composure—you transform your self-defense skills from mere theory into a formidable, holistic system of survival. True readiness is found at the intersection of a sharp mind, a technical skill set, and a body physically capable of answering the call, regardless of where the fight takes place.

When faced with an unavoidable physical confrontation where all avenues of escape have vanished, you must accept the grim reality that fighting is a chaotic and inherently "dirty" battle. In such a crisis, it is vital to utilize every environmental advantage available to gain the upper hand; however, this tactical necessity must always be balanced by the principle of reasonable force. If you are facing a perpetrator who is significantly larger, more aggressive, or if you find yourself outnumbered, you must quickly survey your surroundings for improvised tools. This might mean using dirt to temporarily compromise an attacker's vision and breathing, or utilizing a leather belt, sturdy sticks, or poles to maintain a safe distance.

These tools should be used to inflict only the force required to neutralize the immediate aggression and facilitate your escape. Crucially, you must remain disciplined enough to apply only the force necessary to stop the threat—and no more. The moment the threat is neutralized, the legal justification for force ends. The consequences of overstepping into excessive force are severe; it can instantly turn the tables, transforming you from a victim seeking safety into a defendant facing the authorities. In the eyes of the law, your actions will be scrutinized for their proportionality. By remaining calm and exercising restraint even in the heat of a fight, you ensure that your defense remains both physically effective and legally defensible, protecting your future just as much as your life.

In 2025, while securing a facility as part of my post-retirement career, I encountered an aggressive trespasser who immediately charged toward me, shouting threats of physical violence. In that high-tension moment, I was well-equipped to escalate: I held a heavy-duty flashlight that could serve as a formidable blunt force instrument, and I was carrying a concealed firearm. However, true tactical proficiency is defined by restraint rather than escalation. Instead of resorting to immediate physical force, I executed a controlled retreat, maintaining a critical reactionary gap while keeping my eyes locked on the subject. I used firm verbal commands to direct him toward the exit, prioritizing de-escalation while ensuring I remained just beyond his reach.

Had I chosen to exert physical force to neutralize the perpetrator in that moment, the consequences could have been catastrophic. A heavy-duty flashlight used as a weapon can easily cause permanent injury or even death if it strikes a vulnerable area. Had I struck him, the tables would have turned instantly; I would have been forced to justify my actions to a court of law, potentially transforming from a professional performing his duties into a suspect facing criminal charges for injuring or killing an unarmed individual. This realization underscored the importance of my restraint. By managing the distance to buy time and utilizing my radio to summon assistance, I allowed the situation to resolve itself when my partner arrived and the sound of police sirens forced the perpetrator to flee.

The entire encounter was captured by the building's surveillance system, providing me with an invaluable "game tape." I analyzed the footage meticulously, scrutinizing my footwork and positioning to ensure that my actions were not only effective but legally defensible. In the security profession, few scenarios are as daunting as being confronted in the dark by a hostile individual with a significant size advantage. My safety and my legal standing depends entirely on a calm mind, the disciplined use of distance, and the professional maturity to recognize that the best fight is the one you manage to avoid.

Proper footwear is a critical yet often overlooked element of personal safety and situational readiness. While I admit there is an undeniable comfort in wearing sandals or flip-flops in public, especially during the sweltering summer months, they are a significant liability in an emergency. In terms of tactical mobility, such footwear makes it nearly impossible to run effectively, maintain balance on uneven terrain, or pivot during a struggle. For women, high heels are arguably the most restrictive, as they virtually eliminate the ability to flee from a dangerous situation and provide a precarious foundation during a physical encounter.

From a tactical perspective, exposed toes are a glaring vulnerability. A predatory individual looking for an advantage will notice your lack of protection and may stomp on your feet to inflict instant, debilitating pain. As I have emphasized before, a street fight is a "dirty" game devoid of rules; a perpetrator whose goal is to harm you will consider your mobility a fair target. You must be prepared to adopt the same mindset: if an attacker's toes are exposed, a heavy, calculated stomp can inflict significant injury, creating a vital window of opportunity for you and your loved ones to escape and contact the authorities.

I may be in the minority on this issue, but I prioritize function over fashion whenever I step outdoors—even if I am just tending to the front lawn. I consistently wear well-fitting clothing and sturdy sneakers or hard-top shoes, such as steel-toe work boots, to shield myself against the aforementioned risks. Hard-top shoes not only protect against stomps but also turn your own feet into more effective defensive tools. Furthermore, well-fitting attire ensures a full range of motion for running or fighting. Practically speaking, if I am forced to remove my leather belt to use as an improvised weapon, I need to know that my trousers will remain secure rather than falling to my ankles and further compromising my ability to move. Dressing for the "worst-case scenario" ensures that your wardrobe never becomes your greatest weakness.

In most jurisdictions, the law empowers law-abiding adults with no felony convictions to carry non-lethal tools—such as pepper spray and conducted energy devices, commonly known as stun devices—as a primary line of defense. However, simply possessing these items is not a substitute for readiness; a tool is only as effective as the person wielding it. I strongly encourage everyone to evaluate whether these options align with their lifestyle and comfort level. Carrying a defensive tool without a deep, practiced understanding of its mechanics and the "Rules of Engagement" is a liability, not an asset.

When it comes to pepper spray, the environment is your greatest ally or your most dangerous enemy. It is essential to develop a constant awareness of wind direction before a crisis ever occurs. Deploying an aerosol or gel spray into a headwind will almost certainly cause a "blowback" effect, contaminating your own eyes and lungs. In that moment of self-inflicted incapacitation, you grant the perpetrator a massive tactical advantage, effectively blinding yourself while the threat remains active.

Similarly, deploying a stun device requires more than just a finger on the trigger. If used incorrectly—such as failing to maintain a proper reactionary gap or failing to achieve proper probe spread—you risk the device being ineffective. In a close-quarters struggle, a poorly managed tool can easily be wrestled away, allowing the aggressor to turn your own defense against you. The bottom line: if you choose to carry, you must commit to the training. You must learn not just how to fire the tool, but how to retain it under pressure and when the legal threshold for its use has been met.

When utilized with precision, pepper spray serves as a formidable tool for personal defense, capable of instantly de-escalating a dangerous encounter by inducing involuntary eye closure and intense respiratory distress. This physiological reaction effectively neutralizes a perpetrator's vision and focus, granting you a critical, though brief, window of time to retreat to safety and seek help. In fact, screaming loudly for help or specifically instructing someone to call 911 is known to be an effective tactic to draw attention to the situation and potentially deter an attacker. For many, carrying pepper spray—especially while jogging or walking at night—is a practical step that provides a significant sense of security and general peace of mind during daily routines. However, if you decide to carry such a deterrent, it is wise to do so in a way that remains easily accessible under pressure. There are several mounting options to facilitate this, such as belt clips, keychains, or specialized athletic holsters. Another effective strategy is to simply have the canister ready in your hand as you jog or approach your intended destination, ensuring no time is lost if a threat emerges. Shuffling through a bag or deep pockets to find your canister during an emergency is highly counterproductive; not only are you unable to locate the tool when you need it most, but you also risk losing sight of the perpetrator and wasting the precious seconds required to escape. At the same time, it is equally important to store your pepper spray safely to ensure it won't be triggered accidentally inside your pockets or purse, which would result in an unfortunate and incapacitating self-exposure.

While various formulations exist, there is a strong tactical argument for favoring pepper gel over traditional aerosol sprays. Because the gel formula is significantly heavier and more viscous, it travels in a concentrated stream that is far less susceptible to wind drift or "blowback," which occurs when a fine mist is carried back toward the user. Furthermore, gel is often preferred for its localized impact; unlike aerosols that atomize into a cloud and can contaminate an entire room, gel sticks to what it hits, making it a safer choice for use in confined indoor spaces or crowded environments. The optimal conditions for deployment occur when you have a clear, unobstructed line of sight to a threat at a distance of roughly 3 to 10 feet, providing enough space to react without being within a perpetrator's immediate reach. It is most effective when used as a proactive deterrent to stop an approach rather than a reactive measure once a physical struggle has already begun.

Conversely, there are several scenarios where using pepper spray can be dangerous. You should avoid deployment in high-wind conditions—particularly if you are using an aerosol—as the irritant can easily blow back into your own face, leaving you incapacitated. It is also wise to exercise extreme caution in poorly ventilated or small, enclosed spaces like elevators or vehicles, where the chemical cloud can affect everyone present, including yourself. Furthermore, before deciding to carry any self-defense tool, you will need to check with your local and state law to see if it is legal for you to carry pepper spray and or stun devices, as every jurisdiction has different laws and regulations. For instance, some areas restrict the size of the canister or the strength of the formula, and certain locations like government buildings or airports may prohibit them entirely. Ultimately, the decision to carry a specific type of deterrent is a personal one that should be informed by your environment and comfort level. If you choose to incorporate it into your safety kit, it is vital to research the specific rules in your area and consider practicing with an inert trainer to ensure you can deploy it effectively under the stress of a real-world confrontation.

Unlike pepper spray, which offers the advantage of range, a stun device is a contact weapon that requires the electrodes to be pressed firmly against the perpetrator's body—ideally on a large muscle group or through thin clothing—to deliver an incapacitating shock. This fundamental requirement means that for the device to have any physical effect, the perpetrator must be within your immediate personal space. Operating at this "zero-range" is inherently high-risk; if you are close enough to touch them, they are close enough to grab, strike, or overpower you. Relying solely on a contact-based tool means you have effectively surrendered the "reactionary gap," the crucial distance that allows you to evade or flee before a physical struggle begins.

However, a stun device can be highly effective when used as a psychological deterrent to prevent a confrontation from escalating to physical contact. By activating the device at a safe distance, the sudden, brilliant display of electrical arcs and the intimidating, high-frequency crackling sound serve as a clear signal of your intent and capability to defend yourself. This "show of force" can startle a perpetrator and break their focus, creating a vital window of opportunity for you to back away and increase the distance between you.

While using the device as a deterrent, it is essential to pair the visual warning with vocal commands. Screaming for help or loudly instructing bystanders to call 911 not only draws unwanted attention to the perpetrator but also creates a psychological barrier that may cause them to abandon their approach. By leveraging the stun device as a tool for intimidation and communication early on, you prioritize your safety by attempting to end the encounter while you still have the space to escape, rather than waiting until a dangerous physical struggle becomes unavoidable.

Whether you choose to carry pepper spray, a stun device, or a combination of both, it is your responsibility to ensure you are in full compliance with the law. You must meticulously check your local municipal codes, regional regulations, and state statutes to determine if you meet the specific requirements for possession and carry. These laws are often nuanced; for example, some jurisdictions may have strict age limits, restrictions on the maximum chemical concentration of spray, or specific permitting requirements for electronic deterrents. Since regulations can vary significantly even between neighboring cities, staying informed is essential to ensuring your self-defense tools remain a legal protection rather than a potential liability.

Beyond legal compliance, it is highly advisable to seek out professional training courses to ensure you are proficient with your chosen equipment. Merely owning a device does not guarantee safety; true effectiveness comes from being well-trained on how to deploy it under the intense physiological stress of a real-world encounter. A quality training program will teach you proper grip, aiming techniques, and situational awareness, as well as the critical "when" of self-defense—helping you understand the ethical and legal boundaries of using force. By combining a clear understanding of the law with practical, hands-on experience, you can carry these tools with the confidence and discipline necessary to protect yourself effectively.

The United States remains one of the few nations where the constitutional right to keep and bear arms is extended to both citizens and lawful permanent residents, provided they satisfy all federal and state legal requirements. However, this constitutional protection does not grant a universal right to carry firearms in public spaces. While "open carry" states permit individuals to carry firearms openly without a license, many other jurisdictions strictly prohibit the practice or require a specific concealed carry permit to do so legally.

Recent data from the FBI and the Pew Research Center for early 2026 indicates that approximately 31% to 32% of U.S. adults personally own a firearm, while 42% of adults live in a household where a gun is present. Furthermore, nearly 47% of current non-owners can envision themselves owning a firearm in the future, signaling a sustained national interest in ownership (www. pewresearch.org).

Deciding whether or not to own a firearm is a significant personal choice that requires careful consideration. If you choose to own or carry one, it is imperative to conduct diligent research to ensure you meet all legal requirements in your specific jurisdiction. Equally important is the commitment to formal training; owners should take comprehensive courses to learn how to safely operate and maintain their equipment, understand the legal parameters for the use of force, and fully grasp the gravity of the consequences involved.

Beyond operation and legality, the safe storage of a firearm is paramount. If a child or an unauthorized individual gains access to a weapon and causes harm to themselves or others—whether accidentally or intentionally—the gun owner will be held legally and civilly accountable. Ultimately, every gun owner bears absolute responsibility for every bullet that leaves the barrel of their firearm, regardless of their original intentions.

Yet, acknowledging the gravity of carrying a weapon is only half the battle; the other half is cultivating the discipline to avoid ever having to use it. While being prepared for conflict is a virtue, the ultimate expression of tactical wisdom is the realization that the best fight is the one that never occurs. De-escalation and avoidance are not signs of weakness, but of superior judgment; they represent the understanding that no ego-driven confrontation is worth the potential legal, physical, or emotional fallout. When faced with a potential skirmish, your primary objective should always be to preserve your safety and your future. If there is a path to walk away, a door to exit, or a way to diffuse the tension through silence or a calm word, take it. In the realm of self-defense, a successful escape is a total victory. This mindset is particularly vital in the modern landscape of high-stress environments, such as the open road. As the cost of living climbs and the rapid integration of artificial intelligence threatens job security, many people are operating with a dangerously short fuse. When you encounter an aggressive driver—someone who cuts you off or tailgates you—recognize that you are likely seeing the boiling point of their personal frustrations. In these moments, take a deep breath, consciously slow down, and create distance between your vehicle and theirs. Road rage is a volatile phenomenon, and in today's world, you simply do not know who might be carrying a firearm or who is desperate enough to use it. Swallowing your pride is a small price to pay to ensure you arrive home to your family.

To ensure that your defensive skills are available to you when avoidance fails, you must bridge the gap between theory and reality through consistent practice. One of the most effective ways to do this is by engaging in light technical sparring at approximately 10% strength with a trusted partner. At this controlled speed, you can focus on the mechanics of a move without the cloud of adrenaline or the fear of injury. This low-impact repetition allows techniques to be etched into your nervous system, transforming conscious thought into instinctive muscle memory. By slowing down the practice, you give your brain the space to memorize the nuances of timing and distance, ensuring that if you are ever forced into a corner, your body will know exactly how to react before your mind even has a chance to panic. These concepts are not isolated survival tactics; they are the connective tissue of a holistic approach to personal safety. True security is a spectrum that begins with the mental discipline of avoidance, extends to environmental awareness, and ends with the physical capability to defend one's life. The philosophy that the best fight is the one that never happened is the foundation of this spectrum. When you choose to walk away, you are practicing strategic avoidance. Physical altercations are inherently unpredictable; even a trained fighter can trip or be blindsided. By removing yourself, you maintain total control over your outcome.

This strategy is put to the test most frequently in daily life. Refusing to engage with an aggressive driver is a vital exercise in risk-benefit analysis. Engaging in road rage offers zero reward and carries a potential death sentence. By creating distance, you are defending your peace to protect your life. However, sometimes the world brings the fight to you regardless of your efforts to avoid it. This is where instinctive readiness through muscle memory becomes vital. Practicing at 10% strength programs your "internal bodyguard." In a moment of true danger, your logical brain often shuts down, but by etching moves into your system through deliberate repetition, you ensure that your response is governed by muscle memory rather than panic. This creates a powerful psychological edge: knowing you can defend yourself makes it easier to remain calm and walk away, as you no longer feel the need to prove your strength.

Reflecting the adage to 'prepare for the worst and hope for the best,' true personal safety is a layered endeavor: the mind avoids the conflict, the temperament de-escalates the environment, and the body serves as the final line of defense. By integrating these habits, personal protection ceases to be a matter of luck and becomes the byproduct of a deliberate, disciplined life.

Chapter 2

Situational Awareness

Every environment has its own unique charms, beauty — and hidden challenges. In high-crime or economically distressed neighborhoods, residents often develop a sharp, instinctive awareness of potential dangers simply to survive. They remain constantly alert to subtle cues that could mean the difference between safety and victimization: avoiding certain streets after dark, steering clear of specific colors or clothing that might signal affiliation with the wrong group, or reading body language and group dynamics with practiced precision.

To someone living in an ultra-wealthy enclave like Atherton, California; Scarsdale, New York; Cherry Hills Village, Colorado; or Greenwich, Connecticut, this level of daily vigilance may sound far-fetched or even exaggerated. Yet for millions of Americans navigating rougher, lower-income neighborhoods every day, it is a necessary reality — a hard-earned survival skill shaped by experience.

The truth is that crime can happen anywhere. Criminals are highly mobile. They do not limit themselves to physical streets in troubled areas. They operate just as effectively in quiet suburban neighborhoods, upscale shopping districts, and exclusive gated communities. Moreover, in today's digital age, threats extend far beyond the physical world — into social media, the airwaves, the internet, emails, text messages, and any space where human beings interact. Sophisticated scammers, identity thieves, and predators use online platforms to target victims regardless of zip code, often exploiting trust, distraction, or a false sense of security. This is precisely why situational awareness is imperative for everyone, no matter where you live or how safe your surroundings may appear. It is not about living in constant fear or paranoia, but about developing a calm, consistent habit of observing your environment — both physical and digital — that works equally well on a high-risk street corner or while scrolling through your phone in a luxurious home. Complacency can settle anywhere, especially in seemingly safe, affluent communities where people assume "it won't happen here." True awareness bridges this gap and empowers you to protect yourself and your loved ones in every environment you encounter.

A recent survey[1] still show that a significant portion of Americans — around 40% in some polls — remain afraid to walk alone at night near their homes, one of the highest

---

[1] https://news.gallup.com/poll/544415/personal-safety-fears-three-decade-high.aspx

levels in three decades, even as overall violent crime rates have declined in many cities. This gap between improving statistics and lingering public fear highlights why awareness matters: risks may not be constant, but they are real, and they can strike suddenly when we least expect them.

At any given moment — especially in public places — you are surrounded by good, honest, hardworking people simply going about their daily lives. Yet moving among them may be individuals carrying concealed weapons or harboring harmful intentions, quietly scanning for an easy opportunity to strike.

Think of a completed crime as a triangle. All three sides must be present and firmly connected for the shape — and the crime — to form. The first two sides belong entirely to the perpetrator: their desire to commit the crime and their ability to carry it out. Both of these elements are largely beyond any victim's control. However, just as two sides alone cannot complete a triangle, desire and ability alone are rarely enough to finish the act.

The critical third side is opportunity — and this is the one element that is almost entirely within your control. By practicing strong situational awareness and making deliberate choices, you can deny criminals that opportunity and prevent many crimes before they ever begin. In other words, while you cannot control a criminal's intentions or capabilities, you can dramatically reduce your risk simply by refusing to present yourself as an easy target.

So how exactly do you prevent creating opportunities for crime? It begins with small, consistent habits rooted in strong situational awareness.

One of the most important pieces of advice I have repeatedly shared with my daughters is this: never wear earphones or earbuds when you are in public spaces. Of course, like most young people, they pushed back and tried every way possible to keep listening to their music or podcasts. But the ability to hear is a vital component of situational awareness. Sounds often provide the earliest warning that something is not right — a van's sliding door opening nearby, rapid footsteps approaching from behind, raised voices, or the sudden silence of others around you.

When my daughters were a few years younger, I sat them down and gave them a vivid example of why hearing can literally make the difference between safety and danger.

"Imagine you're walking toward your car in a parking structure after dark," I told them. "You suddenly hear quick, heavy footsteps closing in fast behind you. That sound alone can give you those precious extra seconds to turn, assess the situation, and respond — whether by moving toward a better-lit area, gripping your keys like a makeshift tool, or calling out for help. But if you're wearing earbuds, you might remain completely oblivious until someone is right on top of you — and by then it could be too late."

They listened with frowns of displeasure on their faces, clearly not thrilled with the idea of giving up their music or podcasts in public. Still, they slowly nodded their heads in reluctant agreement.

That conversation stuck with me, and it reinforced something I've come to believe deeply after nearly 30 years in law enforcement: removing your earbuds (or at least keeping only one in) when you're out in public is one of the simplest yet most powerful habits you can adopt. It keeps all of your senses fully engaged so you can detect potential threats early, trust your instincts, and maintain control over the third side of the crime triangle — opportunity.

I still remind my daughters of this today, and I encourage you to do the same with your own family. In a world full of distractions, choosing to truly hear what's happening around you is an act of quiet empowerment that protects not only you, but everyone you love.

If you think the term "situational awareness" sounds too tactical or military and therefore doesn't apply to everyday civilians, you're right about the first part — and completely wrong about the second.

Situational awareness isn't just for law enforcement, military personnel, or security professionals. It's a fundamental life skill for every single person. At its core, it simply means being fully present and tuned in to your surroundings — actively noticing and making sense of what you see, hear, smell, taste, touch, and that subtle "sixth sense" feeling that something isn't quite right.

It's the difference between walking through life on autopilot and moving through the world with calm, confident awareness. Whether you're in a parking garage, crossing a busy street, traveling, or just out for a run, situational awareness helps you spot potential dangers early, make better decisions, and stay safer — without living in fear.

After nearly three decades responding to calls ranging from domestic disturbances to violent assaults and unexpected tragedies, I strongly believe no one should ever let down their guard whenever they are in public places. Everyone should stay off autopilot by keeping their head up and their attention on their surroundings rather than their phone. Avoid predictable routines that make you easy to follow. In transitional spaces such as parking lots, garages, sidewalks, elevators, or ATMs, move with purpose and scan for anything or anyone that feels out of place. Limit distractions — especially earbuds or deep focus on a screen — that dull your ability to notice approaching threats.

Like a broken record, I often reminded my wife and daughters to position themselves strategically in any environment: choose well-lit areas whenever possible, sit or stand with your back protected against a wall or solid object, and always take a few seconds to identify at least two exit routes wherever you are. I also taught them to trust their instincts without hesitation — if a situation or a person simply feels "off," create distance immediately or leave the area altogether. These small, intentional choices are not about living in fear; they are about staying in control and denying criminals the opportunity they need to act.

I still remember one evening as clearly as if it were yesterday. My daughters were in their early teens, and the four of us had gone to catch a movie. As we stepped into the theater, I quietly asked them to scan for the exit doors and choose seats that would give them the shortest, clearest path to at least one of those exits. They rolled their eyes and groaned, "Dad, you're totally killing the vibe. Thanks a lot!"

Years later, on a couple of occasions, they confessed with a smile that they had started doing the exact same thing with their friends — scanning for exits and picking smart seats without being asked. In that moment, I couldn't help but feel a quiet surge of pride. That little lesson had taken root. What felt like nagging at the time had become a natural habit that empowered them to look out for themselves and others.

Fortunately, hearing is only one of the powerful senses we can rely on. From my years as a law enforcement officer, I can tell you that vision is by far the most important and versatile tool we have for maintaining strong situational awareness. Your eyes allow you to gather an enormous amount of information quickly and from a safe distance. They help you establish a baseline of what "normal" looks like in any environment, spot subtle anomalies before they become threats, read body language, detect suspicious behavior, and identify escape routes or safe havens. When you actively use your eyes instead of keeping them locked on a screen, you dramatically increase your ability to stay one step ahead of potential danger.

I've reminded both of my daughters — and I still remind the people I work with today — that constantly gluing their eyes to their cell phones in public is one of the riskiest modern habits. When your head is down and your focus is elsewhere, you surrender a huge tactical advantage. Most perpetrators need to get relatively close to carry out physical harm, and a distracted, phone-focused person makes for an easy, predictable target. By simply lifting your gaze and scanning your surroundings, you make it much harder for anyone to approach you unnoticed.

In my experience responding to countless incidents over nearly three decades in law enforcement, the simple act of looking around has saved lives more times than I can count. For example, as you walk through a parking lot or enter a store, school, place of worship, or shopping mall, take just a few seconds to casually scan the area. You might notice someone lingering too long without a clear reason, or a person whose clothing or behavior doesn't match the environment — such as wearing a heavy jacket on a warm day, pacing nervously, or avoiding eye contact. These small deviations from the baseline can signal potential trouble long before anything happens, giving you valuable time to adjust your path, move toward safety, or quietly notify the authorities if needed.

It's equally important to secure your belongings, avoid openly displaying valuables, and never leave doors, windows, or vehicles unlocked or unattended — even for "just a minute."

Vision also lets you read body language effectively. I've seen many situations where clenched fists, rapid or agitated movements, or the way someone kept glancing at my gun belt revealed their intentions early. In everyday life, if you notice a stranger repeatedly looking at your purse, phone, or belongings while following your general direction, you can create distance or head toward a more populated, well-lit area before they get any closer.

Another practical application of situational awareness is the identification of strategic advantages within your environment. In crowded locations—such as malls, theaters, or transit stations—quickly noting the nearest exits, stairwells, or solid objects that could provide cover ensures that if a crisis erupts, you already have a mental map for escape rather than panicking and searching blindly.

Although I have retired from law enforcement, I continue to work in the security field and frequently escort colleagues to their vehicles. This includes a good friend of mine who often works late into the evening. She, along with others I've escorted, can certainly attest to my repeated, uncompromising reminder: before entering your vehicle—especially at night or in a parking structure, you must scan the area for suspicious individuals. Whenever I noticed their vehicles parked in a dark or isolated spot, I warmly suggested that they should park in a well-lit area of the lot to deny potential predators the cover of darkness.

As we approach, I make it a habit to shine my flashlight through the rear windows to illuminate the back seat and floorboards, encouraging them to always perform this check themselves as the light reveals the interior. I often warn them that one of the most terrifying scenarios is realizing too late that an intruder is hiding in the rear, positioned to choke you or press a weapon to the back of your head the moment you sit down. Taking just a few extra seconds to thoroughly inspect the back seat area can prevent a lifetime of regret. Throughout my career, I responded to countless calls where victims later wished they had taken those brief seconds to verify their surroundings. Ultimately, consistent visual awareness is the simplest and most effective way to ensure that your vehicle remains a safe space rather than a trap.

I strongly believe making brief, calm eye contact with people around you projects confidence and awareness. In my years on the job, I observed that criminals often prefer distracted or submissive-looking targets. A simple scan that includes making eye contact can deter someone who was considering you as a potential victim.

Of course, there are rare situations — such as an active shooter from a distance — that are largely beyond our immediate control. But the vast majority of opportunistic crimes and confrontations happen up close, in everyday settings where strong visual awareness gives you a real, tangible edge.

By deliberately using your eyes to scan your surroundings instead of defaulting to your phone, you transform passive movement into active protection. You stay ahead of the threat, reduce the opportunities you present, and maintain control over the one side of the crime triangle you can influence. These small visual habits, practiced consistently, become a quiet superpower that allows you and your loved ones to live more confidently and safely in any environment.

We should never overlook the quieter senses that quietly but powerfully support our situational awareness. Among them, the sense of smell stands out as one of the most underappreciated yet highly effective tools we possess. Unlike vision or hearing, which require deliberate focus and effort, smell operates almost autonomously — constantly feeding us information with minimal conscious input. It can deliver critical early warnings about our surroundings long before our other senses pick up on danger. A sudden whiff of smoke might alert you to a fire well before flames become visible. The sharp, unmistakable odor of natural gas can signal a dangerous leak that could otherwise go unnoticed. Even subtler scents — strong cologne worn in an unexpected setting, the metallic smell of blood, or an unusual chemical odor — can instantly tell you that something is out of the ordinary and deserves your immediate attention.

I still remember a valuable lesson from my early days as a brand-new officer fresh out of the academy. During my night shift field training, my Field Training Officer (FTO) sat beside me in the patrol car and instructed me to drive with the windows down. At the time, I followed his advice without thinking much of it. Looking back, however, he was absolutely right. By keeping the windows down, we could pick up on the distinct odors of illicit drugs being smoked or the strong scent of alcoholic beverages drifting from vehicles or groups on the street. Those smells gave us valuable hints about where criminal activity might be occurring, helping us decide where to patrol more closely and where to make proactive stops. That simple practice taught me how powerful our sense of smell can be in real-world law enforcement — and how it can give ordinary citizens the same kind of early advantage in everyday life.

The same principle applies when approaching your home or your vehicle. If you detect an out-of-the-ordinary smell as you get closer — whether it's cigarette smoke, unfamiliar cologne, cooking odors when no one should be home, or any scent that doesn't belong — treat it as a serious red flag. Immediately create distance, step back, and take a moment to assess. Walk away from your front door then use your phone to check interior security cameras to see if everything looks normal inside; in the worst cases, a home invasion could be underway or someone may be hiding nearby, waiting to ambush you the moment you unlock the door. Similarly, when walking toward your car — especially at night or in a parking structure — that same unusual scent should prompt you to stop, scan the area carefully, and check for anyone hiding near or inside the vehicle before you approach. Trusting these olfactory warnings and taking those extra precautionary seconds can prevent you from walking into a dangerous ambush.

Our sense of touch also plays a valuable supporting role. The feeling of someone standing uncomfortably close behind you in line, a sudden brush against your shoulder in a crowd, or the instinctive tightening of your muscles when your gut signals danger can all serve as powerful alerts. These subtle physical sensations often reach us faster than conscious thought and can prompt us to create distance or heighten our alertness before we fully process what we've seen or heard.

Even our sense of taste can serve as an important early warning system. For instance, if you're at a bar or restaurant and your drink suddenly tastes off — slightly bitter, overly sweet, or chemically different from what you remember — that unusual flavor can trigger your sixth sense that something might be wrong. Many date-rape drugs or sedatives have a distinct aftertaste or leave a strange residue. Trusting that instinctive "this doesn't taste right" feeling and immediately stopping consumption, discarding the drink, and alerting staff or friends can prevent a potentially dangerous situation.

When we deliberately engage all of our senses — sight, hearing, smell, touch, and even taste — working together with our natural instincts, we build a far more complete and reliable picture of our environment. This multi-sensory approach is the very heart of situational awareness. It transforms you from a passive participant moving through life on autopilot into an active guardian of your own safety. By staying tuned in to these constant streams of information, you spot anomalies earlier, read people and situations more accurately, and — most importantly — you deny potential criminals the one element they need to succeed: opportunity.

In my years of law enforcement experience, the vast majority of victims I encountered were not targeted because they were reckless; they were targeted because they were unaware. They had unknowingly given the perpetrator the third side of the crime triangle. But when you actively use every sense you possess, you close that door. You make yourself a harder target. You stay safer — not through fear or paranoia, but through quiet, consistent preparedness. This is how situational awareness becomes more than a concept: it becomes your everyday superpower, empowering you to protect yourself, your family, and those around you while living life with greater confidence and freedom.

In the digital realm, situational awareness is just as critical as in the physical world — and often far more challenging. Threats are invisible, borderless, and can strike instantly from anywhere on the globe. Recent data from the FBI's 2025 Internet Crime Report[2] reveals that Americans alone lost nearly $21 billion to cyber-enabled crimes, with romance scams, investment fraud, and phishing attacks among the most devastating categories. Far too many victims have lost thousands — or even hundreds of thousands — of dollars, had their identities stolen, faced ransomware demands, or endured deep emotional trauma simply because they lowered their guard while communicating online.

The core danger lies in never truly knowing the identity of the person or automated system on the other end of a screen. Scammers expertly impersonate charming listeners, lonely successful entrepreneurs, wealthy investors, or even potential romantic partners. They build trust gradually through social media, dating apps, messaging platforms, or

---

[2] https://www.ic3.gov/AnnualReport/Reports/2025_IC3Report.pdf

seemingly innocent emails. Once they sense vulnerability, they pivot to requests for money — often framed as urgent investments, medical emergencies, travel costs, or business opportunities — or they escalate to more sinister tactics.

Email scams have grown particularly treacherous. Perpetrators send seemingly legitimate messages — fake invoices, account alerts, package notifications, or urgent requests from "colleagues" or "authorities" — that contain malicious attachments or links. Clicking them can install malware or ransomware that hijacks the victim's electronic devices. Ransomware encrypts files or locks the entire system, demanding payment, often in cryptocurrency, to restore access. In other cases, the malware quietly extracts personal information: banking details, passwords, Social Security numbers, photos, and browsing history. This data can then be used for identity theft, further fraud, or sold on the dark web. Phishing emails remain one of the most common delivery methods for such attacks, with billions of malicious messages sent daily and success rates boosted by AI-generated content that makes them harder to spot.

A few years ago, a close friend of mine excitedly shared that she had met a charming Dutch businessman online. For weeks, they exchanged warm, attentive messages. He claimed to be recently divorced, highly successful in international business, and deeply eager to marry her and bring her to Belgium to start a new life together. She was absolutely elated — she couldn't stop talking about their future plans, the romantic trips they would take, and how perfect he seemed. She even showed me his polished online profile, complete with professional photos and a convincing backstory.

While I didn't want to dampen her happiness, I gently expressed my suspicion that he might be trying to scam her. At first, she didn't want to believe it and defended the connection. But she eventually agreed to let me investigate further for her peace of mind. I performed a simple reverse image search on his main profile photo — and the results were shocking. The image belonged to a real-life politician from an entirely different European country. The entire persona, complete with fabricated details and stolen photos, was completely made up.

I carefully presented the evidence to her: side-by-side comparisons, the original source of the photo, and additional red flags I uncovered. Thankfully, she came to her senses and realized the deception before sending any money, personal details, or intimate photos. She immediately cut off contact and avoided what could have been a devastating financial and emotional loss.

Her story is far from unique. Romance scams, also known as confidence or "pig butchering" scams in their more sophisticated forms, continue to devastate victims worldwide. According to the FBI's 2025 Internet Crime Complaint Center (IC3) Annual Report[3], Americans reported losing $929 million to Confidence/Romance scams in 2025 alone — a significant increase from previous years. Many victims suffer losses well into the thousands of dollars, with

---

3 https://www.ic3.gov/AnnualReport/Reports/2025_IC3Report.pdf

some losing life savings, retirement funds, or even taking on debt after being emotionally manipulated over months. Scammers often build deep trust through consistent communication, feigned vulnerability, and promises of love or partnership, only to later invent emergencies, investment opportunities, or travel needs that require urgent financial help.

In the physical world, we rely on all our senses — sight, hearing, smell, touch, and even taste — to detect danger as it approaches. We can read body language, sense tension in the air, or notice something that simply feels wrong. In the digital world, however, those senses are largely stripped away. There is no smell, no touch, and no taste — only pixels on a screen, words in a chat, or a voice that may not belong to a real person. Without these natural warning systems, we must depend entirely on our wit, critical thinking, and that inner "sixth sense" — the instinctive feeling that something is not quite right — to avoid traps and stay safe.

Modern romance scammers understand this vulnerability and exploit it masterfully. They leverage advanced tools such as AI-generated conversations, deepfake images and videos, voice cloning, and emotionally scripted interactions to create deceptions that feel remarkably authentic. Operating from anywhere in the world, they hide behind fake profiles on dating apps, social media platforms, messaging services, and email. Predators no longer need to be physically near their targets. They can strike from halfway across the country or on the opposite side of the globe, using these technologies to build false intimacy and then exploit it without mercy. What once betrayed scammers through poor grammar or inconsistent stories can now appear polished, caring, and eerily human, steadily eroding the traditional red flags that once helped people stay alert.

Scammers are particularly skilled at sensing and targeting moments when people are most emotionally fragile. They often strike when someone is intoxicated, lonely, heartbroken, or emotionally devastated — precisely the times when judgment is impaired and the desire for connection or comfort overrides caution. In these vulnerable states, individuals are far more likely to lower their guard, share personal details, send money, or make impulsive decisions without proper thinking. What begins as a comforting late-night conversation can quickly escalate into requests for financial help, "emergency" transfers, or the sharing of sensitive information. The consequences can be irreversible: drained bank accounts, compromised identities, destroyed credit, or profound emotional trauma that lingers long after the scammer disappears. This is why maintaining strict situational awareness is especially critical during times of emotional distress or intoxication. If you are feeling overwhelmed, heartbroken, or under the influence, the wisest choice is often to step away from online communication entirely — at least until you are clear-headed and emotionally grounded. In those fragile moments, your "sixth sense" is easiest to silence, and scammers know exactly how to take advantage of that temporary weakness.

Everyday people can protect themselves by consciously extending the same principles of situational awareness from the physical world into their digital lives. This means slowing down, questioning everything, and verifying claims before acting. Never click on suspicious links or open attachments, even if they seem to come from a friend or a familiar company. Always verify any request for personal or financial information through an independent channel, such as a phone call to a known number. Be extremely cautious about sharing your location, daily routines, vacation plans, or photos that reveal where you live or when you are away from home, as criminals often use this information to plan burglaries or targeted attacks. Use strong, unique passwords for every account and enable two-factor or multi-factor authentication wherever possible. Regularly review your bank statements, credit reports, and privacy settings on social media. Teach your children and family members not to accept friend requests from strangers or share intimate details and locations online. Most importantly, if something feels "off" — whether it is an urgent request for money, a sudden emergency story, a message designed to create panic, or an offer that seems too good to be true — pause, verify independently, and trust your instincts.

One careless click or overshare can open the door to fraud, identity theft, ransomware, cyberstalking, or financial ruin just as easily as leaving your front door unlocked in a dangerous neighborhood. By deliberately applying situational awareness online — relying on sharp judgment and that sixth sense when your other senses cannot help you — you close the digital door on many threats and dramatically reduce your risk of becoming a victim. In today's interconnected world, staying safe means being just as vigilant behind a keyboard or smartphone screen as you would be walking down a dark street. If it feels wrong, it probably is. Trust that instinct and protect yourself accordingly.

These seemingly simple actions — practiced consistently in both the physical and digital realms — compound into a powerful, layered defense. By deliberately denying the third side of the crime triangle in every environment, you make it far more difficult for motivated offenders to succeed against you or your loved ones. In today's world, where the physical and digital realms have merged more deeply than ever before, situational awareness is no longer confined to one sphere. As artificial intelligence becomes increasingly advanced, the lines between online and offline life continue to blur: deepfakes appear in video calls, AI voices mimic loved ones, and a single careless click on your phone can expose your physical home, finances, and family to global threats. Everyday people like you and me can dramatically lower our risk of victimization by adopting these habits across both worlds — no special training or expensive equipment required, just consistent, mindful awareness practiced one day at a time.

Situational awareness must evolve from a conscious effort into an autonomous habit — something that operates quietly in the background of your daily life, much like breathing or checking for traffic before crossing the street. When it becomes second nature, you no longer have to remind yourself to scan your surroundings or question a suspicious message; your mind does it instinctively. This automatic vigilance is especially crucial in our blended physical-digital reality, where threats can shift instantly from a stranger on the sidewalk to a sophisticated AI-powered scam in your inbox. Building this habit requires repetition and intention at first, but once ingrained, it provides constant, reliable protection without draining your mental energy. The earlier you commit to making situational awareness an unconscious reflex, the safer and more confident you will feel navigating both worlds.

In conclusion, situational awareness serves as the ultimate bridge between the physical and digital realms, acting as a constant, quiet guardian of your safety. By fully engaging your senses—from the keen vigilance of your eyes to the honed intuition of your "sixth sense"—you effectively dismantle the crime triangle by removing the critical element of opportunity. Whether you are navigating a dimly lit parking structure or vetting a suspicious email, the goal is to transition from a passive participant into an active protector, empowering your family to move through the world with the confidence of the truly prepared.

Start small today. The next time you step outside or reach for your phone, take a deliberate breath, lift your head, and actively scan your surroundings. By practicing this unified approach, these protective measures will eventually become a natural reflex, granting you the peace of mind that comes from knowing you are doing everything within your power to protect what matters most.

Chapter 3

Trust: A Dangerous Weakness

I'm a firm believer that the people capable of causing you the most profound damage—both financially and romantically—are almost always the ones who occupy your inner circle. Trust is a luxury that, if left unchecked, becomes a dangerous illusion of comfort, blinding you to the red flags your instincts are desperately trying to wave. In the financial world, blind trust often serves as a smokescreen for exploitation; however, the sting is even more piercing when that betrayal enters your personal sanctuary. Consider the devastating scenario of a best friend who betrays your confidence to engage in an affair with your spouse. This is a cold realization of the "two-way street" of betrayal: while a friend may initiate the hurt, a spouse is a willing participant in the destruction of your trust. In one swift stroke, the two people you relied on most for emotional and social security have collaborated to dismantle your peace. To save your sanity, you must recognize that total, unquestioning trust can be a form of mental vulnerability. Protecting yourself doesn't mean living in a state of constant suspicion, but rather maintaining enough psychological distance to see people as they truly are, not just as you wish them to be. By tempering your heart with a layer of objective awareness, you ensure that your instinctual "internal radar" stays sharp enough to detect the subtle shifts in behavior that precede a betrayal, whether that threat is aimed at your bank account or your home.

This shift in perspective is often necessary because the victims who suffer the most are rarely the ones who saw it coming; they are the ones who felt the most secure. Looking back on my years walking beats and responding to calls, I've sat across from countless people who said, "I never thought this could happen to me," or "I trusted them completely." When we trust someone, we instinctively exhale. We stop watching and we stop questioning, and that moment of relaxation is often exactly when we become someone's opportunity. It is a pattern I've seen play out in neighborhoods where "everyone knows everyone," and even in my own life when I foolishly followed a stock analyst's advice without a single question, assuming their credentials equaled sound counsel. It cost me real money and a painful lesson. You might want to consider asking yourself occasionally, even with those you feel most comfortable around, whether that comfort is based on current evidence or simply on long-term familiarity.

Part of the challenge is that genuine trust is often easily manufactured by those with a motive to deceive. However, some individuals possess natural traits—warmth, humor, and a disarming presence—that allow them to bypass the defenses of even the most cautious people. In my experience, some of the most dangerous individuals are also the most charming, and I can attest to this through firsthand experience. During my four years as a detective in a Sexual Assault Investigation Unit (SAIU), I conducted countless interviews and interrogations of alleged child molesters. A chilling commonality among them was that they were almost universally charming, warm, and appeared inherently trustworthy. These individuals not only successfully gained the trust of their intended victims, but they also fooled the victims' parents and legal guardians with their natural, disarming characters. They didn't look like monsters; they looked like the kind of people you would want as neighbors or friends. They utilized these positive characteristics to groom the entire family unit, systematically building a sense of security before exploiting it.

This predatory charm is so effective because many manipulators understand the nuances of human nature better than most—their very survival and success depend on an ability to mirror your language and make you feel uniquely valued. While they are busy making you feel "seen," they are actually mapping out your psychological and emotional vulnerabilities. I fell for a version of this myself with financial analysts whose polished speeches and supposedly proven records convinced me I was in good hands. I felt a profound sense of reassurance that, in hindsight, was entirely manufactured to keep me from conducting the comprehensive research needed to answer the difficult questions I already had. By creating an atmosphere of unearned comfort, they effectively silenced my internal alarm system, allowing my desire for security to override my need for due diligence.

To protect your sanity and your assets, it is helpful to consciously look beyond the initial presentation. You might consider making it a habit to ask for independent references, verify track records, and pay close attention if trust is being offered to you too quickly or too intensely. Real trustworthiness is like a slow-growing tree; it reveals itself over time through consistency and actions. It isn't a gift that can be handed to you upfront in a single, charming encounter.

This "betrayal blind spot" is a human reality because the mind genuinely resists the idea that someone we love could mean us harm. We explain away warning signs and tell ourselves we are overreacting, essentially turning our loyalty into a wall between us and the truth. I did something similar with my investment losses—even after early signs appeared, I held on, telling myself the analyst knew better than I did and they had a professional reputation to keep. That loyalty to someone I hadn't truly vetted cost me more than the initial loss. You might want to gently practice what I think of as honest observation—allowing yourself to see a person's behavior clearly, without the filter of affection distorting what is right in front of you.

When we decide someone is "safe," our internal threat detection system effectively goes to sleep. We stop gathering new data and stop noticing inconsistencies. I have spoken with many people who, looking back, could identify dozens of moments where something felt slightly off, but they dismissed those feelings as irrationality. That instinct they silenced was trying to protect them. I silenced my own instincts when investing, telling myself that my discomfort was just a lack of knowledge. In truth, unease is useful data. You might consider making a quiet habit of observing people even after you have grown comfortable with them, because trustworthy people remain consistent—and inconsistency is one of the most honest signals you will ever receive.

We often have to fight against our own social conditioning to maintain this awareness. From childhood, many of us are taught that skepticism is unkind or that following our instincts is the same as being paranoid. I watched that conditioning harms good, decent people who had never been given permission to trust their own discomfort. The investment world has its own version of this—a culture that makes everyday people feel foolish for questioning experts. You might want to quietly give yourself permission to ask questions without apology and to understand that any person or system that discourages your questions is telling you something very important about itself.

It is worth noting that every predator or con artist I encountered throughout my career always took the time to build trust first. This "grooming" or rapport-building is a deliberate strategy designed to get you to lower your guard. Some of these processes take months or even years, because a predator knows that deep trust, once established, is extraordinarily difficult to break even with evidence. I think about the trust I placed in that analyst simply because he remembered my name and made me feel valued. It was a technique, not a relationship. You might want to pay particular attention to anyone who seems unusually invested in earning your trust early on, as genuine people tend to let trust develop naturally.

This need for verification has only increased in our digital age, where the distance of a screen makes it far too easy to trust profile pictures or polished personas that cannot be verified at a glance. I have seen this manifest in the most heartbreaking ways with seniors and lonely individuals who fall prey to online romance scammers. These predators spend months manufacturing a deep, emotional connection, only to eventually drain their victims of massive life savings under the guise of a shared future or a sudden, fabricated crisis. In these cases, the victims aren't just losing money; they are losing the security they spent a lifetime building, all based on a relationship that was entirely constructed.

You might want to develop a simple habit of verifying the identity of anyone you meet in a digital space before allowing an emotional or financial tie to take root. Protecting your personal information and your heart from these "manufactured" realities is a vital form of protecting your sanity. In a world where your data and your vulnerability are currencies others are eager to spend, independent verification is your most reliable defense.

The urgency of this caution is reflected in recent events, as the following cases from 2025 and 2026 highlight the staggering financial and emotional toll of romance scams.

These instances demonstrate that predators often target the most vulnerable—the widowed, the lonely, and the elderly—to dismantle their life savings. I encourage you to search the internet using keywords like "international romance fraud indictment," "senior citizen romance scam losses," or "pig butchering scam tactics" to understand the sophisticated methods used to weaponize human emotion. The following scenarios represent real-world cases:

Case 1: The Professional Platform Deception

• Synopsis: A woman in her 60s lost her entire life savings—totaling $800,000—after meeting an individual on a professional networking site who claimed to be a high-level executive in the energy sector. Over the course of nearly a year, the scammer manufactured a deep emotional bond, discussing marriage and a future together. He eventually claimed he was "wrongfully imprisoned" abroad and required urgent legal funds.

• Adjudication: While the specific suspect in this case fled jurisdiction, related members of the fraud ring were arrested and faced charges across multiple regions for similar predatory behavior.

Case 2: The International Fraud Syndicate

• Synopsis: A 63-year-old man was indicted for orchestrating an international scheme that defrauded elderly victims across the country. The group created fake online personas to "woo" victims before directing them to wire millions of dollars into bank accounts held under the names of shell companies.

• Adjudication: The individual was arrested in early 2026 and faced federal charges of wire fraud and conspiracy. The maximum penalty for such charges can reach up to 20 years in prison per count.

Case 3: The Dating App Manipulation

• Synopsis: A predator targeted vulnerable individuals on popular dating apps, creating a false identity to seek a relationship. In reality, he was living a double life and manipulated multiple victims into sending him tens of thousands of dollars for "living costs" and "travel expenses," with absolutely no intention of repayment.

• Adjudication: The individual pleaded guilty to multiple counts of fraud by false representation and was sentenced to three years in prison in early 2026.

Case 4: The Fatal Betrayal

• Synopsis: A sophisticated group targeted senior citizens nationwide, grooming them through romantic pretenses before draining their bank accounts. One victim was so distraught by the total financial loss and the psychological betrayal of the "relationship" that the stress tragically resulted in their death.

• Adjudication: In late 2025, three members of the criminal ring were sentenced to over 20 years in federal prison for their roles in the conspiracy and the resulting fatality.

Case 5: The Widow's Financial Liquidation

• Synopsis: A widow was targeted shortly after the death of her husband by a predator who used her grief to build a "safe haven" of trust. Once the emotional perimeter was breached, the scammer fabricated a series of financial emergencies that coerced the victim into liquidating her assets and even losing her home.

• Adjudication: While the investigation into the specific perpetrator remains open, the victim's testimony was used by federal authorities to launch a national public awareness campaign to combat the growing epidemic of elder fraud.

As these cases make painfully clear, the cost of misplaced trust is rarely limited to the initial financial loss; it carries a heavy psychological weight of self-doubt and shame that can haunt a person for decades. When the news cycle moves on, the victims are left to navigate a fractured sense of reality, often struggling to ever trust their own judgment again.

I share these reflections and these tragic accounts to suggest that a little thoughtful caution beforehand is a far smaller burden than the long, agonizing recovery that follows a serious betrayal. Ultimately, the effort required to verify, question, and pause is nothing compared to the monumental effort of rebuilding a life after your trust has been weaponized against you.

Ultimately, I'm not suggesting you go through life suspicious of everyone—that is no way to live. Instead, think of trust not as a light switch that is fully on or off, but as something you extend in small increments based on what you actually observe over time. Trustworthy people welcome questions and do not ask you to ignore your red flags. After my own financial losses, I made a quiet promise to verify before I trust and to listen to my instincts before I dismiss them. You might want to consider doing the same in whatever area of your life feels most relevant. Watch behavior over time rather than accepting words at face value, and please be gentle with yourself if trust has already cost you something—that lesson, as painful as it is, now belongs to you.

One of the most consistent errors I watched people make — civilians, colleagues, and honestly myself included — was the silent assumption that a title, credential, or institutional affiliation is the same thing as trustworthy character. It is not, and I cannot say that plainly enough. A badge tells you someone passed a background check and an academy. A medical license tells you someone completed a course of study. A Series 7 tells you a broker passed a regulatory exam. None of those documents tells you a single thing about what that person will do when your money is on the table and no one is watching. I learned this the hard way as a retail investor, sitting across from a polished financial advisor whose office wall was covered in framed certifications and whose handshake was firm and whose recommendations cost me a significant portion of what I had saved. He was credentialed, well-reviewed, and entirely focused on his own commissions. The credentials were real. The fiduciary duty I assumed came with them was not. I had also seen it from the other side of a badge — officers who abused their authority, detectives who cut corners, supervisors who protected their rank above the people they were supposed to serve. The uniform did not make them trustworthy. It made them appear trustworthy, which is a very different thing. Any system, institution, or professional designation can be used as a prop in the same way a charming personality can — to lower your guard before the real transaction begins. You might want to make a habit of separating the credential from the person and quietly evaluating both, because the title on the door has never once stopped anyone from making a bad choice behind it.

Long before your conscious mind forms a coherent argument for concern, your body is often already filing a complaint — and after enough years conducting interrogations and sitting across from victims in small rooms, I came to respect that physical intelligence more than almost any other investigative tool available to me. A reluctance to return a phone call you can't quite explain. A tightening in the chest before you sign something that looks fine on paper. A poor night's sleep after a conversation that seemed pleasant on the surface. These are not signs of weakness or irrationality. They are your nervous system processing information that your logical mind has not yet organized into words. During interviews, victims would regularly tell me some version of the same thing: "I knew something was wrong, I just couldn't put my finger on it." They had felt it in their bodies weeks or months before the evidence caught up. I experienced it as an investor — a vague, persistent discomfort about a position I was holding that I kept talking myself out of by deferring to the analyst's expertise. That discomfort was not anxiety. It was data. I simply chose not to file it properly. You might want to start treating physical unease as a signal worth recording rather than a feeling worth suppressing. When your gut fires a quiet alarm, consider writing it down — the date, the situation, what you noticed physically. Over time, you may look back and find that your body was consistently accurate long before any concrete evidence arrived. Your instincts are not infallible, but they are not random either, and they deserve a hearing before you dismiss them in favor of someone else's confidence.

What rarely gets discussed after a serious betrayal — and what I watched quietly devastate people long after the initial damage was done — is what that experience does to a person's capacity to trust going forward. The wound does not heal cleanly. In my experience, victims tend to break in one of two directions, and both of them carry their own danger. The first is total withdrawal — an emotional fortress so thoroughly sealed that no one gets close enough to cause harm, but no one gets close enough to help either. I have spoken with fraud victims who stopped opening bank statements, stopped answering calls from financial institutions, stopped engaging with any system that reminded them of how they were hurt. That kind of shutdown does not protect you; it simply makes you invisible to both predators and legitimate support alike. The second pattern is in many ways more dangerous: the emotionally hungry overcorrection, where the need for connection that was weaponized during the betrayal doesn't disappear — it intensifies. Loneliness and shame are powerful conditions, and I watched predators find people in that exact state and move quickly. I have seen victims of romance fraud fall into a second scheme within a year of the first, because the vulnerability that was exploited originally had not been examined — it had simply been amplified by the hurt. As a cop, I saw this cycle repeat itself in domestic situations and financial fraud cases more times than I can count. As an investor, I felt a quieter version of it — after losing money on a bad recommendation, I became briefly susceptible to the next confident voice that promised to recover my losses, which is precisely when I needed to slow down the most. If you have been badly betrayed, you might want to resist the urge to simply wait for time to pass. Understanding what made you vulnerable in the first place — with honesty and without self-blame — is not a luxury. It may be the most important protective work you ever do.

One of the most valuable things you can do with the hard-won awareness this chapter is trying to build is to share it — not as a lecture, and not in a way that frightens, but in a way that quietly prepares the people around you who are most at risk. In my years in law enforcement and in the years since, the victims who haunted me most were not strangers. They were people whose families had no idea the danger was there until it was far too late to do anything useful about it. An aging parent living alone, recently widowed and newly active on social media. A teenager navigating online friendships with the full emotional intensity of that age and none of the pattern recognition that only comes from experience. A recently divorced sibling who is just beginning to meet people again and whose need to believe in a new chapter makes them generous with trust in ways they wouldn't normally be. Talking to an elderly parent about romance scams is genuinely uncomfortable — it can feel patronizing, and they may resist any implication that they are susceptible. But I can tell you, as someone who has sat with victims after the fact, that the discomfort of that conversation is a fraction of what you will carry if you don't have it. Approach it not as a warning but as shared intelligence: "I've been reading about something that's affecting a lot of people right now, and I want us both to know what to watch for." With teenagers, the framing is different but the urgency is the same — online relationships accelerate emotional investment faster than any verification can keep pace with, and the social pressure not to seem suspicious of someone you like can override every instinct a young person has. Giving the people you love explicit permission to slow down, to ask questions, to come to you without shame if something feels off — that conversation may be one of the most lasting acts of protection you can offer anyone.

Detection, as critical as it is, only gets you halfway there. Knowing what to do once you suspect something is wrong is a practical skill most people have never been given — and in its absence, I have watched people stay trapped in harmful financial arrangements and damaging personal situations far longer than they should have, simply because they did not know how to move without making things worse. The most important thing I can tell you, drawing on both my time in law enforcement and my own experience as an investor who had to extract himself from a bad advisory relationship, is this: do not confront a suspected predator until you are ready. A person who has been deliberately building your trust over months or years will have a prepared answer for every question you raise, and a premature confrontation gives them the opportunity to adjust their position, move assets, cover their tracks, or redouble their emotional pressure before you have gathered any real clarity. What I would suggest instead is that you begin creating quiet distance — slow down any financial transactions, become less available, reduce the personal information you share going forward — without offering any explanation that signals what you are thinking. At the same time, begin gathering documentation calmly and methodically: bank records, written communications, transaction histories, anything that establishes a timeline. If the relationship is professional, consult an attorney or an independent advisor before you make any visible move. If it is personal and you have any concern about how the other person might respond to being confronted, speak to a victim's advocate or a trusted law enforcement contact first. Most predators — financial and personal alike — are counting on three things: your reluctance to make a scene, your fear of being wrong about someone you care about, and your emotional attachment to the version of them you believed in. Exiting quietly and deliberately, rather than dramatically and without a plan, is how you protect what is left without giving them one final advantage on the way out.

In light of these staggering realities, I have often found that the most important protective work I do isn't out on the street or in an interrogation room, but at my own dinner table. I have frequently sat my daughters and my wife down to remind them to be exceptionally cautious with the people they allow into their lives. I tell them plainly that when someone is being "too nice," it is rarely a random act of grace; they are being nice for a reason, and too often, that reason carries a hidden, malicious intent. It is a difficult conversation to have, and quite frankly, it hasn't always been well-received. In fact, my wife rolled her eyes on a number of occasions to express her disagreement. I tell her that she can extend trust if she prefers, but must verify and then verify again. When I was a rookie fresh out of the police academy, a senior officer told me something that has stayed with me forever: "Believe half of what you see and none of what you hear." Looking back on twenty eight years of experience, I couldn't agree with him more. It is a philosophy that doesn't dampen a loved one's spirit so much as it arms them against those who would use their kindness as a handle to grab.

This need for vigilance is why we must be especially wary of "The Familiarity Trap," a burden I try to help my family avoid by encouraging them to evaluate people based on their present actions, not just their past history. My insistence on this often fuels the "paranoid" label my family gives me, but the logic is sound: the longer you have known someone, the more invisible credit you silently extend to them. Ten years of shared history can purchase a person dozens of free passes on behavior that would have stopped you cold coming from a stranger. I saw it in financial crimes where the most devastating losses weren't caused by unknown fraudsters but by the trusted bookkeeper or the childhood friend. Familiarity is a comfort, but you must check, every so often, whether the trust you are extending today is based on who a person is right now or simply on the accumulated weight of who they used to be. Don't let a long history blind you to a new reality that requires you to verify.

Furthermore, we must extend this scrutiny to the silent assumption that a title, credential, or institutional affiliation is a substitute for character. It is not. A badge, a medical license, or a financial certification tells you someone passed a test; it tells you nothing about what they will do when your money is on the table and no one is watching. I learned this the hard way as a retail investor with a polished advisor whose office wall was covered in framed certifications but whose heart was focused only on his own commissions. Any professional designation can be used as a prop to lower your guard. You might want to make a habit of separating the credential from the human being and quietly evaluating both, because a title on the door has never once stopped a bad choice from being made behind it.

In addition to this objective evaluation, you must learn to listen to your own biology, because long before your conscious mind forms a coherent argument for concern, your body is often already filing a complaint. A reluctance to return a phone call, a tightening in the chest, or a poor night's sleep after a "pleasant" conversation are not signs of "paranoia"—they are your nervous system processing data. In my years conducting interrogations, victims regularly told me, “I knew something was wrong, I just couldn’t put my finger on it.” They had felt it in their bodies weeks before the evidence caught up. You might want to start treating physical unease as a signal worth recording rather than a feeling worth suppressing. Your instincts are not random; they deserve a hearing before you dismiss them in favor of someone else’s confidence.

This is critical because, beyond the immediate incident, we must also consider what a serious betrayal does to a person’s capacity to trust going forward. The wound rarely heals cleanly. Victims often retreat into an emotional fortress where no one can hurt them, but no one can help them either. Even more dangerous is the "emotionally hungry" overcorrection, where the need for connection is amplified by the hurt, making the person even more susceptible to the next predator. I have seen romance fraud victims fall into a second scheme within a year for this very reason. If you have been badly betrayed, resist the urge to simply wait for time to pass. Understanding what made you vulnerable—with honesty and without self-blame—is perhaps the most important protective work you will ever do. Such a process requires you to revisit that difficult rule: trust is earned, but safety is maintained by those who verify and verify again.

Ultimately, the most valuable thing you can do with this hard-won awareness is to share it—not as a lecture, but as a quiet preparation for those you love. Talking to an aging parent or a teenager about these risks is genuinely uncomfortable, but that discomfort is a fraction of what you will carry if you remain silent. My reminders to my wife and daughters about the "reason" behind someone's sudden kindness aren't meant to make them fearful, but to make them formidable. Knowing how to detect a threat is half the battle; the other half is knowing how to exit quietly and deliberately if a suspicion arises. By teaching the people you love to ask questions, to verify before they commit, and to come to you without shame if something feels off, you are offering them a lasting form of protection that no predator can easily dismantle.

In the end, the most sobering lesson twenty eight years of law enforcement has taught me is that the greatest threats to our security rarely arrive with a snarl; they arrive with a smile. Whether it is a charming new acquaintance, a credentialed professional, or a "familiar" face we have known for a decade, the mechanism of betrayal is always the same: it requires the dismantling of your natural defenses through the manufacture of trust. Trust, in its purest form, is a beautiful thing, but in a world where predators use kindness as a tool and charm as a mask, it is a luxury that requires a secondary safety—verification.

Protecting your finances and your family doesn't require you to live in a state of constant, suffocating fear. Instead, it requires you to shift your perspective from blind faith to objective awareness. It means recognizing that a title is not a character reference, that a long history is not a guarantee of future integrity, and that your body's quiet "gut feelings" are often the most accurate data points you possess. As I tell my wife and daughters, staying vigilant doesn't make you cynical; it makes you formidable.

We owe it to ourselves, and to those we love, to move through the world with our eyes wide open. By extending trust in small, earned increments and maintaining the discipline to "verify and verify again," you ensure that your inner circle remains a true sanctuary rather than a target. The effort of asking the hard questions today is a small price to pay to avoid the monumental burden of rebuilding a life tomorrow. Remember the words of that senior officer: believe half of what you see and none of what you hear. It isn't just a rule for rookies—it is a blueprint for a secure life.

Chapter 4

Protecting You from Yourself

Let's be honest: most of us are our own most relentless adversaries. We act as judge, jury, and executioner in the courtroom of our own minds, often showing ourselves far less grace than we would offer a total stranger. We are perpetually hyper-critical, fixating on the echoes of past mistakes and the persistent flaws we can't seem to shake. This internal "slow-burn" of self-judgment doesn't just lower our morale; it erodes the very confidence we need to actually address and rectify those imperfections.

In my line of work, I've seen that the most dangerous lack of situational awareness is the one directed inward. When you are blinded by self-loathing or stuck in a loop of past failures, you lose the tactical clarity needed to navigate the present. Acknowledging your flaws is a critical step in "peeling the onion" of your own character, but there is a distinct difference between objective self-analysis and destructive self-sabotage. To grow, you have to stop being the aggressor in your own head. You must learn to view your mistakes not as permanent stains, but as forensic data—lessons that inform your future movements so you don't trip over the same stone twice. After all, you cannot successfully defend your personal safety from external threats if you are busy dismantling it from within.

As human beings, we are wired with a wide range of emotions, but two of the most volatile and potentially destructive are anger and hatred. These emotions are part of our biological hard-wiring—remnants of ancient survival mechanisms designed to protect us from threats. However, in the modern world, if these impulses are left unchecked, they quickly mutate into a toxic force. It is incumbent upon each of us to master these internal fires rather than allowing them to master us.

When anger and hatred are permitted to spiral out of control, they have a profoundly detrimental impact; they cloud our judgment, dissolve our logic, and poison our most precious relationships. Throughout my career in the field, I've seen that an uncontrolled temper is often the first "breach" in a person's character—the point where the structural integrity of their life begins to fail. To prevent this breach, you must learn to identify your own internal "smoke" before the fire takes hold. This means paying clinical attention to your physiological triggers: the sudden tightening of your chest, the clenching of your jaw, or the "tunnel vision" that narrows your focus until you can only see the object of your rage. These are your body's tactical alerts, signaling that you are about to lose your clearance for logical thought.

I vividly recall the haunting repetition of apologies from perpetrators as I escorted them to my patrol car. Their words were almost always variations of a desperate theme: “I'm so sorry. I just lost it,” or “I screwed up big time—I didn't mean for it to go that far.” In those moments, I rarely responded to their spontaneous statements, but I could sense the heavy weight of their realization. They weren't just regretting the handcuffs or the impending legal battle; they were experiencing the gut-wrenching regret of having surrendered their self-control to a momentary flare of temper. They had allowed a few seconds of rage to dismantle years of effort, and as the iron door of the patrol car slammed shut, they finally understood that "losing it" meant losing everything.

In the heat of these moments, I advocate for a "street-level" defensive tactic: the Three-Second Rule. When you feel that physiological surge of anger, you must implement a mandatory tactical pause. Three seconds of deep, controlled breathing acts as a circuit breaker, allowing your heart rate to drop and your logical mind to re-engage before you take an action you can never take back. Learning to regulate these internal fires is not just about being a better person—it is a fundamental requirement for maintaining your own stability and safety. If you cannot govern the storm within, you will never be able to navigate the challenges waiting for you outside.

To effectively protect yourself from within, you must Identify the primary fuel source for anger and hatred: the Ego. In the field, I've seen the ego act as a catastrophic "security breach." It is the invisible force that whispers that you cannot "lose face," that you must have the last word, or that you must prove you are right at all costs.

In tactical terms, an unchecked ego prevents you from executing a strategic retreat. Whether you are in a heated argument on the street or holding a losing stock, the ego is what keeps you anchored to a sinking ship. It forces you to stay in a "losing trade" long after the objective data has signaled a total failure.

I've processed countless individuals who ended up in the back of my patrol car simply because their pride wouldn't allow them to walk away from a trivial insult. They viewed "backing down" as a sign of weakness, failing to realize that the true weakness was their inability to govern their own self-importance. In the legal and financial worlds, the "indifferent auditor" doesn't care about your pride; it only cares about the damage you cause while trying to protect it. To stay safe, you must learn to kill your ego before it kills your future.

As a retail investor navigating the stock market for over three decades, I have spent countless hours battling the internal storm that inevitably follows a bad trade. Whether it was the sting of losing thousands of dollars or the hollow ache of missing out on a massive run-up, the psychological toll was often heavier than the financial one. I found myself consumed by a blistering anger, directed squarely at my own failure to identify the structural weaknesses of certain stocks before the trap was sprung.

In those moments, the market feels less like a financial system and more like a personal adversary. I would obsess over the details I missed—the subtle red flags in a balance sheet or the shifting industry trends—only to have my oversight confirmed when the negative news finally hit the newswire. Seeing a stock plummet and pull my account down with it felt like watching a slow-motion collision I should have been able to avoid.

During these periods of volatility, I had to fight to tame the storms within me just to maintain the clarity needed for my next move. I found myself at a critical crossroads, forced to decide whether to hold the position, cut my losses and sell, or double down to "cost average" in a desperate hope to recover. The pressure was immense; I knew that a follow-up mistake in such a compromised state could trigger a serious financial crisis. Yet, on a number of occasions throughout my years of trading, that exact scenario played out. In essence, I failed to control my emotions—more specifically, my anger—and made successive mistakes on the same stocks that affected my financial safety significantly. Those were the days when I was young and reckless, and as a result, I got destroyed.

Through the lens of a long-time retail investor, I've realized that the "stock market storm" is the ultimate test of emotional regulation. The market is a cold, indifferent machine; it has no regard for your feelings, your ego, or your past successes. In the moments when I allowed anger or self-loathing to dictate my next move, I ceased to be a disciplined investor. Instead, I became an emotional "jumper," reacting to the adrenaline of a crisis rather than the objective reality of the charts.

I've had to learn that a bad trade is not a personal indictment; it is simply market feedback. To survive for thirty years in this game, you must develop a level of tactical detachment. You have to analyze the "crime scene" of a failed trade with clinical objectivity to understand why your strategy failed, then dispassionately apply those lessons to your next position. If you let the hatred of a loss or the regret of a missed opportunity fester, you aren't just losing capital—you're losing the situational awareness required to spot the next big win. Controlling the storm within is the only way to ensure you have a clear, unobstructed view of the horizon.

By the same token, the law is equally indifferent to how or why you lost control of your anger. The legal system doesn't grant passes for "temporary lapses" in judgment. If the probable cause for a crime is present, you will be arrested, and your future will be handed over to the District Attorney's Office to decide whether or not to file formal charges. If they proceed, you will find yourself on a long, grueling ride through the gears of the justice system—a journey that may very well end with you sitting behind bars, reflecting on the irreversible actions you took in a few seconds of uncontrolled rage. Just as a reckless trade can destroy a portfolio, an emotional outburst can dismantle a life; in both worlds, the consequences don't care about your intentions—only your actions.

Needless to say, I am neither a psychologist nor a trained specialist in human behavior. I am simply a man who has spent decades on the front lines of law enforcement, sharing the street-level wisdom I've gathered throughout my career.

My insights aren't derived from textbooks, but from witnessing the raw, unfiltered consequences of human choices.

For that reason, I encourage you to take my words with a grain of salt. While I can offer you a tactical perspective based on thousands of real-world cases, it is ultimately up to you to navigate your own internal landscape. You are the only one who can decide how to manage your emotions and regulate your impulses to ensure you don't fall deeper into self-destruction. In the end, learning to master the "storm within" is your most vital defensive maneuver. It is the only way to protect yourself from making the kind of irreversible mistakes that lead straight into the iron jaws of justice—a system that is indifferent to your excuses and unyielding in its judgment.

In order to protect your dignity, your freedom, and your future, you must master the discipline of emotional regulation. You have to take definitive, proactive measures to prevent a flash of temper from leading you down a path of total destruction. I will be the first to admit that I have never participated in an anger management class myself, so I cannot speak to the specifics of the curriculum. However, my decades in law enforcement have shown me exactly what happens when that education is missing. If you find yourself unable to curb your impulses or if you feel your temper beginning to override your logic, a professional course is an investment you should consider long before a crisis forces your hand.

Ultimately, you are the key person in this equation. You are the only one who can objectively assess your internal warning signs and decide to seek coaching in anger management now—while it is still a choice. It is far better to voluntarily refine your character today than to wait until the law mandates it as a condition of your probation or as a requirement for your release. Don't wait for a judge to tell you that your temper is a problem; by then, the "iron jaws of justice" have already closed, and the damage to your reputation and freedom is already done. Take the lead in your own life before the legal system takes it for you.

While uncontrolled anger is a fast-burning fire, there is a slower, more quiet threat to your safety: the unchecked biases we carry into every interaction. As human beings, we are naturally hard-wired with a wide range of biases. These mental shortcuts are often deeply ingrained, shaped by our upbringing, our environment, and our personal experiences. One of the most dangerous of these is "Confirmation Bias"—the tendency to ignore any data that contradicts our existing prejudices while obsessively searching for information that supports them. Much like a trader who ignores a stock's failing financials because he "wants" to believe in the company, we often ignore the true character of a person because they fit our biased expectations. While many of these biases are minor—influencing small preferences or everyday opinions—others are far more significant and carry a much heavier weight.

When a bias moves from a hidden thought to an outward action, you enter a dangerous legal and social territory. If you allow a deep-seated prejudice to fester and grow, it can quickly mutate into something far more toxic. In essence, when you allow your biases to turn into hate, you have already failed yourself. You have surrendered your logic and your humanity to a destructive impulse.

If you choose to act upon that hatred, the consequences will be swift and absolute. The "wheel of justice" will turn against you with criminal and civil penalties, but the devastation doesn't stop at the courtroom door. The press will dissect your character, and the communities you live and work in will turn their backs on you. You will find yourself crushed in more ways than you can imagine—facing a total loss of reputation, livelihood, and personal freedom.

The law is an indifferent auditor; it doesn't care about your internal justifications—it only measures the legality and the impact of your conduct. To protect your future, you must have the self-awareness to identify these biases within yourself and the discipline to ensure they never manifest in your actions. Mastering your internal "blind spots" is not just a moral obligation; it is a fundamental requirement for survival in a civilized society.

As you can see, anger and hatred are undoubtedly two of your own worst enemies—clandestine predators that live within the very perimeter you are trying to protect. If left untamed, these emotions do more than just cloud your judgment; they consume your identity from the inside out, leaving you vulnerable to the reactive mistakes that lead to financial ruin or legal catastrophe.

To survive the long game—whether navigating the volatility of the markets, the unpredictability of society and the streets, or maintaining the warmth of your home and the stability of your workplace—you must view emotional regulation as a non-negotiable survival skill. These environments are the sources of your livelihood and the foundation of your happiness; allowing a momentary lapse in control to jeopardize them is a tactical failure of the highest order.

Taming these impulses is not an act of suppression, but an act of strategic defense. By mastering the "storm within," you ensure that your decisions are driven by tactical clarity rather than raw impulse. In doing so, you ultimately safeguard your freedom, your reputation, and your peace of mind from being devoured by your own internal fire.

In the landscape of recent years, we continue to see instances where a split-second loss of self-control has led to life-altering criminal consequences. These incidents serve as a sobering reminder of the "iron jaws of justice" that wait for those who allow their internal storms to dictate their actions. I encourage readers to search the internet for legal cases using keywords like "road rage shooting conviction," "aggravated battery property dispute," or "hate crime enhancement sentencing" to witness the severe reality of these outcomes. The following scenarios represent real-world cases:

Case 1: The Commuter's Breaking Point

• Synopsis: During a heavy morning commute, an individual became enraged when another driver inadvertently cut him off. Rather than utilizing a tactical pause, the individual pursued the other driver for several miles, eventually forcing him onto the shoulder. In a state of "tunnel vision," the individual exited his vehicle and fired into the other driver's car, narrowly missing the person but shattering the window.

• Adjudication: The individual was arrested at his place of employment the following morning. Despite having no prior criminal record and claiming he "snapped" due to work-related stress, he was convicted of assault with a deadly weapon and discharging a firearm into an occupied vehicle. He was sentenced to 7 years in state prison and hit with a $500,000 civil judgment for emotional distress.

Case 2: The Neighborhood Dispute

• Synopsis: A long-simmering dispute over a shared property line escalated during a weekend gathering. The offender, fueled by years of unchecked resentment, lost control when a neighbor's pet entered his yard. The offender attacked the neighbor with a heavy blunt-force gardening tool, causing a traumatic brain injury.

• Adjudication: The offender was charged with aggravated battery. While he expressed deep remorse to responding officers—stating he simply lost his temper—the law remained an indifferent auditor. He was sentenced to 12 years in prison and lost his home to pay for the victim's medical restitution.

Case 3: The Customer Service Outburst

• Synopsis: A customer became belligerent over a denied return at a retail store. When the manager refused to override store policy, the customer's anger turned into a physical attack. He produced a folding knife and lunged at the manager, wounding him before being tackled by bystanders.

• Adjudication: The incident was captured on high-definition surveillance and went viral on social media within hours. The public exposure destroyed the defendant's reputation, leading to his immediate termination from his career. He pleaded guilty to assault with a deadly weapon and is currently serving a 4-year sentence. Upon release, his status as a registered felon will effectively end his professional life.

Case 4: The Digital Escalation

• Synopsis: An individual allowed online biases to turn into genuine hatred, engaging in a weeks-long digital feud with a community leader. The offender eventually acted on this hostility, driving to the victim's home to vandalize the property with hate speech and incendiary devices.

• Adjudication: Because the crime was motivated by bias, authorities filed "Hate Crime" enhancements. The offender was convicted in both state and federal courts, resulting in a 15-year federal prison sentence without the possibility of parole.

In every one of these cases, the offender appeared to be a "normal" person—a neighbor, a commuter, a customer—until the moment they surrendered their self-control. They failed to identify the "smoke" of their own physiology, and by the time they realized they had "lost it," the iron jaws of the legal system had already clamped shut.

When your internal alarm system—your physiology—begins to signal that a breach is imminent, you must be prepared to respond. This is where your pre-determined "Red Line" becomes your most valuable asset. By deciding today that no provocation is worth your freedom, you harden your internal perimeter against the most dangerous threat you will ever face: your own impulse.

Beyond the internal fires of anger and hatred, there is another biological impulse that can be just as destructive if left unmanaged: the propensity for addiction. While some might dismiss it as a lack of willpower, behavioral specialists often classify this as an Impulse Control Disorder or a Behavioral Addiction. It functions much like a high-stakes trade—your brain becomes hooked on the "dopamine hit" of the hunt, the purchase, and the hope of a massive future payoff.

In my own life, I have stared into this "deep hole." Since my early 20s, I have been a passionate collector of sports cards, specifically autographed rookie cards. On numerous occasions, I found myself going overboard, crossing the line from a disciplined investor to an emotional "jumper." I would convince myself that I was making a sound tactical investment, only to watch as the "forensic data" of a player's career—the injuries, the benchings, the fizzled potential—turned my high-priced assets into worthless cardstock.

I have seen this addiction dismantle the perimeters of others' lives, and I had to learn to identify my own triggers before I was pulled under. Take my recent activity as an example. Last year, I invested a few hundred dollars in a Caitlin Clark rookie card—a move backed by her historic impact on the WNBA. I also sourced several Munetaka Murakami 2018 BBM #317 rookie cards from a vendor in Japan, banking on his international legendary status. Most recently, I spent $307 on a 1/1 Leaf Autographed card of Fernando Mendoza. With Mendoza being selected first overall in the 2026 NFL Draft by the Las Vegas Raiders just days ago, he has the potential to be a franchise-altering quarterback.

Whether these cards will eventually be valued as "Gold" or "Dust" by the market's indifferent auditor remains to be seen. However, I have learned to regulate the impulse. I no longer buy out of a desperate need to "hit it big"; I buy for the priceless joy of owning a piece of sports history and the tactical thrill of watching these athletes compete. The key is knowing when to stop. You must be the one to govern your own "internal house" before the financial or emotional cost forces a foreclosure you never saw coming.

I point out my own impulses to demonstrate that we all possess a propensity for addiction. Not all addictions are inherently detrimental—some can even be productive or joyful—unless you allow them to spiral out of control. However, some addictions are absolutely unacceptable and extremely counterproductive to every aspect of your personal safety.

Two of the most dangerous addictions are illicit drug use and gambling. During my years in the Patrol Division, I made it a point to go where many others wouldn't — spending time under bridges and along railroad tracks, reaching out to the homeless community. The recurring theme in their stories was almost always the same: drugs or gambling were the catalysts for their demise — though for some, homelessness stemmed from systemic challenges like mental illness or job loss entirely beyond their control. I vividly remember one gentleman who told me he was once a millionaire. He owned a successful furniture business, a home, and a beautiful family — all of it evaporated because of a gambling addiction. He didn't just lose his money; he lost every aspect of his personal safety. By the time he realized he was in a hole, it was too deep to climb out of. Identifying these toxic addictions early and cutting them out with surgical precision is the only way to ensure you don't lose everything you've spent a lifetime building.

It is imperative that you develop the self-awareness to recognize your own propensity for addiction and take immediate, precautionary measures to protect your personal safety from your own impulses. Identifying your "internal vulnerabilities" is a fundamental step in personal security; if you don't know where your defenses are weak, you cannot possibly fortify them.

However, regardless of your personal history or perceived willpower, there are certain "high-threat" activities that must be avoided entirely because of their chemically and psychologically corrosive nature. Illicit drugs and gambling are not just habits; they are systemic traps designed to hijack your brain's reward centers.

Illicit drugs, in particular, represent a total compromise of your situational awareness and physical safety. Once they take hold, they become the primary driver of your decision-making, leading you toward the "iron jaws of justice" or the physical ruin.

Similarly, the gambling industry has evolved into a sophisticated machine for financial destruction. With the surge in the popularity of Texas Hold'em poker and the gamification of mobile betting, the barrier to entry has vanished. What many mistakes for a "skill-based" hobby often mutates into a deep, inescapable hole. These addicts aren't just losing money; they are losing the time, focus, and reputation necessary to maintain a safe and stable life. For many, once the "wheel of addiction" begins to spin at full speed, they find themselves unable to dig their way out until their entire livelihood has been liquidated. In the realm of personal safety, the most effective defense against these traps is a policy of zero-entry—refusing to engage with the threat before it has the chance to breach your defenses.

Drawing from my decades in law enforcement, I wholeheartedly believe the vast majority of victims are exactly who they claim to be—individuals who have suffered immense trauma and provided investigators with the unvarnished truth. However, as a truth seeker dedicated to the facts, I must also acknowledge a darker, more tactical danger: the rare but devastating instances where an individual weaponizes the legal system by fabricating a false accusation.

While serving as a detective in the Sexual Assault Investigation Unit (SAIU), I handled two separate cases where the evidence simply didn't align with the allegations. Through meticulous investigation, I was able to collect sufficient proof—including digital footprints and witness inconsistencies—to show the allegations were fabricated. As a result, I was able to clear two in-custody defendants of all charges. These men were inches away from the "iron jaws of justice" closing on them for crimes they did not commit.

The point here is not to diminish the reality of sexual assault, but to highlight a specific vulnerability regarding your personal safety. Sexual attraction is human nature, but engaging in intimacy requires a high level of situational awareness. In a legal battle that often boils down to one person's word against another's, your freedom often hinges on the presence of objective evidence.

To safeguard your personal safety from a "reputational execution" or a wrongful conviction, you must be tactically smart about your movements. While you cannot and must not secretly audio or video record a private sexual encounter—as doing so without consent is a crime and a gross violation of trust—you should ensure that your interactions leading up to and following the encounter are captured by the "unblinking eyes" of public security cameras.

Whether at a restaurant, a hotel lobby, or a public parking garage, being captured on camera establishes the demeanor and willingness of all participants. In a police investigation, these clips are collected by the investigators and subpoenaed by the court to reconstruct the timeline. If an accusation is later made, video evidence showing mutual comfort and voluntary association before and after the encounter becomes the "silent witness" that can dismantle a false narrative. In the eyes of the law, your best defense is a well-documented reality; if you are truly innocent, these digital receipts are the tools that will protect your personal safety and set you free.

As a truth-seeker and former investigator, I have seen how false allegations can derail a life in an instant. These cases highlight why maintaining a well-documented reality—through situational awareness and digital footprints—is a non-negotiable part of your personal safety. When the "unblinking eyes" of surveillance or objective evidence are absent, the legal system can become a dangerous trap.

The following cases, representing real-world instances, illustrate the devastating impact of falsified allegations. I encourage you to search the internet using keywords like "wrongful conviction exoneration," "defamation lawsuit campus assault," or "criminal penalties for false reporting" to understand how the forensic truth eventually surfaces to dismantle these fabricated narratives.

Case 1: The Stolen Athletic Career

• Synopsis: A 16-year-old high school football standout with a full scholarship to a prestigious university was accused by a classmate of a violent assault. Facing a potential 41-year sentence, the teenager took a plea deal and served five years in prison. He lost his prime athletic years, his scholarship, and was forced to register as a sex offender based entirely on a fabricated claim.

• Adjudication: Nearly a decade later, the accuser admitted she had manufactured the story. With the assistance of a legal innocence project, the conviction was overturned. While the individual eventually achieved his goal of playing professional sports, the "prime of his life" and his reputation had been stolen by the initial false report.

Case 2: The Retracted Media Firestorm

• Synopsis: A major national magazine published an explosive article detailing a horrific gang assault at a university fraternity house. The story ignited a global firestorm regarding campus safety, leading to the vandalism of the property, death threats against members, and the immediate suspension of campus organizations.

• Adjudication: A detailed police investigation found no evidence that the assault ever occurred; in fact, the "lead perpetrator" identified by the accuser did not exist. The magazine was forced to issue a full retraction, and the accused organization later won a multi-million dollar defamation settlement against the publication for the destruction of their reputation.

Case 3: The Fabricated Campus Incident

• Synopsis: A university student accused two fellow student-athletes of a serious assault. Both students were immediately forced to leave the university, losing their scholarships and facing the "crushing" weight of public condemnation. The accuser later admitted she made up the story specifically to gain sympathy and attention from a different individual she was interested in.

• Adjudication: The accuser pleaded guilty to multiple counts of falsely reporting an incident and interfering with police. She was sentenced to one year in prison for her actions, but the professional and educational paths of the accused students had already been severely disrupted.

These accounts serve as a stark reminder that your personal safety perimeter must include a defense against "reputational breaches." By understanding the mechanics of how these false narratives are built—and eventually dismantled—you can better appreciate the necessity of transparency and documentation in your daily life. Truth is the ultimate armor, but in a world of quick judgments, you must be the primary custodian of your own factual reality.

In each of these scenarios, the defendants were saved only when the truth was dragged into the light—often through inconsistent statements or forensic evidence. To protect your personal safety, you must realize that the legal system is an "indifferent auditor." It doesn't know you are a "good person"; it only knows what can be proven.

Always ensure that your public demeanor is captured on camera during social interactions. If the "iron jaws of justice" ever begin to close based on a fabrication, those surveillance clips and digital footprints will be the primary tools used to dismantle the lie and preserve your freedom.

Ultimately, the most sophisticated security system in the world is useless if the person behind the controls is compromised by their own internal volatility. This chapter has demonstrated that personal safety is not merely about surviving a physical altercation; it is a holistic discipline that requires you to survive the persistent threats posed by your own ego, impulses, and biases. Achieving this level of security begins with self-governance, where you stop being the aggressor in your own head and start viewing past failures as forensic data rather than permanent stains. By implementing the Three-Second Rule, you create a mandatory circuit breaker for the "internal smoke" of rage, ensuring that a flash of temper never leads you into the iron jaws of justice. You must also recognize that an unchecked ego is a catastrophic security vulnerability that prevents a strategic retreat, and that the only way to stay safe is to kill your pride before it anchors you to a sinking ship.

Furthermore, protecting yourself means recognizing that addiction—whether to a reckless purchase or to drugs and gambling—is a systemic trap designed to hijack your awareness and bankrupt your future. To guard against the devastating threat of false allegations, act as a truth seeker who knows the legal system is an indifferent auditor; documenting your public movements provides the objective evidence needed to protect your freedom. Ultimately, the markets, the law, and the streets do not care about your intentions—they only measure your actions. By mastering the storm within, you ensure you are never your own adversary, but the disciplined architect of your own survival.

Chapter 5

Temptation: An Internal Threat

In the field of personal safety, we often worry about external predators, but we overlook the internal saboteur. While integrity is the engine that drives us toward our goals, temptation is the internal threat that tries to run us off the road. It is the evil twin of our integrity, pushing us to grab what we want by any means necessary, completely blind to the wreckage it leaves behind. Survival requires acknowledging that your greatest enemy isn't always at the gate; sometimes, it's the impulse sitting right behind your own eyes.

In my three decades in law enforcement, I've come to view every criminal act as a fundamental failure of the perpetrator to neutralize an internal threat. Every crime begins as a seed of temptation that is allowed to override an individual's integrity. However, it is a dangerous mistake to believe that temptation only operates within the realm of the illegal.

The reality is a treacherous spectrum of risk. At one end are the impulses that lead to overt criminal acts—clear breaches of the social contract that result in sirens and handcuffs. At the other end are choices that remain entirely legal in the eyes of a judge, yet are morally or ethically bankrupt. Then, there is the 'gray zone'—those ambiguous choices that sit right on the line.

In terms of personal safety, these 'gray area' failures are often the most insidious because they are silent. While some lapses might fall into oblivion without immediate harm, others act like a slow-moving poison. They can dismantle your reputation, erode your character, and sabotage your future just as effectively as a felony conviction.

The true danger lies in that silence. Because these internal choices don't always trigger an immediate police response, there are no sirens to warn you of the coming crash until the damage is absolute. But don't mistake silence for safety. Throughout my career, I saw tens of thousands of instances where a "silent" temptation eventually turned into a loud, life-altering disaster.

I confronted this reality daily when I was active on the force. Sometimes I responded in full uniform to investigate "gray" situations that had finally boiled over. Other times, these failures landed on my desk in the Sexual Assault Investigation Unit (SAIU). In those rooms, I saw firsthand how a small, seemingly "legal" compromise of integrity could spiral into the total destruction of lives, families, and careers. I interviewed perpetrators who had spent years building fortresses of trust, only to burn them down from the inside because they failed to police their own hearts. The sirens might be delayed, but the wreckage is very real.

To show how these internal threats manifest in real-world "gray zones" that turn into catastrophic "black zones," consider the following scenarios represent real-world imstances. They follow a hauntingly familiar pattern: a position of trust or mentorship used as a cover for a failure of internal discipline. I encourage you to search the internet using keywords such as "grooming by trusted mentors," "abuse of authority cases," or "position of trust sexual assault" to see the staggering volume of real-world examples that mirror these patterns.

Case 1: The Youth Sports Mentor

• Synopsis: A respected youth coach spent years building a "fortress of trust" with local families, positioning himself as a dedicated advocate for young athletes. He used his role as a mentor as a tactical tool for grooming, slowly isolating victims under the guise of specialized, one-on-one training sessions.

• Adjudication: The individual was convicted on multiple counts of continuous sexual abuse of a child and sentenced to 25 years to life in prison.

Case 2: The "Trusted Neighbor" Breach

• Synopsis: Mirroring the "family friend" dynamic, a neighbor became a mentor figure to a young student, helping her with school and life goals. The family viewed him as an extension of their home, allowing him to bypass their natural "perimeter" defenses and grant him unsupervised access.

• Adjudication: The individual was found guilty of sexual assault and risk of injury to a minor. He was sentenced to 20 years, with a requirement to serve a decade behind bars followed by ten years of strict probation.

Case 3: The Martial Arts Instructor Betrayal

• Synopsis: A high-level martial arts instructor used his status as a "discipline-builder" to target students. Parents trusted him specifically because his profession was rooted in the concept of safety and self-protection. This is a classic internal threat where the person hired to teach protection became the primary predator.

• Adjudication: The instructor was convicted of multiple counts of sexual assault and sentenced to 15 years in prison.

Case 4: The "Second Father" Figure

• Synopsis: A close family friend, often described as a "second father," provided financial and emotional support for years. He leveraged the family's profound gratitude and his "pillar of the community" status to silence his victim and hide his predatory behavior for a long period.

• Adjudication: The individual pleaded guilty to indecent assault and battery on a child. He was sentenced to 4 to 6 years in state prison and placed on lifetime GPS monitoring.

These cases illustrate the point perfectly: in almost every instance of catastrophic failure, the perpetrator was not a "stranger in the bushes." They were people who were already inside the perimeter. They were mentors, coaches, and trusted friends. Their downfall wasn't a lack of willpower to achieve their goals; it was a total failure to neutralize the most dangerous breach of all: Temptation as an Internal Threat.

Building on that reality, we must recognize that this internal threat is not limited to physical or predatory behavior; it frequently manifests as unrestrained greed. This is the hunger for illicit monetary gain—a "silent alarm" that begins with the smallest compromise of character. It starts on the low end of the spectrum with petty larceny or the "victimless" padding of an expense report, but if left unchecked, it escalates into systemic embezzlement.

When the internal threat is allowed to fester, the stakes grow exponentially. It evolves into high-level bribery, organized robbery, or the ultimate cold-blooded calculation: murder for a life insurance payout. In these instances, the perpetrator hasn't just committed a crime; they have completed a total internal takeover. They have allowed the desire for a "payday" to completely dismantle their humanity and their future. Whether the motive is lust or gold, the result is a total breach of the life you've worked so hard to secure.

In my experience, the only effective way to prevent falling victim to temptation is to neutralize the internal threat the moment it appears. You cannot wait until you are in the heat of the moment to decide your values; you must defeat the desire to act against your integrity as soon as it crosses your mind. This requires maintaining a "Clear Red Line"—a set of non-negotiable moral boundaries that you refuse to cross under any circumstances.

Think of this Red Line as your internal tripwire. In law enforcement, we know that once a perimeter is breached, the cost of defense goes up exponentially. The same is true for your character. If you allow yourself to "negotiate" with a small temptation, you are essentially softening your defenses for a larger one. You open a door that becomes increasingly difficult to close.

To maintain your personal safety, your moral compass must be calibrated long before the storm hits. By establishing a definitive Red Line today, you remove the volatile element of "choice" when temptation eventually strikes. You don't have to struggle with what to do in the face of greed or impulse because the decision has already been hard-coded into your integrity. Without that line, you aren't truly living in safety—you are simply waiting for your defenses to crumble.

I have spent years drilling this concept into my daughters. When they were young, I frequently reminded them: never take what is not yours. I taught them that finding money on the street isn't a "lucky break"—it is a test of character. Taking it is not just morally wrong; it is a tactical failure of empathy that actively deprives the rightful owner of the chance to recover what they lost.

A few months ago, I had the opportunity to put my own "Red Line" into practice. As I was leaving a grocery store, I noticed several twenty-dollar bills scattered on the asphalt next to an old white sedan parked in a handicap stall. Without hesitation, I gathered the cash and counted it—exactly two hundred dollars. Instead of walking away, I took up a position against the grocery store wall, maintaining a line of sight on the vehicle. I waited.

Approximately ten minutes later, an elderly man approached the car, his face clouded with anxiety as he frantically patted his pockets. When he reached the door, I stepped forward and asked what he was looking for. With visible distress, he explained that he had lost the money he intended to send home to his relatives in Vietnam. Once he confirmed the exact amount, I returned the cash. The relief on his face was all the confirmation I needed.

I shared this incident with my family not to boast, but to reinforce a cold reality: Integrity isn't a theoretical concept. Had I allowed the "internal threat" of greed to override my Red Line, a family thousands of miles away might have missed the funds they needed to survive.

I also reminded my daughters of a very modern danger. In today's society, "social experiments" are a staple of digital content. YouTubers and influencers are constantly filming in public, waiting for someone to fail a test of character for the sake of viral content. I told them plainly: imagine the life-altering embarrassment of keeping that money, only to have your lapse in integrity broadcast to the entire world. In a world of ubiquitous cameras, a "private" choice can become a public execution of your reputation in seconds.

We re-emphasized our family's standing orders: our moral compass is non-negotiable. We do not take what is not rightfully ours. There is no room for debate, no "gray zone" justification, and absolutely no room for negotiation. When your Red Line is absolute, you are protected—not just from the cameras, but from the internal threat that seeks to dismantle your soul.

It is easy to look at a two-hundred-dollar find and say it was simple to be righteous. You might ask: "What if it was a briefcase filled with two million dollars? Would you still give it back, or would you disappear with the life-changing wealth?"

My answer is that it would be even easier to walk away from the briefcase. Why? Because as a veteran of law enforcement, I know the math of the "black market." In the real world, two million dollars in cash doesn't belong to a lottery winner; it belongs to crime bosses, drug cartels, or organizations that kill without a blink. Taking that money isn't a "lucky break"—it is a death warrant.

This is why the internal threat of temptation must be squashed at the very onset. If you allow the "hunger" for gain to take root, you aren't just compromising your integrity; you are gambling with your life and the lives of those you love. I am not willing to spend the rest of my days looking over my shoulder, being tracked and hunted, and dragging my family into a world of violence and fear. No amount of paper is worth the permanent loss of my freedom.

The answer for me will always be: “No way!”

Now, ask yourself the same question. What would you do? Would you trade your peaceful life, your reputation, and your children’s safety for two million dollars? If you don’t squash that internal threat the second it enters your mind, the temptation will begin to negotiate with your common sense. In the end, you’ll find that the "easy money" is the most expensive thing you’ll ever own. Preserve your safety by making your decision today: your peace is not for sale.

The fact of the matter is that we must accept the hard truth: "Easy money" always comes with a heavy string attached. Whether that string is a pair of handcuffs or a target on your back, the cost of compromising your integrity is always higher than the payout. When the internal threat of greed is not squashed at the onset, it leads to a catastrophic breach of trust.

The following cases, representing real-world instances, illustrate how even those in the highest positions of power were dismantled because they allowed a "payday" to override their Red Line. I encourage you to search the internet using keywords such as "public official bribery conviction," "corporate embezzlement federal prison," or "political racketeering sentencing" to see how the legal system ultimately audits these failures of character.

Case 1: The Foreign Influence Bribery

• Synopsis: A high-ranking government official accepted hundreds of thousands of dollars in bribes—including gold bullion, luxury vehicles, and stacks of cash—in exchange for using their political influence to benefit foreign interests and interfere in active criminal investigations.

• Adjudication: The individual was convicted on over a dozen federal counts. In early 2025, they were sentenced to 11 years in federal prison. The presiding judge noted that the official had "lost their way," trading the public trust for personal enrichment.

Case 2: The Digital Currency Misappropriation

• Synopsis: The founder of a multi-billion-dollar cryptocurrency exchange succumbed to the temptation of misappropriating massive amounts of customer funds. This capital was used to fund a lavish personal lifestyle, make illegal political contributions, and cover losses at a private hedge fund.

• Adjudication: The individual was convicted of multiple counts of fraud and conspiracy. In 2024, they were sentenced to 25 years in federal prison and ordered to forfeit over $11 billion in assets.

Case 3: The Legislative Bailout Scheme

• Synopsis: A powerful legislative leader orchestrated a $60 million bribery scheme to pass a billion-dollar corporate bailout. The "dark money" involved was used to pay off the official's personal debts and settle private lawsuits, prioritizing greed over the citizens they were elected to serve.

• Adjudication: The official was convicted of racketeering conspiracy and sentenced to 20 years in prison, the maximum sentence allowed under federal law.

Case 4: The Defense Contractor Corruption

• Synopsis: A defense contractor bribed scores of high-ranking military officers with cash, luxury travel, and illicit gifts in exchange for classified information. This inside access allowed the contractor's company to defraud the government out of millions of dollars.

• Adjudication: After years as a fugitive, the contractor was sentenced in late 2024 to 15 years in prison and ordered to pay $20 million in restitution. The careers and freedom of dozens of high-ranking officers were destroyed in the wake of this internal breach.

Each of these individuals had achieved what many would consider the pinnacle of success. Yet, they lost their reputations, their legacies, and ultimately their freedom because they fell victim to their own internal temptations. In every case, the root cause was simple, unadulterated greed. They traded their lives for a "payday," failing to realize until it was too late that no amount of money is worth the loss of our freedom.

There is no doubt in my mind that sex and money are the two most lethal catalysts for a catastrophic breach of character. They are the primary engines behind almost every "gray area" failure that eventually turns into a "black zone" disaster. For those with a compromised moral compass, these temptations act as predatory internal threats that wait for a single moment of weakness to strike.

When you fail to squash these impulses at the onset, you are not just making a "mistake"—you are inviting a parasite into your life that will eventually consume your reputation, your career, and your freedom. Whether the goal is the illicit thrill of power over another or the hollow high of an unearned payday, the end result is a total dismantling of the safety you have worked so hard to build.

The following cases, representing real-world instances, illustrate how quickly these temptations can turn into a life-altering crash for those in trusted positions. I encourage readers to search the internet using keywords like "federal agent civil rights violation conviction," "educator invasive recording sentencing," or "insider trading corporate merger fraud" to further understand the legal mechanisms used to prosecute these breaches of trust.

Case 1: The Badge and Authority Betrayal

• Synopsis: A veteran federal agent used his position of authority to coerce and assault victims during the course of his official duties. He operated under the delusion that his badge and his expertise in the law made him untouchable, allowing his predatory internal threats to operate unchecked within the very system he was sworn to uphold.

• Adjudication: The individual was convicted of multiple counts of sexual battery and deprivation of rights under color of law. In 2024, he was sentenced to over 10 years in federal prison.

Case 2: The Voyeuristic Educator

• Synopsis: A high-ranking school administrator and mentor used his privileged access to campus facilities to install hidden recording devices in private areas. His failure to neutralize a voyeuristic temptation led to a massive breach of trust within the student body and the broader community.

• Adjudication: He was convicted of multiple counts of invasive visual recording and sentenced to 8 years in prison, along with a permanent revocation of his professional credentials.

Case 3: The Political Deception Scheme

• Synopsis: While serving in a high-profile national legislative office, an individual engaged in a complex web of financial deception. This included the misappropriation of campaign funds for personal luxury items and the execution of fraudulent credit card schemes. He viewed his public office as a vehicle for illicit monetary gain rather than a commitment to public service.

• Adjudication: After a high-profile investigation, the individual pleaded guilty to wire fraud and aggravated identity theft in late 2024. He faces a significant prison term and was ordered to pay massive restitution to his victims.

Case 4: The Silicon Valley Insider Leak

• Synopsis: Several tech professionals exploited confidential information regarding upcoming corporate mergers and acquisitions (M&A) to execute illegal stock trades. They operated under the false belief that because the information was "internal," they could exploit it without consequence to generate millions in illegal profits.

• Adjudication: The defendants were convicted of securities fraud and conspiracy. In 2023, they were sentenced to various prison terms ranging from 18 to 36 months, along with millions of dollars in fines and forfeitures.

Each of these individuals—agents, educators, politicians, and engineers—shared a common flaw: they believed they could negotiate with their temptations. They ignored their "Red Lines," thinking the illicit payout or thrill was worth the risk. By the time they realized the "payday" was a trap, their perimeters had already collapsed, leaving their lives and reputations in ruins.

In the end, they all lost. They fell victim to their own internal threats, proving once again that greed and lust are not just "bad habits"—they are the enemies of your freedom. We must emphasize this hard truth: no amount of money and no momentary impulse is worth the loss of your life's peace.

Preserve your personal safety by squashing the threat the moment it enters your mind. Once you let it in, you are no longer in control.

These are lessons we must learn from to harden our stance against temptation and reinforce our iron-clad integrity. In the world of security, we talk about "hardening a target" to make it too difficult for an intruder to breach, and that same tactical principle applies directly to the human soul. When you study the public failures and private collapses of others, you aren't merely looking at their shame; you are identifying the specific gaps in their armor so that you can proactively reinforce your own. To maintain an iron-clad moral compass, you must realize that integrity is a daily drill rather than a one-time decision—it requires a constant state of operational readiness. These high-profile collapses prove that the threat is real and that no one is "too successful" or "too smart" to be destroyed by their own unchecked impulses.

Ultimately, your "Red Line" must be non-negotiable, because once you begin to negotiate with a temptation, you have already lost the battle; the only way to secure a definitive win is to refuse the conversation entirely. Let these stories serve as the psychological reinforcement for your own boundaries and use them to remind yourself that the "easy" path is almost always a trap designed to strip you of your freedom. By committing to these lessons today, you ensure that your personal safety remains intact and your integrity remains beyond reproach. No matter the bait—be it sex, money, or power—your peace of mind and your freedom are the only assets that truly matter. You must keep your compass calibrated and your perimeter secure, refusing to ever trade your future for a momentary lapse in judgment.

While greed and lust are slow-burning internal threats, my experience has shown me another temptation that is more immediate and far deadlier. In the legal world, this is known as acting in the "Heat of Passion." This occurs when a person is struck by a provocation so shocking to their conscience that their rational mind is momentarily hijacked by a blinding, uncontrollable rage. In these split seconds, the "Red Line" isn't crossed through a slow negotiation; it is obliterated by a sudden, violent surge of emotion.

These are the instances that frequently lead to "black zone" tragedies: catching a spouse in the midst of an affair or, most viscerally, discovering a predator in the act of molesting one's own child. In these moments, the temptation isn't for pleasure or profit—it is for immediate, violent retribution. The "Internal Threat" here is the loss of self-control. While the law may sometimes recognize the extreme provocation involved, the result is often the same: a life destroyed in an instant of unbridled anger. Hardening your stance against temptation means preparing even for these extreme scenarios, ensuring that your commitment to the law and your own freedom remains stronger than the most primal of impulses.

To understand the true weight of the "Heat of Passion," we must look at how instantaneous decisions—often born from deep emotional trauma or protective instincts—can lead to a total loss of freedom. While the legal system may weigh the level of provocation, the internal threat of unbridled rage often leaves a trail of wreckage that no court can fully undo.

The following scenarios represent real-world instances where individuals were pushed to the brink by shocking circumstances and chose immediate, violent action over the restraint of the law. I encourage readers to search the internet for legal cases using keywords like "heat of passion," "crime of passion," or "extreme emotional disturbance" to further understand the devastating legal and personal consequences that follow these split-second lapses in judgment.

Case 1: The Parent's Retribution

• Synopsis: Upon discovering that a trusted associate had severely harmed their young child, a parent tracked the individual down and engaged in a violent physical assault that resulted in the person's death. Though acting out of a primal protective instinct, the parent bypassed the legal system to exact "street justice."

• Adjudication: The parent was charged with voluntary manslaughter. Despite the defense arguing extreme provocation, the defendant was sentenced to 8 years in prison. The court noted that while the provocation was gut-wrenching, the law does not permit citizens to act as judge, jury, and executioner.

Case 2: The Marital Betrayal

• Synopsis: A spouse returned home unexpectedly to find their partner with another individual. In a state of shock, the spouse retrieved a weapon and fired upon both parties. This is a classic "Heat of Passion" scenario where a stable individual's moral compass was momentarily shattered by a sudden emotional crisis.

• Adjudication: The individual pleaded guilty to attempted murder. Despite having no prior criminal record, the defendant was sentenced to 15 years in prison. This case highlights that a single moment of lost control can override a lifetime of good character.

Case 3: The Vigilante Grandparent

• Synopsis: After a predator who had harmed their grandchild was released on a legal technicality, a grandparent confronted the individual at their home. The confrontation escalated instantly, and the grandparent killed the individual.

• Adjudication: The defendant was convicted of manslaughter. Due to the defendant's age and the nature of the provocation, the court showed some leniency, yet still handed down a 5-year prison sentence. A single moment of rage cost this individual their final years of peace and freedom.

Case 4: The Workplace Breaking Point

• Synopsis: A dedicated employee discovered that a colleague had been embezzling funds and framing them for the theft. During a heated confrontation, the colleague mocked the employee's predicament, triggering a violent assault that left the colleague permanently disabled.

• Adjudication: The employee was convicted of aggravated battery and sentenced to 4 years in prison. This serves as a reminder that even when you are morally "right," acting out in uncontrolled anger makes you legally "wrong."

These examples are a sobering reminder that the most dangerous internal threat isn't always a slow-moving desire for money or sex; often, it is the sudden, explosive urge for vengeance. These individuals were pushed to their absolute limits, but by failing to control the "Heat of Passion," they allowed a temporary circumstance to dictate their permanent destiny.

They traded their entire lives for a few seconds of retribution. As we harden our internal perimeters, we must realize that our self-control must be at its strongest when our provocation is at its peak. No matter how "justified" the anger feels in the heat of the moment, the loss of your freedom is a price you can never afford to pay.

To survive a "heat of passion" moment, you must treat your emotions like a high-stakes emergency that requires an immediate manual override. When you are hit with a shock that makes your blood boil—whether it is a deep betrayal or a threat to your family—your brain's logical side can shut down. To prevent a tragedy, you must practice a "tactical pause." Force yourself to take a slow, deep breath for at least five seconds before you move or speak. This small window of time allows your rational mind to catch up with your emotions, moving you away from a blind "fight or flight" reaction and back to a place where you can weigh the life-altering consequences of your next move.

If you find yourself in the horrific position of catching a predator harming your child, your primary mission must be to save and protect your child, not to lose yourself in the pursuit of vengeance. You must prioritize getting your child to safety and providing them with immediate care, then step back and let the law handle the punishment of the perpetrator. By staying within the lines of the law, you remain present and free to support your child through their recovery. If you choose a path of violence, you risk being removed from your child's life at the very moment they need you most. Justice is best served when the criminal is behind bars and you are still home to guard your family.

The same logic applies to the deep pain of discovering an unfaithful spouse. As devastating as that betrayal feels, you must refrain from throwing away your own life and freedom just to appease a momentary temptation to inflict harm. No matter how much pain they have caused you, that person is not worth your future, your reputation, or your liberty. Visualize the "aftermath" of a violent choice: the cold steel of handcuffs and the reality of a prison cell. Remind yourself that the moment you lash out physically, you stop being the victim and instead become a defendant. By choosing restraint, you ensure that you remain free to walk away and rebuild your life, while acting on your anger only ensures that you lose everything.

Ultimately, the best defense is to physically remove yourself from the situation as quickly as possible. Disengaging from the person who provoked you isn't a sign of weakness; it is a smart, tactical move to preserve your life and your liberty. You have to decide right now—long before a crisis ever happens—that your default response to any shock will be to call the authorities and let the legal system do its job. Hardening your character means accepting the hard truth that while justice can be a slow process, revenge is a fast track to losing your freedom. By keeping your "Red Line" in place even when your heart is racing, you protect yourself from the most dangerous enemy in the room: your own uncontrolled impulse.

In conclusion, maintaining a secure perimeter around your life requires more than just physical locks and alarms; it requires a relentless, iron-clad commitment to neutralizing the internal threats that reside within the human heart. We have identified the three deadliest temptations—Money, Sex, and the Heat of Passion—as the primary catalysts for a catastrophic breach of character. These are not merely moral lapses; they are predatory internal threats that, if not squashed at the onset, will inevitably dismantle your personal safety and destroy the stability of your family.

When you fall victim to these temptations, you aren't just risking your own reputation—you are gambling with the safety and well-being of your loved ones. A choice driven by greed or lust can lead to legal ruin, financial collapse, and the permanent loss of the trust that holds a home together. Similarly, acting in the heat of passion can physically remove you from your family at the very moment they need your protection most, leaving them to navigate the world alone while you face the consequences behind bars. Your family's security is anchored to your self-control; when you lose your grip on your integrity, you leave your perimeter wide open to chaos.

To safeguard your freedom, you must view your integrity as a non-negotiable "Red Line." True character is forged in the silent decisions to stay righteous and preserved in moments of extreme provocation when you choose the law over your own impulses. Let the wreckage of those who traded their lives for a "payday" or a moment of rage serve as your psychological reinforcement. No amount of money, no illicit thrill, and no act of retribution is worth the devastating cost to your life and the lives of those you love. Keep your moral compass calibrated, stay vigilant against your own internal threats, and never trade your lifelong freedom for a momentary lapse in judgment.

Chapter 6

The Mouth:

A Breach in Your Personal Safety

In the previous chapter, we explored how temptation and unchecked emotions can act as clandestine predators, compromising our personal safety from within. In this chapter, I want to introduce you to an organ that, while small, is capable of causing an endless amount of trouble—impacting your legal standing, your financial stability, and your physical security. Without the context of the chapter's title, some might have guessed I was referring to an organ located much lower on the body; however, the culprit is far more visible. That organ is none other than the human mouth—a biological puppet frequently controlled by its master: the Ego.

To understand why this organ is so dangerous, we must first look at the “forensic evidence” of our own lives. The mouth is often the primary point of breach in our personal safety. In my years on the street, I have seen more conflicts ignited by a reckless tongue than by a physical strike. A single phrase like “What you looking at?” in the wrong environment has ended lives, not because it was profound, but because it forced the other person’s ego into a public dominance contest they felt they had to win with fists, blades, or bullets. What starts as a muttered insult or a challenging glare quickly escalates because neither party wants to appear weak in front of witnesses. The mouth doesn’t just provoke—it broadcasts vulnerability and invites retaliation in environments where respect is currency and disrespect can be fatal. One careless sentence can turn a minor slight into a life-threatening situation, compromising your physical safety in seconds.

This is because whenever anger begins to take root, the ego feels the first bruise. Long before a situation escalates into physical violence or reckless behavior, the mouth is deployed to do the ego’s dirty work. It acts as the vanguard of our insecurities, rushing forward to defend, attack, or deflect before the rational mind can intervene. As human beings, we all experience this surge of emotion, but the line that separates the disciplined from the dangerous is impulse control. The ego hates silence because silence feels like surrender. It demands action, and the mouth is its quickest, most accessible tool. When you let the ego win this early battle, you surrender control over your personal safety perimeter before the real threat even fully materializes.

When the ego takes control, the mouth becomes a reckless tool that acts without a strategic goal, leaving you to manage the long-term damage of your own words. Whether it is turning a minor misunderstanding into a bridge-burning conflict or revealing sensitive information during a negotiation that inadvertently hands your leverage to an opponent, an ungoverned tongue is a massive liability. Those impulsive comments or emotional outbursts—whether recorded on a digital device or remembered by colleagues—become permanent marks against your character, transforming a momentary vent into a lasting professional or social disaster. A few unguarded words can destroy your reputation, derail your career trajectory, and create an atmosphere of distrust that follows you into every room you enter.

Furthermore, this tactical error destroys intimacy and professional stability. Words are free to use, much like the air we breathe; however, unlike air, words can cut with surgical precision if we don't watch what we say. Our mouths argue to win rather than to resolve, prioritizing being "right" over being safe or kind. This keeps old wounds fresh and blocks emotional healing. Surveys of mental health professionals and divorced individuals consistently show that communication problems and toxic arguments are cited as a primary factor in roughly 65% of divorces. In those cases, the mouth didn't just speak; it systematically dismantled the foundation of the home, destroying financial security through division of assets, emotional safety for everyone involved, and—most tragically—the stable environment children need to grow up without carrying forward the same vulnerabilities. The collateral damage ripples outward, leaving fractured families and compromised personal safety for years.

The stakes are equally high at the workplace—the very source of our income and livelihood. We must watch our egos and our mouths with clinical precision to prevent catastrophic outcomes. When left unchecked, the mouth will voice every grievance that poisons the atmosphere rather than offering solutions. Research indicates that around 80% of workplace conflicts stem from poor phrasing or communication breakdowns rather than malicious intent. Together, the ego and the mouth form a dangerous duo. They share unverified information, exaggerate successes, or betray confidences. One of the most common security breaches is the habit of bad-mouthing employers, colleagues, or clients. Comparing ourselves aloud to others is a public broadcast of our own insecurity, fostering resentment and signaling to everyone around us that we are a liability rather than an asset. A single regrettable statement, or a confidential vent that inevitably circles back through the grapevine or digital trails, can permanently undo years of built-up goodwill, cost promotions, or lead to sudden termination. In tight-knit industries, that reputation for toxicity travels faster than you do—directly threatening your financial stability and forcing you into survival mode where every future opportunity becomes harder to secure.

To protect your personal safety, you must view your words with the same clinical scrutiny you apply to your financial investments or your home security. In a high-stakes environment, the mouth should only be opened when it serves a strategic purpose. Every word you utter is a piece of data that can be used by an indifferent auditor—be it a rival, a scam artist, or the legal system—to dismantle your life. Learning to silence the puppet is not just a matter of manners; it is a fundamental survival skill that ensures your ego doesn't write a check that your freedom can't cash. The disciplined individual treats conversation like operational security: need-to-know only, with minimal leakage.

Since my daughters entered their teenage years, I have made it a priority to ingrain in them a clear tactical principle: if you have something constructive or kind to contribute, speak freely. But if the intent is to disparage or bad-mouth someone, the most effective move is silence. Nothing of value can ever be harvested from the seeds of gossip or mean-spirited criticism. In the context of personal safety, this is about protecting their social and emotional perimeter. Bad-mouthing is low-leverage behavior—it creates unnecessary friction, invites retaliation, and labels the speaker as untrustworthy. I also taught them to engage in a three-step internal audit before speaking in public: consider what they want to say, how they should express it, and the potential ramifications. Once words are released, the damage is often irreversible. Building this habit early helps them avoid the drama and conflicts that can escalate into threats against their physical or emotional safety later in life.

I have practiced these same principles throughout my law enforcement career. I vividly recall a moment when colleagues were discussing a probationary officer's progress and asked for my assessment. Before I could speak, another officer joked, "Since when does Eric have anything bad to say about anyone?" It sparked a good-natured laugh, but it also reinforced my commitment to the adage: “Praise in public; criticize in private.” Even when brutal honesty is required for accountability, keeping constructive criticism behind closed doors preserves team integrity and gives your words greater weight as a truth seeker rather than gossip. This discipline was especially important for me as a non-native English speaker. I remained acutely conscious of both my word choice and pronunciation, regularly checking with dispatchers to ensure my radio traffic was clear. On the radio or in the family living room, the goal remains the same: make your mouth a bridge for clarity rather than a fuse for conflict. A misunderstood transmission or careless comment in the field can turn a routine call into a life-or-death situation.

While some can govern their speech under pressure, others surrender the controls to their ego entirely. This surrender causes the mouth to spit out careless, harsh, or dishonest words—verbal projectiles designed to wound the other person just to soothe a bruised sense of self. These outbursts trigger unnecessary arguments, dissolve trust, and can permanently dismantle friendships, marriages, and careers in a matter of seconds. What feels satisfying in the heat of the moment often leaves behind a trail of damaged relationships and eroded credibility that takes years to repair, if it can be repaired at all. Without a strong social perimeter, you become isolated and more vulnerable to external threats.

Think of the mouth as a weapon with no safety switch. If the ego is the one pulling the trigger, the collateral damage is almost always self-inflicted. Let’s pause for a moment and look at the forensic evidence of your own life: how many times has a single sentence, uttered in the heat of a bruised ego, cost you something that took years to build? If we are being honest, we have all paid a last word tax at some point. The question is, can you afford to keep paying it? My bet is that eventually your emotional and social credits will run dry, and a reputation for having loose lips will follow you into every room you enter.

Just as dangerous as the words we use to attack are the words we use to appease. In our attempts to please others or avoid short-term discomfort, we often overpromise or say yes too readily, creating a cycle of stress and disappointment that erodes our credibility. Casually agreeing to verbal financial arrangements without proper documentation frequently leads to costly disputes and destroys trust when one party eventually backtracks. What begins as a friendly handshake deal ends in resentment, legal fees, or severed ties because the mouth committed resources the disciplined mind would have protected with clear boundaries and written agreements. These financial breaches can leave you exposed and unable to maintain the resources needed for true personal safety.

Beyond the confines of the home and office, the mouth remains a primary gateway to both physical and financial ruin. Boasting about income, high-end possessions, upcoming travel plans, or predictable daily routines effectively broadcasts your status as a high-value target for robbery, sophisticated scams, or "fair-weather" friends seeking loans. In the realm of negotiations, the mouth often betrays the mind; saying a number first or revealing too much eagerness almost always leaves significant money on the table. Similarly, volunteering damaging information unnecessarily in legal settings can forfeit your defense before it even begins, handing the opposition the very evidence they need to dismantle your case.

In the modern era, the "mouth" has evolved. It now extends far beyond spoken words to include texts, social media posts, emails, and voice notes. A reckless rant fired off in a moment of heat creates a permanent, searchable record that adversaries, future employers, or courts can weaponize years after the fact. The ego thrives on the instant dopamine hit of venting or “telling it like it is,” but the consequences are slow-moving and far more enduring—often resurfacing at the worst possible moment to undermine your long-term security.

As a matter of operational security, I maintain a strict personal rule: never discuss private financial matters with anyone other than a trusted, certified professional. However, I am human and subject to the same ego-driven slips as anyone else. I admit that during enthusiastic discussions regarding trading strategies with friends, I have occasionally let specific financial details slip through. While these instances were harmless in the moment, I recognize them as tactical errors—breaches in my own perimeter that I must consciously correct to prevent future, more significant occurrences.

Most critically, reckless comments or public confrontations can escalate into physical violence in an instant. Casually revealing your location invites burglary or worse. Issuing threats in a moment of anger can trigger severe legal consequences or dangerous retaliation. Even justified whistleblowing, if done without proper operational security, can put your life or your family's at risk.

The core truth is that the mouth often acts before the mind catches up. Impulse, emotion, and habit drive most of what we say and consume, and the consequences almost always outlast the fleeting moment of satisfaction. Developing a brief tactical pause before speaking or eating is one of the highest-leverage habits you can adopt to protect your personal safety.

Train yourself to recognize the early warning signs of an ego bruise: a tightened chest, a rising vocal pitch, flushed skin, or the sudden urge to interrupt, one-up, or lash out. When these alarms trigger, deploy the tactical pause—even two to five seconds of silence can shift control from the reactive ego back to your strategic mind. In negotiations or heated conflicts, that silence often pressures the other party to fill the void, sometimes leading to concessions or de-escalation. Far from projecting weakness, strategic silence communicates control and confidence.

I have used this approach successfully even after personal setbacks, such as losses in the stock market. In those moments when my ego felt battered, I would lock my office door and go completely dark—no calls, no messages, no interaction—until I regained composure. Isolating the misfire protected my relationships and reputation from unnecessary collateral damage.

Adopt these operational rules for speech: speak only to resolve, de-escalate, gather intelligence, or advance a clear objective—never merely to win, soothe your ego, or perform. Default to thoughtful questions over statements when emotions rise. Never volunteer damaging information. Replace complaining and gossip with deliberate silence or solution-oriented language. Treat all digital communication with the same discipline—once sent, it becomes permanent evidence.

Over time, a reputation for discretion and measured speech becomes its own powerful perimeter defense. It deters opportunists and builds alliances with those who value reliability. Loose lips, on the other hand, signal unreliability and invite exploitation.

Regardless of how you feel in the moment, remember that silence is often the most effective shield you possess. The mouth is the most accessible breach point because it feels low-cost and high-reward in the heat of the ego's bruise. But in a dangerous, indifferent world, words are ammunition with no recall function.

Mastering the mouth is not the end of personal safety—it is the visible frontline. True security requires integrating this discipline with deeper control over the mind, body, and environment. The undisciplined tongue is usually just the symptom of an unguarded inner perimeter.

Despite its potential for destruction when manipulated by the ego, the mouth remains one of the most vital organs we possess. It serves as the primary gateway for human connection, the tool we use to communicate complex ideas, share affection, and de-escalate tension. When governed by the mind rather than the ego, it ceases to be a point of vulnerability and instead becomes our most versatile asset—capable of building rather than destroying, and turning a potential security breach into a fortress of personal discipline.

However, the breach in our perimeter doesn't just occur through what we say; it occurs through what we consume. From a physical health perspective, the mouth serves as the primary intake valve for our biological engine. Unfortunately, what we allow through that valve—poor dietary choices, tobacco, alcohol, and stress-driven overeating—remains a leading cause of chronic illness and premature death. The undisciplined mouth undermines the body from both ends: reckless verbal output generates chronic psychological stress, which is often followed by reckless physical intake as a misguided form of self-soothing. Arguments at home or tension at work send many people straight to comfort food, cigarettes, or the bottle, compounding mental strain with physical deterioration that weakens your overall perimeter of safety. When your body is compromised by poor health, your reaction time, mental clarity, and physical resilience—the very foundations of personal safety—begin to erode.

I must admit, I am guilty as charged. Over a twenty-eight-year career—the majority of which was spent in the patrol division—the relentless pace of back-to-back calls for service dictated my lifestyle. In that high-pressure environment, I frequently ate on the go, habitually grabbing unhealthy fast food simply because it was the most convenient option available. While I took pride in the fact that I never smoked and rarely touched alcohol, those "convenient" caloric choices eventually forced a serious forensic reality upon me.

Despite my clean living in other areas, the cumulative effect of a poor diet led to a diagnosis of diabetes and high cholesterol. I learned the hard way that you cannot outrun a bad diet, nor can you ignore the long-term consequences of using your mouth as a disposal for stress-induced cravings. This was a critical internal breach; I was so focused on guarding against external threats on the street that I allowed a silent predator to compromise my health from within.

Discipline must be a 360-degree commitment—it applies to what comes out of your mouth in the form of words and, just as crucially, what goes into it as fuel. Ignoring this internal security flaw can quietly dismantle your physical resilience, reaction time, and mental clarity, ultimately hindering your ability to defend yourself or your loved ones when it matters most. A friend of mine, a dedicated bodybuilder, once told me: “The body is like a machine; you have to ‘work it’ and maintain it properly to make it better.” While his perspective was rooted in aesthetics and strength, the tactical truth is universal. If the "machine" is poorly fueled and neglected, it will inevitably fail when pushed to its limits. True personal safety begins with the realization that your own body is the primary piece of equipment you bring to every encounter.

As you can see, when the mouth and the ego are left unchecked, they form a destructive partnership capable of dismantling every perimeter of your personal safety—legal, financial, social, and physical. However, the mouth is not inherently an enemy; it is an incredibly vital tool for our livelihood and survival. It is the primary mechanism through which we communicate our needs, share our deepest affections, and project our character to a world that is always watching and listening.

Because the stakes are so high, it is imperative that we move beyond mere "talking" and learn to speak with civility and eloquence. Eloquence is not about using big words; it is about the disciplined alignment of the mind and the tongue. Words are a unique resource—they cost nothing to produce, yet they possess a value that can be life-changing. When we use them freely to extend kindness, generosity, and a deep understanding of other people's circumstances, we are not just being "nice"; we are strategically building a world that is safer and more cooperative.

Mother Teresa once said, “Kind words can be short and easy to speak, but their echoes are truly endless.” She couldn't have been more accurate from a tactical or human perspective. A single moment of verbal restraint or an unexpected word of encouragement can de-escalate a potential conflict, heal a fractured relationship, or build a bridge where there was once a wall. By mastering the mouth, you transform it from a point of vulnerability into your most versatile asset—a source of strength that nourishes your body and secures your future.

I encourage you to reflect on a difficult truth: quite often, we reserve our most polished and polite language for colleagues and strangers, yet fail to extend that same courtesy to our own family members. Perhaps we let our emotional guard down too far at home, or perhaps we arrive exhausted, having "spent" our entire reserve of patience on the outside world. This emotional burnout often leaves us grumpy, dismissive, and lacking in empathy toward the very people we care about most.

Unfortunately, I too have fallen into this trap. There have been times when I simply shut down, failing to engage in any substantive communication with my wife and daughters for days at a time. I have come to realize that this "verbal withdrawal" is just as significant a failure of discipline as an angry outburst; while one is a loud explosion, the other is a silent erosion of trust. True personal safety isn't just about surviving a high-stakes threat on the street; it is about protecting the peace and structural integrity of your own living room. It is precisely within the home where we must use our mouths most intentionally for the betterment of the family and the health of the marriage.

I have been told by those wiser than myself that in a romantic relationship, the mouth serves as the primary architect of intimacy. They suggested that while saying “I love you” regularly and genuinely keeps the emotional connection alive, the true strength of a partnership is found in the specifics. I've learned that expressing targeted appreciation—noticing how hard your partner worked on a particular task or affirming their unique strengths—builds a foundation of confidence and loyalty that generic praise cannot reach. I've come to value how daily check-ins and the sacred space of "pillow talk" ensure that you remain a unified team, even through the most stressful seasons of life. Perhaps applying those lessons is how our marriage has lasted for 36 years and is still going strong.

Furthermore, I've learned that we must use our words to manage the inevitable friction of living together. Saying "I was wrong," without qualification or excuse, is one of the most powerful phrases in a marriage; it acts as a tactical de-escalation that prevents small conflicts from festering into permanent wounds. Communicating needs and boundaries clearly prevents resentment from building in the shadows, while consistently using "we" language instead of "you vs. me" signals a shared purpose rather than a competitive rivalry. By vocalizing gratitude for small sacrifices—a meal prepared, a chore handled—and speaking well of your spouse to others, you reinforce a positive cycle of mutual respect. When you choose to use your mouth as a tool for affirmation rather than an outlet for your own exhaustion, you aren't just being a "nice" spouse—you are fortifying the very center of your world and ensuring your home remains a true sanctuary.

Reflecting on years of public service, I've realized that the mouth is a powerful, dual-purpose tool. On the street, I had to monitor not only what I said but how I delivered the message every single day, under every conceivable level of stress. Eventually, through sheer repetition, this discipline became second nature. Speaking professionally, courteously, and with a purposeful kindness wasn't just a department policy; it became an effortless part of my character. I'm no expert on psychology or linguistics—I'm just an ordinary person who had a front-row seat to human nature in its rawest forms. From that vantage point, I realized that the same mouth that possesses the power to destroy also has the capacity to heal, build, inspire, and protect. The difference isn't found in a person's vocabulary; it is found in their intention, timing, and self-awareness.

Throughout my decades in law enforcement, I was often struck by the unique skills of my peers. I noticed that some of my colleagues possessed a remarkable ability to speak eloquently and intelligently without having to rely on an overpowering command presence; they could control a room through the sheer clarity and composure of their words. I have always been fascinated by people who possess that level of verbal mastery, and I often found myself wishing I could communicate with that same effortless grace.

This fascination led me to study the art of communication more closely. I often watched politicians and dignitaries delivering speeches at political rallies or graduation ceremonies, mesmerized by how they could move an audience with just their voice. I made it a point to show those videos to my daughters, encouraging them to watch and learn from these excellent speakers so they could develop their own sense of eloquence. I am confident that these speakers made it to the top of their professional careers not only because of their intellect and dedication, but also because of their ability to articulate their vision. All forms of communication, especially verbal, are so incredibly important in earning the respect of others that I believe everyone must make a deliberate effort to master the art of speaking.

I don't claim to have academic degrees in communication; my lessons were learned on the pavement and in the heat of real-world interactions. From that grounded perspective, I realized that the same mouth that possesses the power to destroy also has the capacity to heal, build, inspire, and protect. The difference isn't found in a person's vocabulary; it is found in their intention, timing, and self-awareness.

In our daily lives, your voice acts as the primary lock on your front door. I've observed that simply carrying yourself with a calm, steady vocal clarity in an awkward or tense situation signals that you are fully present and not easily manipulated. Being direct isn't about being rude; it's about clarity as a form of protection. This looks like the strength to say a firm, "No, I'm not interested," to someone who is pushing your boundaries, or in a chaotic public moment, pointing to a specific bystander and saying, "I need you to call 911," which cuts through the confusion and gets results.

Building on this foundation of clarity, using your mouth as a shield is ultimately a matter of internal conviction. It's about the self-worth required to say, "I'm going now," without feeling the need to invent an elaborate story to justify your exit. It's also about the bravery to look someone in the eye and ask a clarifying question like, "Is there a reason you're walking so close to me?"—a simple move that instantly shifts the power dynamic by showing you aren't oblivious to your surroundings. Whether you're coaching a child on how to speak up when a situation feels "weird" or setting clear expectations in a new friendship, your words create the invisible fence that keeps your life and your peace of mind from being intruded upon.

Beyond survival, I've observed that the mouth is the engine of respect and influence. In my career, I saw that unshakeable credibility isn't built through a badge, but through speaking the truth consistently, even when it's uncomfortable. True integrity is demonstrated when you defend someone's reputation in their absence or disagree with grace and logic rather than raw emotion. By acknowledging others by name and practicing active listening—reflecting back what you've heard—you show a level of respect that commands a reciprocal response, even from opponents. Admitting a mistake publicly and quickly doesn't diminish your power; it transforms vulnerability into a unique kind of authority that people trust.

In the context of achievement and career, your verbal discipline dictates your trajectory. Talent alone rarely opens as many doors as the ability to pitch an idea with clarity and confidence. I've learned that saying, "I don't know, but I'll find out," builds far more professional capital than bluffing ever will. In negotiations, those who remain calm and assertive secure the best outcomes, while those who use inclusive "we" language build loyal communities rather than just oneself.

Perhaps most importantly, I've learned that the mouth is central to happiness, mental wellbeing, and family. On the job, I saw how much weight a person's internal story carries. I've found that verbalizing gratitude daily—even just to yourself—actually helps rewire the brain toward positivity. Changing our language from "I have to" to "I choose to" shifts the mindset from being a victim of a burden to having ownership over our lives. I've learned that asking for help is a sign of wisdom, not weakness, and that telling your own story with self-compassion accelerates healing from the traumas we all face.

This same intentionality is what protects the family. In my own home, I've seen how telling my children "I'm proud of you" for their effort, rather than just the outcome, builds a growth mindset. Speaking your family's values aloud regularly gives children an internal compass to navigate a complicated world. Using a calm voice during a conflict isn't just about being "nice"; it models emotional regulation for the next generation. Every word you speak is a choice, and those choices compound over a lifetime. They dictate the quality of your relationships, the reach of your reputation, and the depth of your safety. Ultimately, your mouth broadcasts your character to the world—make sure the message you are sending is the one you intend for others to follow.

In conclusion, the mouth is the most active and high-stakes gateway to your entire security apparatus. Throughout this chapter, we have seen that personal safety is rarely compromised by a single catastrophic event; rather, it is eroded through a series of small, ego-driven leaks—reckless outbursts, a lack of dietary discipline, or the failure to vocalize boundaries. When we allow the ego to pull the strings, our words become projectiles that dismantle our legal standing, professional reputation, and the structural integrity of our families. Conversely, by reclaiming control from the ego and applying a tactical pause, we transform our speech into an operational asset.

True mastery of the mouth requires a dual commitment: guarding what goes out to protect your social and legal perimeter, and monitoring what comes in to ensure your physical machine remains resilient and ready. Whether it is the self-respect required to walk away from a toxic argument, the clarity to pitch a bold vision, or the humility to offer a sincere apology at home, your verbal output is the primary architect of your life's quality.

As you move forward, view your speech not as a stream of consciousness, but as a series of strategic choices. Discipline is not a restriction of your freedom; it is the very thing that secures it. By choosing eloquence over impulse and silence over gossip, you build a reputation that acts as a natural deterrent to opportunists and a magnet for respect. Let your mouth be the fortress that protects your peace, the bridge that connects you to others, and the ultimate broadcast of a character that is disciplined, purposeful, and profoundly safe.

Chapter 7

Saving Your Sanity

Each of us travels a unique path through life. For some, the journey is tranquil, like a calm sea under a clear sky; for others, it is defined by relentless turbulence and storms. My own journey is perhaps not unique in its beginning—millions have walked similar paths of displacement—but the internal toll it took is deeply personal. As with any voyage, the good times have crystallized into cherished memories. Conversely, the bad times have left scars that are both deep and permanent.

To understand the importance of mental resilience, you must understand the moment my personal safety collapsed. In either 1979 or 1980, I escaped Vietnam by boat. I was only thirteen or fourteen years old at the time. After three nights and two days on the Pacific Ocean, the boat motor stopped working, leaving us adrift and at the mercy of the currents.

While we drifted with the wind, I looked around and saw nothing but the horizon. I couldn't believe how vast, how massive the ocean was, and how tiny our vessel truly was. Our boat was like a speck of sand, and I was much smaller than that—perhaps the equivalent of a grain of dust in a boundless void.

By that third night, we had exhausted our food, our water, and our last hope of rescue. I remember the constant cool breeze and the salty smell of the ocean filling the air—a hauntingly peaceful backdrop to the grim reality we faced. In that hollowed-out state, I became convinced that death was only a moment away. I found myself calmly negotiating with the end, wondering which exit would be the easiest. Should I simply fall asleep and let the sea claim me as the boat sank? Or should I grab a wooden plank and cling to life until hypothermia, exhaustion, or the predators of the deep took me? I pondered these grim choices in the dead of night, surrounded by a darkness so absolute I could not see my own hands in front of my face.

By what I can only describe as the grace of God, around three in the morning, a ginormous Norwegian merchant ship appeared like a ghost in the blackness. The Norwegian blasted their horns, the sound ripping through the darkness and shattering the silence of our despair. Suddenly, their massive spotlights lit us up, blindingly bright, as their heavy wakes shook our small boat violently. We rocked precariously until the Norwegian crew skillfully tied us to their massive ship, finally tethering us to life.

They took us to Osaka, Japan, where I spent a year in a refugee camp before receiving authorization to fly to the United States. When I finally landed in California, I had to learn a new language and assimilate into a completely foreign culture. I was broke—at one point literally surviving on the kindness of United States Catholic Charity (USCC) volunteers and the strength of a single "red penny" I found on a sidewalk. Yet, I deeply appreciated the tranquility of my new life in which I didn't have to think about choosing the manner of my own death.

I vowed then to stay within the realm of peace, hoping one day I would become a teacher. However, life has a way of shifting your trajectory. Nine years after arriving in California, instead of standing in a classroom, I was sworn in as a police officer. I realized that the scars of my past didn't just haunt me; they drove me toward a profession where I could face death to protect others.

I have lived and worked in California for over 45 years now, yet the memory of that fourteen-year-old boy standing on the precipice of death still haunts me. While I have managed to continue my journey, I am acutely aware of how easily such trauma could drive a person into the depths of insanity. These permanent scars have taught me that protecting your mind is just as critical as protecting your body; if you do not find a way to save your sanity, the weight of the past will eventually sink the ship of the present.

I'll be honest with you—nobody warned me about this part. When I was working in law enforcement, I assumed that staying alert was just a mechanical part of the job. You did it, you went home, and you switched off. Except it doesn't quite work that way, at least not for me. Over the years, I found that the mental habit of constantly scanning, assessing, and processing my surroundings didn't clock out when I did. It followed me to family dinners, to vacations, and to quiet Sunday mornings. I was always running a background check on the room.

However, the most perilous manifestation of these scars occurred during the most high-stakes moments of my career. Whenever I found myself conducting dangerous searches for armed suspects, or fighting for my life against suspects whose biceps were the size of my head, the trauma from my childhood journey across the Pacific would resurface and mess with my mind. In the middle of life-or-death moments, a dark thought would often creep in: If I die right now, at least I got to live many years past that night on the ocean. While it may sound like a form of peace, these thoughts were extremely dangerous. They distracted me from the immediate threat and affected my sanity during moments that required absolute, life-saving focus. The scars weren't just memories; they were active psychological hazards that tested my survival instincts all over again.

At first, I thought this hyper-vigilance and these intrusive thoughts were just the price of experience—the natural byproduct of a career spent paying attention. But eventually, I had to be honest with myself: there's a massive difference between being appropriately aware and being mentally exhausted by your own haunted vigilance. I've seen colleagues burn out not from the physical demands of the job, but from the relentless inability to mentally leave the "street" behind. I've felt that weight personally, carrying the heavy armor of a protector long after the uniform was taken off.

What I've come to understand—and this took me longer than I'd like to admit—is that the goal isn't to think about safety less, but to think about it more efficiently so it doesn't quietly consume you. Fortunately, I was able to outlast these internal and external dangers, and I retired after 28 years of service. Now, everyone is wired differently. Some people naturally compartmentalize better than I ever could. What drained me might not drain you at all. But if you've ever felt tired in a way that sleep doesn't fix, it might be worth asking yourself whether your mind is working overtime, fueled by old scars, just trying to keep you safe.

Looking back, I have no doubt that my journey across the Pacific Ocean and my law enforcement career made me who I am, both the good, the bad and the ugliness in me. Drawing from my experience, I understand that it is imperative that we all have to nurture our mind to save our sanity. We have to take time out from the chaos of life to reflect and reset ourselves. As resilient as we think we are, it doesn't take much for a person to go insane. For instance, back in the early 1990, there was a beautiful talented and very popular Vietnamese singer hailing from Southern California, who had everything anyone could ever want. Years later, she was seen being homeless, refusing help from loved ones and friends. Rumors had it that while performing at a concert in Canada, she witnessed a fatal shooting which affected her to the degree that she lost her mind. She remained homeless until this day, despite colleagues and fans countless attempts to help.

If a person with every possible resource can lose their sanity due to a single traumatic event, we must all be vigilant in protecting our own. Recognizing our vulnerability is the first step in ensuring that our past experiences—whether on a boat in the Pacific or a dark alley on patrol—don't eventually become our permanent undoing. By nurturing our minds, seeking professional help when the weight becomes too heavy, and setting intentional boundaries, we ensure that the ghosts of the past never sink the ship of the present.

Beyond the mental strain, there is a physical toll that often goes unmentioned in any training manual: your body keeps score, whether you're paying attention or not. I learned this the hard way during stretches in my career where I was running on adrenaline for weeks at a time. I thought I was fine because I was functioning, but my body was quietly accumulating the cost of that sustained tension. The fight-or-flight response is a remarkable biological survival mechanism, but in law enforcement, the option of "flight" is often nonexistent. While most people naturally run away from danger, law enforcement is required to run toward it. This creates a unique physiological burden; your body prepares to flee or fight, yet you must override that instinct to remain composed, tactical, and present.

When that system runs constantly in the background like an engine that never idles, it wears the machinery down. To counter this, you must find a way to bring your body back to a "baseline" calm. For me, this meant controlled breathing and quiet reflection, but for you, it might mean physical exercise, a creative hobby, or simply disconnected time in nature. You might consider techniques like mindfulness, engaging in community service outside of work, or even just setting a firm rule to leave "the job" at the door when you arrive home. The method matters less than the commitment to doing it. If you ignore the mind-body connection altogether, it becomes a debt that eventually comes due with interest.

This realization led me to understand the necessity of setting healthy boundaries around my "safety thinking." For a long time, I believed constant vigilance was a virtue, but I eventually carried that intensity into every corner of my personal life. My wife eventually stopped me cold when she said, “You’re here, but you’re never really here.” I was so committed to watching for what could go wrong that I was missing everything that was going right. Learning to give myself permission to relax in safe environments was one of the hardest things I’ve ever done; it felt like dropping my guard. However, a mind with no off-switch eventually becomes unreliable. You must ask yourself: Is your awareness serving your life, or is it slowly replacing it?

Building on this, it is crucial to recognize how trauma shapes our perception. In law enforcement, you carry the scenes you've witnessed and the stories of people on their worst days. These experiences often go underground and influence your behavior, making you quicker to assume bad intent or slower to trust. For a while, I told myself this was just "wisdom," but it was often old fear wearing the disguise of professional judgment. If you find yourself overwhelmed, shocked by a specific event, or simply feeling that your mind is stuck in a "zombie mode" to a degree that you can no longer find peace, it is imperative that you seek professional help. There is no shame in seeking a mental tune-up. Whether it is through counseling, support groups, or trauma-informed therapy, getting a professional perspective can prevent your sanity from drifting far beyond the point of repair. You deserve the same care and attention you would give to any other vital part of your health.

Being a small retailer playing the stock market where information was currency, I know firsthand that the more you knew, the better equipped you were. But somewhere along the way, the sheer volume of available information stopped being an asset and started becoming a problem. I remember a period after I retired where I found myself consuming news almost compulsively—analysts' reports, safety alerts, and legal updates. In retrospect, I think I was feeding an anxiety that had mistaken itself for diligence. A steady stream of threat-focused media creates a distorted picture of reality. It makes rare events feel routine and turns ordinary environments into imagined danger zones. That distortion doesn't make you safer—it makes you more reactive, more exhausted, and less accurate in your actual threat assessment.

I worked a lot of hours throughout my law enforcement career and continue to do so in post-retirement, not because I am desperate for money, but because I don't like to waste time doing nothing. Whenever there are opportunities to work, I sign up. Nonetheless, I do take time out to unwind my mind with hobbies I have always enjoyed, such as checking out my sports card collection, writing books, or playing guitar and letting my voice scare the nocturnal insects (and annoy the neighbors) throughout the night. While these activities worked for me in my efforts to save my sanity and re-energize my body, they may not work for you. You owe it to yourself to find ways to nurture your mind and remove yourself from the chaotic cycle of work, just enough to save your sanity.

If there's one thing my career taught me about resilience, it's that it is built—it doesn't just arrive. I was not naturally a resilient person; I was actually fairly anxious as a young officer. What changed things for me was competence. The more genuinely skilled I became—at de-escalation, at defensive tactics, at reading situations accurately—the quieter my fear became. Not because the world got safer, but because I trusted myself more within it. Confidence that comes from real preparation feels different in your body than confidence that comes from simply telling yourself everything will be fine.

However, resilience is a double-edged sword. While it acts as the shield that saves your sanity in the heat of battle, it can become counterproductive if you push it to the extreme without rest. There is a dangerous threshold where "toughing it out" stops being a strength and starts becoming a slow erosion of the self. When we over-rely on our ability to absorb trauma without processing it, we aren't actually being resilient; we are simply delaying a collapse. If pushed far beyond its natural limit, this forced resilience can backfire, causing the mind to snap under a pressure it was never meant to hold indefinitely. This is how the pursuit of strength can ironically drive a person toward the very insanity they were trying to avoid.

To save your sanity in an unpredictable world, you must fundamentally change how you relate to the unknown. Many of us suffer from a form of mental exhaustion brought on by the impossible task of trying to control every variable and eliminate every doubt. This pursuit is unsustainable because uncertainty isn't a flaw in our lives—it is a fundamental part of the human experience. In reality, almost every major decision we make must be built on the shifting ground of incomplete information.

The secret to preserving your mental health is learning to be prepared without needing to be certain. There is a profound, freeing distinction between these two states. Preparation is about having the tools and the mindset to handle whatever comes; needing certainty is a trap that keeps your mind in a state of high-alert anxiety until an outcome is guaranteed. Since life offers no guarantees, that anxiety never ends. To protect your internal peace, you must recognize that the line between stability and collapse is often thinner than we'd like to admit. Acknowledging your own vulnerability isn't a sign of weakness—it is your greatest defense. It allows you to build a foundation that won't shatter when the unexpected happens.

To safeguard your sanity, you might consider "auditing" your relationship with control. Ask yourself: "Is my mind focused on building real strength, or am I just exhausting my sanity trying to control the uncontrollable?" True preparation provides a foundation of mental clarity, but a relentless struggle against every unknown variable only serves to drain your spirit and fracture your peace. By making the intentional choice to accept what is out of your hands while fortifying what is within your reach, you shield your mind from the corrosive effects of chronic stress. Resilience isn't a gift that suddenly arrives; it's a conscious strategy you must choose every day to protect your mental well-being. Do not wait for peace of mind to find you—save your sanity by making the intentional shift to embrace uncertainty today.

I'm going to say something that would have made the younger version of me uncomfortable: prioritizing my mental health has made me sharper and more effective at personal safety, not "soft." For a long time, I operated under the quiet assumption that toughness meant pushing through, sacrificing sleep, and running on a volatile mix of stress, coffee, and professional pride. Having seen that approach play out across a twenty-eight-year career, I can tell you the results are rarely sustainable.

Throughout my career, I came to deeply respect fear as a vital source of information—a silent partner that, when understood, can save your life. Real fear is a biological radar; it hones your senses and heightens your alert, allowing you to detect lurking dangers or potential mistakes before they manifest. I've been in situations where a sudden, unexplainable feeling made me pause or change course, and that momentary hesitation turned out to be the only thing standing between safety and disaster. When your mind is clear, fear acts as a sharp lens, bringing the hidden risks of a situation into sudden, vivid focus.

However, I've also learned that not everything that feels like fear is an honest signal. To save your sanity, you must learn to distinguish between a protective instinct that alerts you to a real threat and a "lying" anxiety that simply clouds your judgment. Often, a mind that has been under constant pressure begins to mistake its own shadows for enemies, causing you to see potential mistakes where none exist and react to dangers that aren't there.

Learning to tell the difference is a life-long discipline. By slowing down before reacting and asking yourself if you are responding to a genuine detection or a nervous system that is simply "crying wolf," you save yourself from the exhaustion of living in a state of false alarm. Protecting your sanity means knowing when to lean into that heightened alert to avoid a lurking trap, and when to recognize that your mind just needs to rest.

Getting hit with a major incident—whether a physical threat on the street or a crushing financial blow—can cloud your judgment and bruise your sanity. In the aftermath, you inevitably start blaming yourself for a failure to anticipate the danger. I felt this deeply just this past month with my investment in PayPal. After conducting extensive research, I felt certain the stock was undervalued, only to be hit with a serious downturn. I spiraled into self-blame, obsessing over my failure to recognize a "value trap," and the mental weight of that mistake began to feel like a heavy fog threatening my peace of mind. However, I've learned that I cannot let one bad read become my permanent undoing; I have to consciously tell myself to pause, breathe, and move forward.

I've had my share of incidents throughout my life—some professional, some personal, and some that don't fit neatly into either category. What I can tell you from experience is that the aftermath of a genuinely high-stakes situation is its own distinct challenge. After my first significant incident on the job, I did what many do: I filed it away, declared myself fine, and moved on. That approach worked for a while, but those unaddressed experiences eventually surfaced in dreams, overreactions, and a constant background tension. I've learned that moving forward in a healthy way requires moving through the experience, not around it.

That means allowing yourself to feel whatever comes up—the anger, the shaken confidence, and the questions about what you could have done differently—without rushing to bury it. It means being willing to talk to someone if the weight becomes too heavy, without treating it as an admission of weakness. Recovery is not a race, and the timeline is different for everyone. Give yourself the same grace and care that you would encourage someone you love to give themselves. You deserve no less than that.

If I've learned anything across decades of law enforcement and ordinary living, it's this: personal safety is a marathon, not a sprint, and your mind is the most important piece of equipment you carry. For years, I operated under the assumption that vigilance meant constant, high-level stress. However, I eventually realized that exhausting your mind in a frantic attempt to control every variable actually makes you less safe. A fatigued brain is slow to react and prone to tunnel vision. True personal safety is built on a foundation of mental clarity. By nurturing your sanity and finding a sustainable balance, you aren't "letting your guard down"—you are sharpening it.

Mastering the mind allows you to replace panicked scanning with calm, deliberate observation. This mental shift makes you freer, more decisive, and ultimately much more effective at protecting yourself. When you protect your sanity, you ensure that your "internal radar" remains clear and ready to detect a real threat the moment it appears. Therefore, the balanced safety lifestyle is not a fixed destination; it is an ongoing conversation with yourself. It requires a regular check-in where you ask: "Is my mind clear enough to protect my life, or is my stress level clouding my judgment?" This balance shifts with age, environment, and what you've recently endured. There is no universal formula, but the priority remains the same: keep your primary safety instrument—your mind—in peak condition. You are a unique person with a unique history and set of circumstances. My experiences are offered here simply as one person's honest account—a starting point for your own reflection, not a rigid blueprint. Find the safety habits that work for you. Test them honestly, adjust as you go, and wherever possible, make sure that the life you are protecting is a life you are truly living to the fullest.

This is your journey. I've simply shared mine.

Chapter 8

Home Safety

Building upon the foundational principles of financial safety established earlier, I remain a firm and unwavering advocate for real estate as the primary cornerstone of long-term stability. It is my strong conviction that strategic property investment is among the most effective methods available for reinforcing one's financial safety, and it is vital to recognize that homeownership itself is nothing short of a primary real estate investment. While it is true that owning a home introduces additional layers of responsibility and expense—such as property taxes, homeowners insurance, and the inevitable costs of maintenance—these should be viewed as strategic investments in an appreciating asset rather than mere sunk costs. In return for these expenditures, you effectively stop the cycle of wasting money on rent, which offers zero return, and begin actively building home equity with every monthly payment. As the cost of housing naturally increases over time, your equity grows alongside the market value of the property, eventually providing you with sufficient leverage to sell for a significant profit. In my own journey, this path was made possible by the Section 121 Exclusion, a tax law that allowed us to keep up to $500,000 of our profit tax-free when selling our primary residence, provided we lived there for at least two of the five years prior to the sale.

Furthermore, as you transition from homeownership into the realm of real estate investment as a landlord, you can utilize the Section 1031 Exchange. This "like-kind" exchange is a powerful tool for investment properties, allowing you to sell a rental unit and reinvest the proceeds into a new investment property while deferring capital gains taxes. By leveraging these specific tax laws, you ensure that your hard-earned equity is not eroded by taxes every time you move or upgrade your portfolio. Whether you are "trading up" your family home or scaling your rental holdings, these strategies allow your wealth to compound over time, converting a monthly necessity into a powerful engine for long-term financial security. Beyond the practical financial benefits, the emotional reward of homeownership is profound. There is a deep, enduring pride in owning the land beneath your feet and the roof over your head; it serves as a powerful symbol of your personal journey and a tangible manifestation of years of sacrifice and hard work. Unlike a rental, which remains a temporary arrangement subject to someone else's terms, a home you own is a sanctuary that you have earned. It stands as a monument to your resilience and a physical testament to the fact that you have transitioned from a life of financial uncertainty to one of established stability.

However, hand-in-hand with the pride of homeownership is the solemn responsibility to protect your home—your castle—and its occupants. This stewardship extends far beyond routine maintenance; it is about the active defense of your loved ones from potential intruders. To ensure the safety of my own family and the security of our home, I have diligently installed a robust security system and a comprehensive surveillance camera network. This system allows me to monitor our surroundings remotely via my cell phone, tablet, or laptop, providing real-time alerts whenever movement is detected. I have designed this network to be exhaustive, covering a full 360-degree view of the exterior as well as key areas of the interior. While I am committed to total vigilance, I am equally committed to the dignity of my family; therefore, I have carefully excluded areas where privacy is expected, such as bathrooms and my daughters' bedrooms. To reinforce this layer of protection, I installed the surveillance application not only on my own devices but on those of my family members as well. We have collectively developed a disciplined habit of checking our feeds to ensure the exterior and interior of the home are clear before we ever pull into the driveway or step through the front door. This level of vigilance is perhaps a residual side effect of my former career in law enforcement, but I view it as a necessary precaution in an unpredictable world. The last thing I ever want is for a loved one to unknowingly walk into the middle of a robbery or, worse, a violent home invasion. In such a terrifying scenario, those inside—potentially held as hostages—would be praying for someone on the outside to notice the anomaly and summon the police. By maintaining this constant situational awareness, we ensure we are never blindsided, treating our home not just as a place of comfort, but as a secured environment where safety is never left to chance.

Technology alone, however, is insufficient; it must be supported by "territorial reinforcement," which is the physical management of your property to deter criminal interest. It is imperative to keep your front porch, side yards, and entry points clear of dense brush or overgrown vegetation. Thick shrubbery creates ideal "blind spots" where a perpetrator can hide and wait for an opportunity to ambush you from behind, forcing their way into the residence as you unlock the door. You must ensure that landscaping does not create hidden pockets that a lens cannot penetrate. Furthermore, while modern cameras have impressive night vision capabilities, they are significantly enhanced by the strategic installation of motion-sensor spotlights. These lights not only act as a primary deterrent by stripping an intruder of the cover of darkness, but they also provide the high-contrast illumination necessary for you to clearly monitor your home at night. While motion-sensor spotlights are excellent for startling an intruder, they should be supplemented by a consistent "dusk-to-dawn" lighting strategy. A common mistake is leaving the exterior of a home in total darkness, relying solely on sensors to catch movement. However, a well-lit perimeter acts as a powerful psychological barrier; criminals naturally prefer the anonymity of shadows and will almost always bypass a home bathed in light in favor of one with dark corners. Low-voltage architectural lighting and well-placed LED floods eliminate the "blind spots" where cameras might struggle to resolve a face, ensuring that your home remains a "hard target" from the street view at all hours of the night.

True security also requires "hardening" the physical entry points of your fortress to delay any attempted breach. Most standard door frames are surprisingly fragile, which is why I recommend replacing the factory screws in your hinges and strike plates with three-inch hardened steel screws that anchor directly into the wall studs. This simple modification makes a door nearly impossible to kick in. Additionally, applying heavy-duty security film to glass windows prevents them from shattering, forcing an intruder to make a great deal of noise and spend precious time attempting to gain entry. For those seeking an even higher level of physical deterrence, the installation of a steel security door outside of your primary front door is a powerful option. While I recognize that these industrial-style doors may detract from the outward beauty or "curb appeal" of a home, their functional benefit is unmatched. Because these doors open outward, it is structurally almost impossible for a perpetrator to kick them in. I chose to install one at my home for the peace of mind it provides, though I understand many homeowners prefer not to for aesthetic reasons. Whether you choose this path or stick to reinforced locks, having a pre-planned sanctuary within the house—a safe room equipped with a solid-core door and communication tools—ensures your family has a final line of defense if the perimeter is ever compromised. Furthermore, because our modern "castles" are increasingly managed through digital networks, you must safeguard your technological perimeter as diligently as your physical one. Since your security cameras and smart alarms rely on your home Wi-Fi, an insecure network is a vulnerability that a sophisticated criminal could exploit to "blind" your surveillance. Protecting your Wi-Fi with complex passwords and hidden network IDs ensures that your digital eyes remain open. By integrating these physical reinforcements and digital safeguards with your surveillance habits, you move from a strategy of mere detection to one of total deterrence.

There is no doubt that your home is your castle, but even the strongest fortress is vulnerable if the gates are opened to the wrong person. In many ways, the most dangerous threats are not the ones that storm the walls, but the ones you unwittingly invite inside—troubles that are neither seen nor suspected until it is too late. While I hold no ill will toward repairmen, handymen, or service professionals, I am a firm believer in the principle of "limited access." You should avoid allowing strangers into your home unless it is absolutely unavoidable. This is an especially critical consideration for female homeowners who live alone, as they can be specifically targeted by those looking for perceived vulnerabilities. Every time an outsider enters your private sanctuary, they aren't just fixing a sink; they are gaining a vantage point to observe your floor plan, your security measures, and your daily routines. When a professional visit is necessary, you must vet the individual with extreme diligence. Beyond a standard background check, make an effort to contact previous customers. However, maintain a healthy skepticism—remember that provided references are often friends or associates biased in their favor. Seek out independent, third-party reviews to cross-reference their history before granting them access to your safe haven. Whenever possible, arrange for a friend or family member to be present during the service call so you are never alone with a stranger.

To minimize these risks, I strongly encourage you to become your own first line of defense by learning to handle recurring household repairs yourself. In our digital age, there is almost no leaky faucet or broken cabinet that cannot be mastered through a bit of study and practice. By becoming self-reliant, you don't just save money; you eliminate the need for an outsider to cross your threshold. Of course, exercise common sense: if a repair involves high-voltage electricity, gas lines, or anything that poses a risk of explosion or serious injury, call a licensed professional. For everything else, your own two hands are your most secure tools. By the same token, while I have no hard feelings against mobile solicitors, I advise my family to exercise extreme caution. If my wife or daughters happen to be seen at the front door, they are instructed to never open the steel security door. It is safer to communicate from behind the locked barrier, remaining acutely aware that a screen door offers no protection against a ballistic threat. Even if a person arrives in a uniform—or claims to be a law enforcement officer—requesting entry to your house or backyard, do not take their appearance at face value. Simply seeing an identification card or a badge is insufficient; in today's world, these items can be easily faked, stolen, or purchased as realistic props to fool unsuspecting victims.

The only reliable way to verify an individual's identity and the legitimate purpose of their visit is to contact their agency or company directly. However, you must be extremely cautious about how you obtain that contact information. Never use a phone number provided by the person standing at your door. If they are an impostor, they may simply give you a number for an accomplice who is waiting to answer the phone and pose as a supervisor or dispatcher to further the deception. Instead, keep the door locked, ask them to wait, and independently find the official phone number through the company's verified website or a trusted directory. Only by initiating the call through a verified, third-party channel can you be certain you are speaking with the actual organization. It is especially alarming when a person claiming to be on official business arrives at your door without a matching company vehicle parked at the curbside. If they arrive on a scooter, a bicycle, or on foot with no visible professional transport, these are significant red flags. Furthermore, if the individual insists that you open the security door so they can speak with you "face-to-face," your internal alarm should be ringing. You must ask yourself: why is this person so intent on removing the physical barrier between you when they can communicate perfectly well through the mesh? There is no legitimate reason for a stranger to demand that you compromise your safety just to talk.

Ultimately, the guiding principle is simple: when it comes to the safety of your family and the sanctity of your home, blind trust is a luxury you cannot afford. In an era of sophisticated deception, skepticism is not paranoia—it is a vital layer of protection. If you find yourself in a situation where you feel you must grant someone your trust, you must do so only on the condition of absolute verification. As the adage "it's better to be safe than sorry" implies, every possible precaution must be taken before allowing anyone to cross the threshold of your home.

The following cases, representing real-world instances, illustrate the necessity of this caution, a review of recent events reveals a sobering list of incidents involving service workers and the risks they can pose to homeowners. I encourage you to search the internet using keywords like "service worker home invasion," "utility worker impersonation scam," or "contractor fraud prosecution" to understand the patterns predators use to bypass domestic perimeters.

Case 1: The Familiar Handyman Invasion

• Synopsis: A handyman who had become familiar with a family through previous work used his intimate knowledge of the residence's layout and security to orchestrate a violent break-in. During the home invasion, the suspect restrained one occupant and physically assaulted another.

• Adjudication: The suspect was apprehended and faced multiple felony charges, including home invasion and aggravated battery. This case highlights the extreme danger of granting interior access to individuals who may later exploit that "inside" information.

Case 2: The Residential Repair Burglary

• Synopsis: A worker hired specifically for residential repairs used his time inside a home to scout for high-value items. Once he identified the location of jewelry and small electronics, he executed a series of thefts totaling over $44,000.

• Adjudication: Forensic evidence linked the suspect to a string of similar residential burglaries across multiple neighboring counties. He was subsequently convicted and sentenced to significant prison time for organized retail and residential theft.

Case 3: The Exterior Maintenance Vulnerability

• Synopsis: While performing routine yard maintenance at a client's home, a service provider was brutally assaulted by an individual from a neighboring property.

• Takeaway: This incident serves as a reminder that even "low-risk" exterior work creates a "blind spot" in your home's security. It exposes both the homeowner and the worker to external neighborhood violence that can spill onto your property unexpectedly.

Case 4: The "Trojan Horse" Remodeling Scheme

• Synopsis: A contractor orchestrated a $1.4 million fraud scheme by using demolition as a tactical weapon. He would begin a project by tearing apart a home's interior to leave it uninhabitable, then effectively held the property hostage, demanding more money to make the home livable again.

• Adjudication: In 2026, the contractor was sentenced to 10 years in prison for large-scale fraud and property damage.

Case 5: The "Urgent Repair" High-Pressure Tactic

• Synopsis: Authorities issued community alerts regarding criminals arriving at homes unannounced, claiming that "emergency repairs" were desperately needed on the roof or foundation. The goal was to create a sense of panic that would pressure homeowners into bypassing their normal vetting process.

• The Strategy: By manufacturing a crisis, these individuals successfully convinced several residents to let them inside the home or provide immediate cash deposits for work that was never intended to be completed.

Case 6: The Utility Impersonation Strategy

• Synopsis: Criminals across several regions have begun using fake high-visibility vests and counterfeit utility gear to gain proximity to private residences. By posing as official technicians, these individuals conduct surveillance or approach front doors without raising the suspicion of neighbors or police.

• The Result: These impersonators use the guise of "official business" to test door locks, peer through windows, or engage homeowners in conversation to determine if they are home alone.

These cases prove that protecting your "castle" is not just about the locks on the doors, but the vigilance of the mind behind them. True home safety requires a layered defense: physical barriers, digital verification, and most importantly, a psychological "Red Line" that refuses to let a stranger pass without verified credentials. Remember, a badge or a vest is just a costume; only independent verification provides the truth.

One of the simple joys of homeownership is the ability to take pride in your property—whether you are tending to the front lawn, manicuring the flower beds, installing updated lighting, or simply relaxing in the yard to enjoy the neighborhood. However, being active in your front yard also makes you visible and accessible. If you are confronted by a stranger passing by, your primary objective should always be de-escalation. While you possess the absolute right to defend yourself, your family, and your home within the framework of the law, a physical confrontation should be your last resort. The logic behind avoiding a physical altercation in front of your residence is rooted in a sobering tactical reality: even if you "win" the fight, you may ultimately lose the peace. Regardless of the outcome, that stranger now knows exactly where you and your family sleep, while you likely know nothing about them. If the individual comes out on the losing end of a confrontation, you haven't just resolved a dispute; you may have created a vengeful enemy with a fixed target to return to. An embittered stranger understands that your "castle" is stationary, which opens the door to a spectrum of retaliatory threats—ranging from the stalking of family members and the vandalism of your vehicles to the shattering of windows or, in the most extreme cases, a drive-by shooting.

This is where the reality of homeownership differs sharply from renting. As a renter, you and your family often have the flexibility to break a lease and move to a different location with relative ease if your safety feels compromised. For a homeowner, it is never that simple. Deciding to move for peace of mind is a grueling, multi-faceted ordeal. It takes significant time to list and sell a home, and prevailing market conditions may not be conducive to a favorable or timely sale. Beyond the financial hurdles, you must weigh the heavy emotional toll of disrupting your children's education and uprooting the communal friendships they have spent years building. By de-escalating and avoiding a physical clash whenever possible, you aren't showing weakness; you are exercising the wisdom of a protector who understands that your home is a long-term investment in stability. Choosing your battles wisely ensures that your sanctuary remains a place of peace rather than a location you are eventually forced to flee.

By the same token, it is paramount that you cultivate and maintain healthy relationships with your neighbors—particularly those immediately adjacent to you, those directly behind your property, and those across the street. The truth is that no one wants to live in the shadow of an adversary. A neighbor who has transformed from a friendly face into a hostile one due to a petty disagreement or a heated confrontation can dampen the joys of homeownership instantly and, in many cases, permanently. It is a deeply tragic situation to feel uncomfortable in your own yard or hesitant to pull into your own driveway after investing a lifetime of savings into your home. Furthermore, this sense of peace begins long before you sign the closing papers. While everyone's home-search process is unique, I cannot overstate the necessity of extreme due diligence. You must remember a fundamental truth: It is always easier to fix your own home, but it is practically impossible to fix your neighborhood on your own. You can renovate a kitchen or repair a roof, but you cannot unilaterally change the culture, the noise levels, or the safety of the streets surrounding you.

To illustrate this point, when my wife and I were looking to purchase our primary home nearly twenty years ago, I didn't rely solely on my professional knowledge. Despite being a patrol officer at the time and already familiar with the general area, we took numerous drives through the neighborhood at all hours of the day and night on my days off. We observed the environment during the early morning commute, the midday school hours, the evening rush, and the dead of night. This allowed us to gain an intimate, unfiltered understanding of the neighborhood's rhythm and the true character of the community. In the same vein, true home safety starts with asking if your lifestyle genuinely fits the existing community. Personally, I have never been much of a party-goer; I have always preferred a quiet, predictable environment. When I noticed that the majority of the residents in the area we were considering were retirees or soon-to-be retirees, I was ecstatic. Even though we were only in our 30s, I chalked that up as a major plus. Another primary concern was traffic safety, as we were about to start a family. We visited the area repeatedly, specifically looking for red flags like signs of reckless drivers, the presence of modified muscle cars, or evidence of street racing. Finding none, we felt confident that our future children would be safe. We exhausted our diligence before we ever signed on the dotted line, and it remains one of the best decisions we have ever made. We are still living in that same house today, enjoying the peace we carefully verified two decades ago. In short, do not rush the process—vet the neighborhood as thoroughly as you vet the house itself, because once you move in, you are wedded to both.

That being said, home safety is an endless process. What might be a concern for one person might not be an issue at all for another; how you prioritize your security is ultimately up to you and your family. Nevertheless, there are universal vulnerabilities that every homeowner should address to maintain a "hard target" profile. For instance, beyond the threat of physical entry, you must consider the "signals" your home sends to those scouting for an easy target. In the age of online shopping, your front porch has become a secondary entryway that requires its own set of defenses. Allowing mail to pile up or high-value packages to sit exposed on your doorstep is a neon sign to "porch pirates" and scouts that the home is either unoccupied or that the residents are not vigilant. These small lapses in stewardship can draw predatory eyes to your property. Investing in a secure, locking mailbox and a reinforced parcel locker is a simple way to deny criminals the opportunity to "test" your home's perimeter. By keeping your porch clear, you maintain the appearance of an active, guarded fortress.

However, we must remember that technology and hardware are only as effective as the people using them. Just as I have trained my family to check the surveillance feeds before entering the home, it is equally important to establish a "Code Word" system for emergencies. In a high-stress situation—such as a stranger attempting to push through the door or an intruder spotted on the feed—seconds are the difference between safety and tragedy. Your family should have a pre-arranged, non-obvious word that, when spoken, triggers an immediate, rehearsed response: retreating to the safe room, locking the interior doors, and contacting emergency services. This ensures that in the heat of a crisis, your loved ones do not hesitate, but act with the precision of a disciplined unit. Finally, remember that the safety of your castle involves more than just defending against human intruders; you must also protect it from the "silent" threats of fire and domestic accidents. True stewardship means maintaining your smoke and carbon monoxide detectors as diligently as you maintain your security cameras. Every floor of your home should be equipped with a fire extinguisher that every family member knows how to operate, and exit paths should always be kept clear. A castle that is impenetrable to outsiders but lacks internal safety protocols is still a vulnerable home. By integrating fire prevention and emergency exit drills into your overall safety plan, you ensure that your sanctuary remains a place where your family is protected from every possible angle.

As previously discussed, the United States remains one of the few nations that recognizes the right of law-abiding citizens and permanent residents to possess firearms. However, the decision to introduce a firearm into the home for self-defense is a deeply personal one—a choice that requires rigorous contemplation and consensus among family members.

If you choose the path of gun ownership, it is imperative that you move beyond mere possession and strive for absolute mastery. This involves not only technical proficiency with the weapon but a comprehensive understanding of the complex laws governing the use of lethal force. You must know, with absolute certainty, the legal thresholds for deployment; a split-second error in judgment can lead to catastrophic consequences. Even a well-intentioned act of defense can trigger exhaustive police investigations, grand jury scrutiny, and harrowing court proceedings that may result in years of incarceration. While firearms can undeniably save lives and serve as a deterrent against violent intruders, the legal and moral weight of using such force is a burden that lasts a lifetime. True security in your sanctuary is derived not just from the tools you keep, but from the wisdom, training, and legal discipline that guide their use.

For me, the decision to own a firearm is straightforward due to my profession, which mandates that I carry one. However, professional carrying is not a "set it and forget it" privilege. To maintain my permit, I am required to qualify at a range three times per year—a requirement that does not include the countless additional hours I spend practicing independently to ensure my proficiency remains razor-sharp.

Owning a firearm carries a massive spectrum of responsibilities, ranging from the technicalities of safe cleaning and secure storage to the legal nuances of "use of force" doctrine. My intent is not to encourage or discourage gun ownership, but rather to prompt a vital self-examination. Ask yourself: If an armed perpetrator breached your home in the middle of the night—or even in the middle of the day—and threatened the lives of your loved ones, how would you respond?

- Do you have a tactical plan in place for such an event?

• Do you have a designated "safe room" or a practiced escape route for your family?

These questions require clear, pre-established answers. When the adrenaline of a real-life threat hits, the ability to think critically vanishes; your survival depends entirely on the plans you made when the world was quiet.

The following cases, representing real-world instances, illustrate the brutal reality of home invasions and the evolving tactics used by violent offenders. I encourage you to search the internet using keywords like "home invasion security camera bypass," "GPS tracking stalking crime," or "residential castle doctrine cases" to see how modern threats are developing.

Case 1: The Calculated Camera Bypass

• Synopsis: Suspects demonstrated a chilling level of premeditation by identifying and disabling exterior security cameras before breaking into a residence. Once inside, they held the occupant captive and subjected him to a brutal assault. The victim ultimately succumbed to severe head injuries sustained during the breach.

• Adjudication: Three individuals were apprehended and charged with murder in May 2025. This case highlights that technology alone is not a shield; if a perpetrator can "blind" your system, your physical response plan is all that remains.

Case 2: The "Target-Specific" Firearm Theft

• Synopsis: In a tragic example of a targeted break-in, four intruders entered a home with the specific intent of stealing a resident's firearms. The resulting confrontation between the armed intruders and the homeowners turned fatal, leading to the death of a 19-year-old resident.

• Adjudication: The suspects were identified and are currently undergoing sentencing as of early 2026. This serves as a stark reminder that if you own firearms, your storage must be so secure that it does not become the very reason you are targeted.

Case 3: The High-Tech Tracking Ambush

• Synopsis: Highlighting a modern "digital stalking" tactic, suspects surreptitiously attached a GPS tracking device to a victim's vehicle. By monitoring the victim's movements, they were able to locate the victim's private residence, lie in wait, and execute a coordinated armed invasion the moment the victim arrived home.

• Adjudication: Authorities have issued widespread warnings regarding these tracking devices. This case proves that your "perimeter" now extends miles away from your front door; it begins wherever your vehicle is parked.

Case 4: The Violent Urban Breach

• Synopsis: A residential neighborhood was shaken by a violent weekend confrontation when a suspect forced entry into a home. The encounter turned deadly almost immediately as the suspect engaged the residents with lethal force.

• Adjudication: The District Attorney filed murder charges against the suspect in late 2025. These urban incidents emphasize that "high-traffic" neighborhoods do not necessarily deter bold, violent offenders.

Case 5: The Multi-Suspect Armed Robbery

• Synopsis: Three individuals coordinated a violent residential robbery, overpowering the occupants through sheer numbers and the display of weapons. The group utilized violence to coerce the victims into revealing the locations of valuables within the home.

• Adjudication: Police apprehended the trio in April 2026. They face a litany of charges including robbery with violence and various weapons offenses. This scenario underscores the difficulty of defending against multiple attackers without a pre-rehearsed family safety plan.

Case 6: The Random Act of Lethal Violence

• Synopsis: In a harrowing case of random violence, an intruder with no prior connection to the family broke in and immediately opened fire, killing a woman inside. A 16-year-old resident was able to retrieve a firearm and stop the threat by killing the intruder. Investigations later revealed the suspect had arrived in a vehicle outfitted with body armor and a significant quantity of extra ammunition, suggesting he was prepared for a prolonged gunfight.

• Adjudication: While the resident acted in self-defense, the investigation revealed the terrifying reality that some predators are not looking for money; they are looking for a high-stakes confrontation.

As you can see, these unfortunate events can happen anywhere, often involving tactics specifically designed to circumvent common security measures. It is vital to plan ahead and be ready to execute those plans to protect your family and yourself—regardless of whether you choose to own a firearm or not. True safety is found in the interval between the threat and your prepared response.

In certain instances, homeowners who have deployed firearms to protect their property, their loved ones, and their own lives have found themselves facing criminal charges rather than being cleared of wrongdoing.

While many jurisdictions recognize the "Castle Doctrine," it is vital to understand that using a firearm for home defense does not grant blanket legal immunity. Law enforcement and prosecutors often initiate arrests when defensive actions exceed the legal threshold of "reasonable force," or if a homeowner discharges a weapon at a suspect who no longer poses an immediate, life-threatening danger. Consequently, if you choose to own a firearm, it is your absolute responsibility to understand your specific state and local laws regarding the use of firearms; ignorance of the law is never a valid defense in a courtroom.

Beyond the physical danger of a home invasion, the judicial aftermath for homeowners can be equally devastating. Legal records illustrate the reality of recent incidents where the line between justifiable self-defense and criminal conduct became a matter of intense litigation. These cases, representing real-world instances, prove that the consequences of a split-second decision can resonate in the courts for years. I encourage you to search the internet using keywords like "shooting at fleeing suspect laws," "manslaughter conviction self-defense rejected," or "objective reasonableness standard use of force" to better understand the legal "tripwires" that exist even inside your own home.

Case 1: The Detached Structure Dispute

• Synopsis: A 24-year-old homeowner was charged with manslaughter after firing at a group of individuals attempting to break into his detached garage. The individual claimed he feared for his safety during the encounter.

• The Legal Conflict: Prosecutors alleged the homeowner fired through a windowless, locked door and continued shooting even as the suspects attempted to flee the scene. A 17-year-old was killed in the encounter. This case highlights that "Castle Doctrine" protections often have strict limits regarding outbuildings and suspects who are retreating.

Case 2: The "Fleeing Suspect" Contradiction

• Synopsis: In a high-profile follow-up to a residential shooting, a judge ruled that a homeowner must stand trial for the death of an intruder. While the homeowner claimed the intruders "came at him" in a threatening manner, the digital evidence told a different story.

• The Legal Conflict: Security footage allegedly contradicted the owner's statement, appearing to show him firing multiple shots at the suspects' backs as they were running away from the property. In the eyes of the law, once the threat is retreating, the legal justification for lethal force often vanishes.

Case 3: The "Accidental" Discharge Rejection

• Synopsis: A homeowner's self-defense claim was rejected by a jury after a fatal struggle. The defendant argued that his weapon discharged accidentally during a physical fight for control over the firearm.

• The Outcome: The court applied an "objective reasonableness" standard. The jury found that his overall actions did not meet the legal threshold for justified lethal force. While he was acquitted of murder, he was convicted of manslaughter—proving that a lack of "intent" does not protect you from the legal consequences of an unreasonable response.

Case 4: The "Necessary in Hindsight" Reversal

• Synopsis: A resident was initially convicted of a felony after firing at a vehicle he believed contained an armed threat. The trial judge originally ruled that while the shooting may have seemed necessary after all the facts came out, it was "objectively unreasonable" at the exact moment the trigger was pulled.

• The Legal Conflict: Although a higher court eventually overturned the conviction and justified the act, the homeowner spent significant time and resources fighting for his freedom. This case serves as a warning that even if you are ultimately found "innocent," the process of proving it can be a life-altering ordeal.

These cases serve as sobering reminders that the legal aftermath of a defensive shooting can be as devastating as the incident itself. They stand as prime examples of why mere firearm ownership is insufficient; you must possess a comprehensive mastery of the specific statutes and "use-of-force" doctrines applicable in your jurisdiction.

In the eyes of the law, a split-second decision is subjected to hours of clinical scrutiny. The razor-thin margin between a justified act of protection and a life-altering felony conviction often hinges on your adherence to these complex legal boundaries. True responsibility begins long before a threat ever appears at your door.

Moving away from the gravity of armed defense, it is important to recognize that one of the most effective ways to transition from individual security to collective safety is through the initiation or active participation in a neighborhood watch program. Usually sanctioned by local police departments and guided by crime prevention specialists, these initiatives bridge the critical gap between residents and law enforcement. During my time on the force, I frequently attended these meetings to interact directly with the community. They provided an indispensable platform to answer questions, address localized concerns, and share specific crime statistics that empowered residents to stay informed. These interactions were consistently positive; my partners and I were welcomed with open arms, fostering a spirit of mutual respect and cooperation that is too often absent in modern society. Looking back, these moments were some of the most rewarding of my career. They proved that when neighbors vigilantly look out for one another and maintain an open, direct line of communication with the police, the community becomes a significantly harder target for criminal activity.

In summary, home safety is a multi-dimensional discipline that integrates financial foresight, physical fortification, and unwavering mental vigilance. This journey begins long before the moving trucks arrive, rooted in the exhaustive due diligence required to ensure a neighborhood aligns with your safety standards. It is maintained through the deliberate "hardening" of your residence—reinforcing entry points, strategic landscaping, and eliminating the shadows through consistent lighting. True security is further sustained by a strict gatekeeping protocol that limits access to strangers, prioritizes self-reliance over unvetted service calls, and demands independent verification for every professional who crosses the threshold. Furthermore, the resilience of your "castle" is exponentially enhanced when you join forces with your community, fostering a collaborative environment where residents and law enforcement act as a unified deterrent. For those who choose to exercise their right to own a firearm as a final line of defense, safety remains inextricably tied to rigorous training and an intimate understanding of the grave legal consequences inherent in the use of force. Ultimately, security is perfected by the human element: the implementation of surveillance habits, emergency code words, and fire safety drills that transform a family into a coordinated defensive unit. By treating your home as both a powerful financial engine and a sacred, secured sanctuary, you transform mere property into a fortress of peace, ensuring that your castle remains a place of safety for generations to come.

Chapter 9

Vehicle Safety

While your home serves as your ultimate castle, your vehicle is a mobile sanctuary—a private extension of your personal space where you likely spend a significant portion of your day. Whether you are commuting to work, running errands, or embarking on a long-distance journey, you naturally maintain a high expectation of privacy and security within that cabin. However, just as we established with home safety, vehicle security is paramount because your car can inadvertently become a "trap in plain view" if you are not vigilant.

The transition from the stationary safety of your house to the fluid environment of the road requires a significant shift in tactical thinking. While your home remains anchored in a neighborhood with which you are intimately familiar, your vehicle is inherently mobile, constantly placing you in proximity to strangers. You can never truly know who is in the vehicles surrounding yours, nor can you fathom their current mental state.

It is an undeniable reality of the human condition that everyone carries some form of personal burden. For some, these are mere inconveniences, but for others, they are monumental crises. While many possess the emotional intelligence to manage their stress, others may be hovering on the precipice of a psychological explosion. In such a volatile state, even a minor, unintentional oversight by another driver—a delayed turn signal or a split-second hesitation at a green light—can serve as the spark that ignites a catastrophic episode of road rage.

Consequently, vehicle safety encompasses far more than the mechanical integrity of your car; it is defined by your ability to navigate the unpredictable human landscape of the open road. Every decision you make—where you choose to park, how you approach your vehicle, and how you interact with the flow of traffic—functions as a critical layer of defense. By applying the same principles of "hardening the target" and situational awareness used to secure your home, you can ensure that your time behind the wheel remains a controlled experience rather than a vulnerability in an increasingly erratic world.

This vigilance is especially vital when considering the sheer volume of firearms in circulation. With approximately 32% of Americans reporting personal gun ownership, the statistical reality is that you never know if the driver you have inadvertently upset is armed. It is important to realize that this figure primarily reflects those who possess firearms through legal channels; when you factor in the presence of illicit or unregistered weapons, the percentage of individuals with immediate access to a firearm becomes significantly higher. You are not only contending with the law-abiding citizen but also with those who may have bypassed legal safeguards entirely.

I will be the first to confess that throughout my forty-plus years of driving, I have occasionally upset others on the road. Whether it was a late lane change or an abrupt stop, I have made the same unintentional errors we all do. However, even when carrying a concealed weapon with a valid permit, my primary objective is always the total avoidance of conflict. My priority is to immediately create distance by turning onto a side street or changing my route to de-escalate the situation before it can breathe. On the rare occasions where eye contact or verbal communication is unavoidable, I am always quick to offer a sincere apology. In the high-stakes environment of the road, humility is a far more effective defensive tool than pride.

Unfortunately, not everyone shares a commitment to de-escalation, and the consequences of that volatility are increasingly lethal. The following scenarios from April 2026 provide a sobering glimpse into the reality of road rage. These events emphasize that in a high-stress driving environment, even a minor traffic dispute can escalate into a life-threatening shootout in seconds.

I encourage you to search the internet using keywords like "freeway shooting forensic investigation," "road rage firearm escalation statistics," or "highway assault open container charges" to understand how law enforcement is grappling with this surge in vehicular violence.

Case 1: The Multi-Vehicle Rollover Shootout

• Synopsis: Occupants of two vehicles engaged in a dispute on a suburban road that escalated when both sides produced firearms and exchanged gunfire while moving.

• The Chaos: During the shootout, one vehicle struck another, causing a high-speed rollover. A third vehicle, carrying a young child, was caught in the crossfire. This case serves as a terrifying reminder that "crossfire" does not respect innocent bystanders or families simply sharing the road.

Case 2: The Commuter Foot-to-Firearm Escalation

• Synopsis: During a busy morning commute near a major transit hub, a physical altercation began when one individual allegedly kicked another driver's car during an argument over positioning.

• The Escalation: The driver parked his sedan, exited the vehicle, and shot the other man in the leg before fleeing. This highlights the "asymmetry of force"—a minor act of physical frustration (kicking a car) was met with lethal force.

Case 3: The Highway Alcohol and Weapon Breach

• Synopsis: An individual was arrested after allegedly firing a handgun at another driver on a major highway during the evening rush hour.

• The Arrest: Police intercepted the suspect and discovered both a firearm and an open container of alcohol. He was charged with assault by pointing a gun, illustrating how impaired judgment frequently fuels the internal threat of rage.

Case 4: The Illegal Turn Freeway Shooting

• Synopsis: A driver reported being targeted after a suspect made an illegal right turn that nearly caused a collision. Rather than acknowledging the error, the suspect pulled alongside the victim's car on the interstate and fired several rounds.

• The Result: While the victim was not struck, the freeway was closed for hours for forensic evidence collection. It proves that even when you are the "victim" of another's poor driving, engaging them can trigger a lethal response.

Case 5: The Rush Hour "Daily Reality"

• Synopsis: State police responded to gunfire on a major interstate during a Monday morning rush hour. Troopers noted that they now investigate multiple incidents involving weapons and road-based disputes almost every single day.

• The Takeaway: This scenario validates that road rage is no longer an anomaly; it is a statistical probability in modern traffic. Your "home field advantage" on your daily commute is an illusion that can be shattered by a single aggressive lane change.

It is a reasonable assumption that whenever we step into our vehicles, our primary goal is to reach our destination without conflict. For the vast majority of our lives, we successfully achieve this. However, the moment we relinquish self-control—allowing an offensive gesture or the erratic behavior of another driver to dictate our reactions—the situation can spiral with terrifying, irreversible speed. In a world where every driver may be a "mobile armory," de-escalation is your only logical tactical choice.

Throughout my law enforcement career, I responded to far too many catastrophic collisions that were entirely preventable. These were not "accidents" in the traditional sense, but the violent conclusions of mid-road disputes. I witnessed massive wreckage caused by drivers who, just minutes earlier, had been ordinary citizens, but were now racing one another to settle a perceived slight. In a desperate attempt to assert dominance and vent their rage through excessive velocity, they transformed their vehicles from modes of transport into high-velocity projectiles. The tragic reality of road rage is that the quest to "win" a roadside argument often ends in a permanent loss of life.

The physics of the road are as unforgiving as they are simple: speed is the ultimate force multiplier of tragedy. In the context of aggressive driving, excessive velocity is a reckless gamble with the laws of motion. As your speed increases, your field of vision narrows, your reaction time is effectively slashed, and the distance required to bring a multi-ton vehicle to a halt expands exponentially. At high speeds, the margin for error vanishes entirely; a minor steering correction that would be harmless at 30 mph can cause a vehicle to roll or spin out of control at 80 mph. I saw clearly on patrol that this ego-driven speed is a dangerous delusion of control. Once a vehicle loses traction, the driver is no longer a pilot—they are merely a passenger in a collision course with fate.

It is vital to never forget that once you engage in these high-speed displays of aggression, you are wielding a multi-ton, blunt-force weapon. This volatility strips away your ability to react and transforms a momentary lapse in judgment into a lethal event. We must constantly pull ourselves back to the foundational promise we made when we first turned the key: our singular mission is to get from Point A to Point B safely and without incident. Anything that distracts from that goal—whether it is a bruised ego or the impulse to retaliate—is a threat to your survival. By driving defensively and mindfully, you honor that original intention, ensuring that your vehicle remains a sanctuary of transport rather than a tool of destruction.

Beyond the mechanics of driving, I have spent years teaching my wife and daughters that the choice of where they park—be it on a public street, within a sprawling parking lot, or deep inside a multi-level parking structure—is a critical tactical decision that directly impacts their personal safety. I've always emphasized that while anyone can be a target, criminals are inherently opportunistic and habitually seek the path of least resistance. From a predator's perspective, whether the motive is monetary gain or sexual gratification, they often perceive a female driver as a "soft target" compared to a physically imposing male who they assume might be more likely to outmaneuver or outmatch them in a violent confrontation.

Consequently, I constantly remind them that selecting a parking space should never be an afterthought. Parking structures and lots often contain "dead zones"—areas with poor lighting, limited lines of sight, and high concrete pillars that provide perfect concealment for a perpetrator lying in wait. I've taught them to evaluate a spot not just for convenience, but for its proximity to exits, its level of visibility to others, and the quality of its lighting. By helping them understand that predators intentionally scout these environments for vulnerability, they can deny an attacker the tactical advantage they need. Hardening oneself as a target begins the moment the decision is made where to leave the vehicle; choosing a spot with high visibility and foot traffic is the first line of defense against being singled out in a moment of isolation.

This same mindset extends to my wider circle of friends. A friend of mine often works late into the evening, and I make every effort to escort her to her vehicle whenever possible. Like a broken record, I am quick to compliment her when she chooses a well-lit area, but I am just as consistent in gently reminding her of the risks whenever I notice her car tucked away in a dark corner of the lot. These aren't just friendly suggestions; they are fundamental habits of survival.

I've stressed to her—and to my own family—that a safety check does not end once you reach the door handle; it begins the moment you start your approach. I constantly remind them to scan their surroundings for anyone loitering near their path or any individual dressed out of place for the environment—such as someone wearing a heavy jacket on a warm night, which can easily serve as a shroud to conceal a weapon or tools of a crime.

Furthermore, it is imperative that we all develop the habit of checking the rear interior of our vehicles before entering. Taking a split second to peer through the window to ensure the back seat is clear is a non-negotiable step. In a dark parking environment, a vehicle can easily become a ready-made blind for someone lying in wait; by the time you've settled into the driver's seat and closed the door, you've effectively trapped yourself in a confined space with a potential threat. Situational awareness isn't a part-time job; it requires a commitment to these small, repetitive actions that ensure you remain in control of your environment.

In line with this proactive mindset, I suggested to my wife and daughters that whenever they suspect something is afoot—whether they spot a suspicious shadow inside the car or sense that someone might be hiding nearby—they should immediately set off their vehicle's panic alarm. This sudden noise serves as a powerful deterrent and allows them to pause from a distance to observe how the situation unfolds. If their suspicions remain, they should never feel pressured to approach the vehicle; instead, they should retreat to a safe, populated area and call for assistance, whether that means requesting an escort from a trusted friend or contacting the authorities. I have told them that when in doubt, they should simply prioritize their safety by leaving the car behind and calling for a ride-share service. Personally, I prefer Waymo for these situations, as its autonomous driving technology eliminates the variable of a stranger behind the wheel, offering an extra layer of security during a high-stress moment.

To complement these defensive measures, I have also encouraged my daughters to carry gel pepper spray and to have it ready in hand as they approach their vehicle. If you choose to carry such a tool, it is imperative that you not only learn the mechanics of how to use it but also practice the tactical nuances of its deployment. This includes understanding environmental factors—such as knowing when to avoid spraying directly into the wind—to ensure the deterrent works against your attacker rather than becoming a hazard to yourself.

Just as Home Safety asks you to think about who may be watching your front door, I must ask you to consider a similarly harrowing scenario: what would you do if you inadvertently entered your vehicle, unaware that an armed perpetrator was hiding in the rear seat? Imagine the moment of sheer terror as you settle in, only to have a voice from the shadows command you to drive. This is not merely a hypothetical exercise; it is a tactical reality that underscores why situational awareness must extend into the very cabin of your car.

In such a high-stress situation, your vehicle is no longer a means of transport—it has become a confined, mobile crime scene where the assailant holds the initial advantage. Once the vehicle is in motion, your options for escape diminish while the perpetrator's control increases. The sad truth is that no two situations are exactly the same, and no single answer will fit every circumstance. Every encounter is dictated by the environment, the temperament of the assailant, and a thousand split-second variables.

When I posed this exact scenario to my wife and daughters, they immediately turned the question back to me, asking what I would do in their shoes. I told them honestly that my personal tactics may not be the best solution for everyone, nor are they guaranteed to get me out of such a dire situation unscathed. However, I shared that there are several measures I would consider to reclaim the advantage.

At the very onset of the situation, my first strategy would be an attempt at de-escalation through compliance. I would offer the perpetrator my car keys, wallet, and phone in exchange for my immediate release. Beyond the items on my person, I would even suggest stopping at an ATM to withdraw a significant amount of cash, dangling a financial incentive to pivot their focus from violence to profit. Would this buy my freedom? I truly don't know, but I would hope that satisfying their greed would resolve the threat. However, the offer is also a tactical ruse; if I managed to arrive at an ATM, I would be hyper-vigilant, looking for any possible opening or distraction to abandon the vehicle and escape.

If those initial offers failed, and it became clear the assailant had no intention of letting me go, I would then be forced to deploy more aggressive, extreme strategies to save myself from what is practically certain death. These are the "cards" I keep up my sleeve for the most desperate of circumstances. For instance, I would consider fishtailing the vehicle violently to off-balance the attacker or using a curbside to intentionally flip the vehicle in an area where I am unlikely to hurt innocent bystanders, pedestrians, or other drivers. The goal is to use the vehicle's momentum to throw the perpetrator against the door or window, potentially disorienting them or causing them to drop a weapon. In fact, I might even consider driving into a deep ditch or off a bridge with my window already rolled down, providing a chance to escape once the vehicle is submerged.

What I hope to gain from these extreme measures is a fleeting chance to escape, a moment to dislodge the perpetrator, or a critical opportunity to draw my own firearm to defend myself. By creating a high-impact or chaotic event, I aim to find the opening necessary to neutralize the perpetrator if they remain armed and continue to pose an imminent deadly threat to my life or the lives of others.

Furthermore, another measure I would consider while scanning for a point of impact is the potential for law enforcement intervention. If I were to spot a police patrol car, I would drive recklessly at a slow speed—just enough to catch the officer's attention—and perhaps strike a curbside or an inanimate object that would not put others at risk. The goal is to force an immediate traffic stop and compel the officer to engage. Ideally, I could then exit the vehicle, alert the officer that I am being carjacked, and point out the armed perpetrator.

Ultimately, the question remains: Would these actions work? I truly don't know. These are incredibly high-risk maneuvers, but I would much rather take my chances by seizing an officer's attention or forcing a chaotic wreck than sit passively and pray for a predator's mercy. In my mind, the risk of a calculated impact or a roll-over is far preferable to the near-certainty of being stabbed or shot from behind once we reach a secluded destination. The objective is to shift the dynamics of the encounter entirely, trading the perpetrator's control for a chaotic event that creates a narrow window for survival.

Nevertheless, I told my wife and daughters that as much as I love them, I cannot give them a definitive "correct" answer. Survival in that moment is a deeply personal choice, and it is a decision they would have to make for themselves based on the variables of the moment. Instead, I emphasized to them that the most effective strategy is to ensure that an encounter never happens in the first place.

It is important to note that I do not suggest these measures to my family or to my readers as a "how-to" guide. These radical actions are simply what I have planned for myself in the event of a catastrophic lapse in judgment. I share them to provoke a necessary thought: what would you do? How would you save yourself or those you love? Ultimately, you are the only one who can decide which risks you are willing to take and which strategies fit your own capabilities.

By taking those few extra seconds to scan the surrounding area and check the back seat before ever opening the door, you eliminate the predator's greatest weapon: the element of surprise. All it takes is a little time and the discipline to diligently look for signs of trouble. I have advised them to make this a lifelong habit—a non-negotiable ritual every time they approach their car. The cold reality of personal safety is that diligent prevention is always a far better alternative than trying to engineer a miracle escape from a life-threatening crisis.

The visibility of your vehicle's interior is a critical tactical factor often overlooked during a routine approach. While factory-standard, non-tinted windows offer the highest degree of transparency, many drivers opt for window tinting for privacy and climate control. However, it is a double-edged sword: while tinting prevents outsiders from peering in, it simultaneously obstructs your ability to clear the cabin before entering. If a perpetrator is lying in wait, those dark windows serve as a veil of concealment, effectively shielding their movements from public view. This creates a "black box" effect where, once you are inside and held hostage, the tinted glass prevents pedestrians and other motorists from noticing your distress or the presence of a weapon.

In the same vein, vehicle height and body style introduce additional layers of tactical complexity. Large-scale SUVs and trucks with high ground clearance or "lifted" suspensions create significant visibility gaps that can be easily exploited. These heights make it difficult to peer into the rear interior from a distance; even as you stand directly beside the door, the elevated beltline of the vehicle can obscure the floorboards and seat gaps. This is particularly problematic for those of us who are "vertically challenged," as the high vantage point required to clear the cabin is physically out of reach. In these instances, you are often forced to get uncomfortably close to the vehicle just to perform a basic safety check, a move that inadvertently places you within the "strike zone" of someone hiding behind the door or within the shadows of the cabin.

By comparison, cargo vans and commercial vehicles without side or rear windows pose the most daunting challenge of all, as they offer zero internal visibility from the exterior. When dealing with these "blind" vehicles, your strategy must shift from passive visual scanning to proactive tactical clearing. If your vehicle is equipped with a key fob that can actuate power sliding doors, I recommend triggering them as you make your approach. The sudden movement and the influx of light can startle a potential intruder and reveal their presence while you are still at a safe distance. If you lack a remote option, you should establish a protocol of opening the side or rear doors while remaining positioned outside the vehicle's frame. By clearing these compartments before you ever climb into the driver's seat, you preserve your "reaction gap," giving yourself the precious seconds needed to retreat and summon help before you are trapped in a confined, windowless space.

Beyond these tactical maneuvers, it goes without saying that your vehicle must be meticulously maintained to ensure total reliability. Minimizing the chances of an unexpected mechanical breakdown is a fundamental pillar of transit safety, particularly when driving through high-crime areas or traversing isolated stretches of highway in the middle of the night. A stalled vehicle in a "no man's land" transforms from a sanctuary into a stationary target. This level of mechanical vigilance is vital for every driver, but it is especially critical for women, as predators are habitually scouting for "soft targets" stranded in vulnerable locations. It is understandable that not everyone has the immediate financial means to address every mechanical issue, but I urge you to try your absolute best to keep your vehicle in peak operating condition. It is not just about convenience; it is about denying a perpetrator the opportunity to find you at your most defenseless.

In an era where new threats emerge as quickly as they can be shared, we must also account for unconventional methods of incapacitation. While I have never personally encountered this on patrol, numerous reports across various social media platforms have issued warnings to drivers regarding the state of their door handles. These reports suggest that perpetrators may coat handles with specialized chemicals or skin-contact toxins designed to make a driver feel disoriented or lose consciousness shortly after touching them.

Although many of these accounts remain officially unconfirmed by law enforcement agencies, it is a matter of tactical wisdom to heed such warnings rather than dismiss them as mere urban legend. In the world of personal security, a "low-probability, high-impact" threat still warrants a degree of caution. Developing the habit of performing a quick visual inspection of your door handles as you approach can mitigate this risk. Look for unusual residues, oily substances, or even small pieces of debris—like a napkin or a coin—stuck in the handle that seem out of place. It takes only a second to look before you touch, but that single second of skepticism ensures you aren't inadvertently introducing a toxin into your system that could leave you defenseless in a matter of minutes.

It is easy to overlook the most basic mechanical safeguards, but you must be mindful of essential emergency equipment, such as a functional spare tire, a working jack, and the proper tools to change a flat. Neglecting these items can leave you stranded and vulnerable in environments where you have little control over your surroundings.

To illustrate this point, I recall a situation from approximately two months ago while I was working a late-night assignment. I noticed a vehicle with a flat tire sitting in a dark, empty parking lot. From a distance, I could see a female driver—a tourist visiting the area—standing outside her car, staring helplessly at the front driver's side tire. Given the isolation and the darkness of the lot, I decided to pull over and offer my assistance.

Upon inspecting the vehicle, I offered to change the tire for her so she could get back on her way. However, when we checked the trunk, we discovered a major oversight: her "spare" was just a plain tire with no rim. Without a wheel to mount it on, the tire was completely useless as a roadside fix.

In this particular instance, fortune was on her side. She happened to break down in a highly affluent area of Palo Alto, near Atherton, California—locations where crime rates are exceptionally low. Because of the relatively safe environment, she was able to wait for friends to arrive and assist her. Throughout my shift that night, I swung by several times to ensure she remained safe. If I remember correctly, she wasn't able to leave until around midnight, at which point she texted me to confirm she was okay and heading home.

This encounter serves as a sobering reminder: had that same mechanical failure occurred on a desolate stretch of freeway or in a high-crime neighborhood, the outcome could have been far more precarious. It is not enough to simply have a spare; you must verify that your emergency kit is complete, that the tire is inflated, and that you possess the necessary tools to perform the task. Proper preparation ensures that a minor mechanical nuisance doesn't escalate into a dangerous security crisis.

Furthermore, I've always reminded my wife and daughters that when they come to a stop in traffic, they must never pull up directly to the bumper of the car in front of them. My rule of thumb is simple: you should always be able to see the rear tires of the lead vehicle touching the pavement. This "escape gap" acts as a critical tactical buffer that ensures you aren't boxed in; if an individual approaches your window with ill intent or a chaotic situation unfolds around you, that space provides the turning radius necessary to steer clear and exit the area without being trapped by the surrounding traffic.

Building on this mindset of physical distance, I have also cautioned my family to be mindful of the digital "breadcrumbs" their vehicles leave behind. While it's convenient to have a "Home" button on a dashboard GPS, I've advised them to never set that destination to our actual front door. Instead, we set our primary location to a nearby landmark or a familiar business a few blocks away. This ensures that if the vehicle is ever compromised—whether by a valet, a car thief, or someone looking to exploit a temporary lapse in security—they aren't handed a direct map to where my family sleeps, effectively protecting our physical perimeter by first securing our digital one.

In addition to these precautions, because a vehicle is only an effective tool for escape if it has the power to perform, I've made it a non-negotiable habit for my daughters to never let their fuel gauge drop below a quarter of a tank—and ideally, to look for a station once they hit the halfway mark. Running on fumes is a significant security vulnerability that limits your options and may force you to stop at a secluded or poorly lit station in a rough neighborhood simply because you have no other choice. By maintaining a constant fuel reserve, you ensure that you always have the "legs" to drive through a dangerous area or bypass a suspicious situation without the fear of being stranded and defenseless.

The necessity of keeping your vehicle doors locked while in motion is a lesson I learned through a jarring, firsthand experience when I was eighteen. Back in the early 1900s, I was driving an old dark gray Datsun sedan through San Jose, California, operating with the typical innocence of youth. On that particular afternoon, my only focus was on the mechanics of safe driving—until I reached the intersection of Roeder Road and Monterey Highway.

As I sat at a fresh red light, the vulnerability of my unlocked cabin was suddenly and violently exposed. Without warning, a burly man wrenched open my front passenger door and climbed in, while his female companion simultaneously entered through the rear passenger door. The man brusquely commanded me to turn left and head north on Monterey Highway. The honest truth is that I was paralyzed by a level of fear I had never known; I was convinced I had just become the victim of a kidnapping.

For several miles, I drove under their direction, my mind racing through the darkest possible outcomes. Fortunately, when we reached a small shopping strip just north of Senter Road, the man told me to pull over. To my immense relief, they both exited the vehicle and walked away without causing me physical harm. While that encounter ended without violence, it fundamentally reshaped my understanding of vehicle security. It taught me that a car at a standstill is not a fortress unless the locks are engaged. In the seconds it takes for a light to change, an unlocked door can transform your private sanctuary into a shared space with a predator, leaving you with zero time to react or retreat. Always ensure your doors are locked the moment you shift into gear; you should never provide a stranger the opportunity to simply "walk into" your life.

In conclusion, vehicle safety is an ongoing exercise in situational awareness that extends far beyond the mechanical health of your car. Your vehicle is a mobile sanctuary, but its security is only as robust as the habits you cultivate. This safety is not defined by horsepower, technology, or even the physical structure of your vehicle—it is defined by your mindset. The moment you step into your car, you are entering an environment that demands constant awareness, restraint, and deliberate decision-making.

From the psychological discipline required to de-escalate a volatile road rage encounter to the tactical precision of "hardening the target" through smart parking and proactive cabin clearing, every choice you make serves to narrow the window of opportunity for a predator. The road is an unpredictable space populated by individuals carrying unseen stress, monumental crises, and, at times, dangerous intent. You cannot control their behavior, but you can control your own. By prioritizing de-escalation over ego, distance over confrontation, and awareness over complacency, you dramatically reduce the likelihood of becoming entangled in a preventable crisis.

The habits outlined in this chapter—maintaining a physical and digital "escape gap," ensuring your doors remain a locked barrier, verifying your emergency equipment, and preparing for mechanical reliability—are not complicated, but they are powerful. These small, consistent actions form cumulative layers of protection that transform your daily commute from a point of vulnerability into a controlled, defended environment. More importantly, they shift you from being a passive participant in your environment to an active manager of your personal safety.

While it is necessary to acknowledge and prepare for worst-case scenarios, your primary objective must always remain prevention. The goal is not to have to outfight a threat, but to deny it the opportunity to materialize. Once a situation escalates—whether through road rage, a vehicle intrusion, or a moment of inattention—your options narrow rapidly, and the margin for error disappears. Ultimately, your goal is to ensure that the element of surprise—the criminal's greatest weapon—is never used against you.

In the end, vehicle safety is not just about reaching your destination; it is about how you choose to get there. By remaining vigilant, disciplined, and prepared, you honor the foundational promise of every journey: to arrive safely, without incident, and without becoming a part of someone else's worst decision. Stay aware and stay in control, ensuring your sanctuary remains intact for every mile you travel.

Chapter 10

Travel Safety

Traveling is undoubtedly one of the most enjoyable experiences for most people, offering a unique window into the diverse cultures of our world. While I do not consider myself a globetrotter by trade, my journey through life has taken me across several continents—from the bustling energy of Asia to the familiar landscapes of North America and, most recently, the historic streets of Europe. Each of these trips has reinforced a vital truth: when you leave your home turf, you are playing an "away game" where the rules, the risks, and the predatory tactics can change in an instant.

In these unfamiliar environments, your standard baseline of security must be elevated. You are no longer navigating the predictable patterns of your neighborhood; instead, you are often viewed as a "high-value target" simply because you are a visitor. Predators in tourist hubs are experts at profiling distraction—watching for the traveler who is too focused on their GPS, struggling with heavy luggage, or overwhelmed by a language barrier. These moments of disorientation are the openings they wait for.

To travel safely, you must adopt a mindset of "strategic invisibility." This means blending in with the local environment, maintaining a high level of situational awareness even while enjoying the sights, and establishing a "tactical itinerary" before you even leave your hotel room. By understanding the specific risks associated with different regions and maintaining the same "aggressive realism" we applied to digital safety, you can ensure that your travel memories are defined by the beauty of the destination rather than the trauma of a preventable incident.

Traveling is an incredible experience, even when operating on a shoestring budget. My own history with international travel started with a dose of youthful invincibility back in 1988, when a group of friends and I decided to drive across the border to Ensenada, Mexico. We were packed into a small, aging sedan like sardines; somehow, six or seven of us managed to cram inside. Being the smallest guy in the group, I spent the duration of the trip perched sideways on the raised floorboard hump between the front and back seats—a seating arrangement that was as uncomfortable as it was tactically poor.

Our trip began with a comedy of errors. While still on the highway, our driver was so oblivious to his surroundings that he failed to notice a Highway Patrol vehicle pacing us in the very next lane. When the sirens finally flared, we erupted into such uncontrollable laughter at his cluelessness that the officers became suspicious. They were convinced we were under the influence of marijuana, but we were simply high on the excitement of the road. Had we actually been smoking, they would have detected that unmistakable sweet aroma instantly. Despite the speeding ticket and the cramped quarters, we crossed into Tijuana and pushed deeper into Ensenada, fueled by the reckless confidence of teenagers.

However, the tone of the trip shifted drastically once we arrived. After a few drinks at a local spot, I made the classic traveler's mistake: I wandered off on my own. In an unfamiliar city, at night, and under the influence, I quickly became separated from the group. I spent the night alone, and the next morning, I began navigating my way back to our hotel. I was in a relaxed, observant state, enjoying the morning air and the local scenery. From a distance, I spotted our old sedan crawling through the streets. I assumed my friends were just out on a casual search for me, so I kept walking at a leisurely pace, waiting for them to catch up.

The reality was far more grim. As the car pulled alongside me, the laughter from the day before was gone, replaced by sheer panic. My friends were shouting for me to get in immediately. The moment I jumped into the sedan, the gravity of the situation hit me: they weren't just looking for me; they were being actively pursued by a group of local individuals. We didn't wait for explanations. We pushed that aging sedan to its limit, navigating the chaotic streets until we reached the safety of the border.

Looking back through the lens of a law enforcement professional, I recognize just how precariously close we came to a disaster during that trip to Ensenada. My "casual stroll" was a textbook display of total situational unawareness in a high-risk environment. The core takeaway from that experience—one that has anchored my mindset for decades—is that while traveling is undeniably enjoyable, it is imperative to maintain constant, 360-degree awareness. You must respect the reality that not every neighborhood is designed with your safety in mind. In every major city, there are "dead zones" or "no-go areas" where a lack of local knowledge can lead a traveler straight into an ambush. We were fortunate to make it back to San Diego unscathed, but that trip served as my first real lesson in the volatility of travel: in an unfamiliar place, the line between a lighthearted adventure and a life-altering crisis is thinner than you think.

This hard-won lesson became the foundation for my planning when I took my family on a vacation to Europe in 2025. Before we even stepped onto a plane, I conducted comprehensive tactical research to identify the "no-go" zones in Barcelona, London, and Paris. To my surprise, the list of areas to avoid was extensive and often overlapped with popular tourist routes. I turned to firsthand accounts and investigative videos on YouTube, which served as a total eye-opener. Seeing the sophisticated tactics of pickpocketing rings, the predatory nature of aggressive street scams, and the sheer hostility of certain districts made me feel incredibly uneasy. That unease didn't fade once we landed; instead, it sharpened my focus into a professional edge. Throughout the trip, I was constantly "on"—scanning crowds, mapping exits, and operating with the same level of vigilance I used during my years in uniform. I didn’t truly feel a sense of relief until we arrived at Heathrow Airport to head home. It may seem like a high-stress way to vacation, but in the modern era, being a "relaxed" tourist is a luxury you simply cannot afford if you want to guarantee your family's safety.

To make these concepts as practical as possible, I have distilled these observations into a more comprehensive approach to travel safety, beginning with what I call YouTube Reconnaissance. Most travelers spend hours looking at glossy travel vlogs that showcase beautiful sunsets and five-star meals, but as a protector, your research must go deeper. You should specifically search for common scams or dangerous districts in your destination city. Watching raw footage of how pickpocketing rings operate in Paris or seeing the physical layout of a "no-go" zone in Barcelona before you arrive is invaluable. This visual data allows you to recognize a predatory setup in real-time, long before you walk into the middle of it. By the time you step off the plane, you should already have a mental map of the areas where your "safety switch" needs to be flipped to its highest setting.

Furthermore, you must embrace a mindset of Aggressive Realism when interacting with strangers in high-traffic hubs. This isn't just a catchy term; it is who I have become because of what I witnessed throughout my twenty-eight-year law enforcement career. When you spend nearly three decades seeing the darkest side of human nature and the consequences of misplaced trust, you lose the ability to view the world through rose-colored glasses. In high-traffic environments, "friendly" is often a tactical distraction. Whether it is someone offering to help with your luggage, a stranger pointing out a "stain" on your jacket, or an overly persistent street performer, you must recognize these as choreographed techniques designed to break your focus so a secondary predator can strike. It may feel cynical to rebuff a seemingly kind gesture, but in a high-risk area, your priority is the security of your family and your assets, not social politeness. You are not there to make friends; you are there to maintain a secure perimeter.

By the same token, understand that the Burden of the Protector means you may not relax in the traditional sense until the trip is over. Whether you are traveling alone or with your family, you must accept the responsibility of being the ultimate safeguard. If you are alone, you are the sole protector of your own life and assets; if you are with family, you are the shield for those who may not see the dangers you do. Honestly speaking, I didn't truly enjoy any of my trip because I simply could not let my guard down. I was constantly scanning for lurking trouble, and in doing so, I failed to experience the relaxation that was the original purpose of the vacation. However, that is just me being me—full of flaws and unable to switch off the instincts that kept me alive for nearly thirty years. As I experienced in Europe, I didn't feel a true sense of ease until I reached the departure gate at Heathrow. While your loved ones enjoy the sights, your job is to be the radar—constantly scanning the environment, identifying out-of-place individuals, and knowing your escape routes. If you return home feeling a massive sense of relief, it isn't a sign of a bad trip; it's a sign that you successfully managed the risks of traveling and fulfilled your duty in a foreign land. In the modern era, being a vigilant traveler is the only way to ensure that safety remains intact.

During my 2025 family trip to Europe, I had to lean into my instincts as a protector to ensure our safety, which required a strict division of labor. I made it clear to my daughters that I could not effectively be both the "Radar" and the "Navigator." When you are the designated Protector, your head must be on a swivel, scanning 360 degrees for threats; you simply cannot fulfill that role if your chin is tucked into a map or a GPS screen.

To solve this, I assigned the Navigator role to my youngest daughter, Ally. She was more than happy to accept the challenge, which freed me to maintain my "Aggressive Realism" and keep a constant lookout while the rest of the group handled the logistics of the route. I also reminded the family of our emergency protocol: a process where, once initiated by any of us, everyone must immediately stop talking, tighten our formation, and move toward me. There was no room for a lengthy "Why?" or a "Hold on a second." In a foreign land, a group that moves with disciplined, non-verbal cohesion becomes a "hard target" that most predators would rather avoid.

The brutal reality of traveling is that you are often far from the familiar layouts of your own neighborhood and community. You lose the "home-field advantage" of knowing where things get sketchy. The following cases, re[resenting real-world instances, illustrate these travel-specific dangers. I encourage you to search the internet using keywords like "tourist distraction theft ambush," "express kidnapping tactics," or "moped robbery high-end neighborhoods" to see how quickly a vacation can turn into a survival situation.

Case 1: The Transit "Dead Zone" Ambush

• Synopsis: A traveler was ambushed by a group in a transit station located on the periphery of a high-crime district late at night. The attackers utilized the seclusion of the station to beat the victim and leave them for dead.

• The Takeaway: This highlights the danger of "dead zones" where police presence is thin and predators feel emboldened. Navigating unfamiliar transit hubs at night requires a "Radar" who is not distracted by schedules or maps.

Case 2: The "Friendly" Direction-Giver Trap

• Synopsis: A family was brutally assaulted after an individual approached them under the guise of offering directions. While the family was distracted by the "helpful" stranger, three other accomplices moved in from behind to physically overpower them.

• The Takeaway: This is a classic example of why viewing "friendly" gestures with a lens of Aggressive Realism is a survival necessity. The "Navigator" might be fooled by the help, but the "Radar" must see the setup.

Case 3: The Perimeter Breach

• Synopsis: A backpacker became a target the moment they separated from their group and unknowingly crossed from a designated resort path into an area controlled by local criminal elements. The victim was subsequently kidnapped and held for days.

• The Takeaway: A single street or path can be the border between a vacation and a nightmare. Maintaining group cohesion and staying within vetted perimeters is vital when you don't know the local "lines."

Case 4: The "High-End" Magnet

• Synopsis: A tourist was hospitalized after resisting a violent robbery by a moped-borne gang in an upscale shopping district. Despite the "safe" reputation of the neighborhood, the visible wealth of travelers acted as a magnet for predators.

• The Takeaway: No neighborhood is 100% safe. Situational awareness must never be toggled "off" just because the surroundings look expensive or refined.

Case 5: The Archaeological Stalker

• Synopsis: A traveler was stalked through a famous historic site by individuals who waited until she reached a secluded area of the ruins to strike. The predators used the complex layout of the site to mask their movements until they had the victim isolated.

• The Takeaway: This validates the instinct to constantly scan for "lurking trouble" even when surrounded by beauty and history. Secluded spots in public landmarks are high-risk transition points.

Case 6: The "Transition Point" Kidnapping

• Synopsis: After leaving a high-end restaurant, a businessman was targeted for an "express kidnapping." He was followed from the building and assaulted as he attempted to hail a taxi on the street.

• The Takeaway: This highlights the danger of the "transition point" between a secure building and a vehicle. Predators watch for that moment of distraction when you are focused on transportation rather than your surroundings.

Case 7: The Daylight Swarming Tactic

• Synopsis: A group of predators used swarming tactics to overwhelm a visitor in a crowded public square during broad daylight. The attackers relied on the "bystander effect," knowing that a crowd of strangers is unlikely to intervene in a fast-moving assault.

• The Takeaway: "Safety in numbers" is a myth if the crowd is composed of indifferent strangers. True safety comes from a cohesive, disciplined group that moves as one unit.

In fact, prioritizing travel safety is imperative even when staying within the borders of the United States. It is a common mistake to assume that domestic travel is inherently safer than going abroad; the reality is that the U.S. contains just as many—if not more—"dead zones" and high-risk environments than most people are willing to admit.

As a law enforcement professional, I know that your sense of "home-field advantage" can be your greatest liability. When you are in your own country, you are more likely to let your guard down, mistakenly believing you understand the local dynamics. However, the same predatory patterns of ambush, distraction, and regional volatility exist from San Francisco to New Orleans. In every major American city, there are invisible lines that, once crossed, place you in a "no-go" area where help is far away and the environment is hostile to outsiders.

The following cases, representing real-world instances, serve as tactical evidence for this point. They are not merely news stories; they are documented failures of situational awareness and reminders that whether you are in Paris, France, or Chicago, Illinois, the rules of Aggressive Realism must remain in full effect. These incidents illustrate that the "Away Game" begins the moment you leave the safety of your own doorstep. I encourage you to search the internet using keywords like "unprovoked urban assault," "alleyway ambush forensics," or "vehicular weaponization incident" to see how these threats manifest in domestic environments.

Case 1: The Daylight Urban Slashing

• Synopsis: A visitor in a supposedly affluent metropolitan neighborhood was stalked and slashed from behind in broad daylight. The perpetrator struck without warning, targeting an individual who appeared to be in a relaxed state of mind.

• The Takeaway: This reinforces the point that predators do not always wait for the cover of darkness. They often strike in "safe" neighborhoods when they perceive a lapse in a target's situational awareness.

Case 2: The Alleyway Ambush

• Synopsis: A woman walking along a busy city street was suddenly dragged into a secluded alleyway and viciously assaulted by a predator. The attacker utilized a "dead zone"—a pocket of space just a few feet away from public view—to execute the crime.

• The Takeaway: This highlights that within major hubs, the presence of a single bystander or a passing motorist is sometimes the only thing between a victim and a tragedy. You must constantly scan for these hidden pockets of vulnerability.

Case 3: The Weaponized Vehicle

• Synopsis: Dozens of people were injured when a driver intentionally weaponized a vehicle against a crowd gathered outside a nightlife venue. The incident turned a high-density public space into a mass-casualty scene in a matter of seconds.

• The Takeaway: This serves as a grim reminder that "public space safety" requires scanning for more than just individual muggers; you must be aware of the "mobile shields" and threats posed by vehicles in areas where pedestrians congregate.

Case 4: The "Vetted" Rental Breach

• Synopsis: A traveler was drugged and assaulted by staff at a private homestay that was marketed as a secure, professional accommodation. The victim had lowered their guard based on the establishment's professional appearance and positive online reputation.

• The Takeaway: This validates the necessity of Aggressive Realism. Just because an establishment has a high rating doesn't mean you can ever fully let your guard down. Your internal perimeter must remain intact even behind "vetted" doors.

Case 5: The Transit Hub Swarm

• Synopsis: A traveler was swarmed and beaten by a "flash mob" near a major transportation center during the day. Despite being surrounded by people, the victim found no help as the group used overwhelming numbers to complete the assault.

• The Takeaway: This proves that "safety in numbers" is a myth if the crowd around you consists of indifferent bystanders rather than a cohesive, protective unit. In transit hubs, your group must maintain tight formation.

Case 6: The Tourist District Robbery

• Synopsis: Despite being in a heavily policed, world-famous tourist district, a visitor was targeted for high-value items and physically assaulted when they hesitated to comply. The local predators used their superior knowledge of the winding streets to escape instantly.

• The Takeaway: Even in "safe" zones, you are playing an "away game" against local predators who know the terrain better than you do. Hesitation in a confrontation often escalates the level of violence used against you.

Whether you are traveling across an ocean or just across the state line, the fundamental principles of safety remain the same. The "Away Game" requires a higher level of internal discipline precisely because you cannot rely on the familiar patterns of your home life. By recognizing that every trip is a tactical excursion, you ensure that you remain a "hard target" regardless of your zip code.

In my twenty-eight years in law enforcement, I learned that a street can tell you its life story if you know how to read the signs. Identifying a "dead zone" before you are physically entangled in it is a survival skill every traveler must master. You start with the overt signs—the broken windows, the aggressive graffiti marking territory, and the accumulated trash that signals a lack of community pride or police oversight. But as a professional, I look for the subtle signs: the absence of the "vulnerable." If you find yourself on a street where there are no women, no children playing, and no elderly people sitting on porches, you have entered a space where only the predators and the prey remain. This is where you will likely experience unwanted encounters. Those groups of young men standing on the corner aren't just killing time; they are performing reconnaissance. They are gauging your pace, your confidence, and your level of distraction. If their conversation stops and their eyes track you in unison as you pass, the interview is over and you've just been selected. You need to recognize that silence for what it is: the quiet before an ambush.

My experience in Ensenada was a failure of movement; I treated a high-risk transit like a casual stroll. In the world of tactical travel, you must focus on your transitions. The most dangerous moments of your trip aren't usually while you're sitting in a restaurant or sleeping in your room; they occur during the transitions—stepping out of a hotel lobby, exiting a train station, or entering a vehicle. This is the "moment of disorientation" where a predator waits for you to pause and look at your phone. You must also be wary of the transport trap. Just because an app tells you a car is coming doesn't mean the environment inside that car is safe. Before you slide into a rideshare, verify the driver's identity and the plate, but more importantly, check the child locks on the rear doors to ensure you aren't being walked into a mobile cage. Never share your live location or "follow me" features until you are securely inside with the doors locked. Move with purpose from point A to point B; if you don't look like you're wandering, you're much harder to catch. With the advancement of autonomous vehicles and availability of Waymo, I would prefer to use these rather than any other mode of transportation. Unlike a human driver who may be part of a local setup or whose child locks might be compromised for predatory reasons, an autonomous vehicle provides a vetted, trackable, and neutral environment that removes the human-predator element from the transition.

The term “Go invisible" and “Strategic invisibility”are phrases that I frequently recommended to victims of robberies and larcenies back when I was still active and taking their incident reports. It is the deliberate effort to broadcast a "nothing to see here" signal to any predator profiling the crowd. Predators are constantly hunting for the High-Value Target—the tourist wearing a $10,000 watch as seen in the London headlines, or the traveler parading bright, branded shopping bags from high-end designers through a crowded transit hub.

To achieve strategic invisibility, you must dress down to the local baseline. Hide the jewelry, swap the designer carry-all for a generic backpack, and maintain calm, rhythmic movements. You want to be the person the predator's eyes skip over because you look like you belong, you appear to have nothing of value, and you look like you might be more trouble than you're worth. Throughout my career, I've seen that the best way to win a fight is to never be invited to one in the first place—simply by being the most uninteresting person in the room.

Unfortunately, the consequences of ignoring this principle are made tragically clear by recurring patterns of targeted theft in high-traffic shopping districts. These areas are primary destinations for travelers, making them "fishing ponds" for those unfamiliar with the local terrain. I encourage you to search the internet using keywords like "follow-home robbery ring," "purse snatching shopping center arrest," or "parking lot transition point ambush" to see how predators profile their targets. The following cases represent real-world instances:

Case 1: The "Prolific" Shopping Center Snatcher

• Synopsis: Authorities apprehended a suspect linked to a string of robberies in a busy commercial corridor. The perpetrator targeted individuals leaving markets and malls, specifically watching for those carrying high-end bags, and used physical force to wrest property away before fleeing in a waiting vehicle.

• The Takeaway: Predators loiter in "safe" commercial zones specifically to identify targets who are advertising wealth through their accessories.

Case 2: The Jewelry Store Transition Ambush

• Synopsis: A coordinated robbery at a high-end retail outlet resulted in a swift arrest after security tracked the getaway car. This incident underscores the "Transition Point" danger—the moment a person moves from a "safe" interior with security guards to an open, unmonitored parking lot.

• The Takeaway: Your security perimeter often collapses the moment you step through an exit door. The parking lot is a "dead zone" where you are most vulnerable.

Case 3: The "Follow-Home" Robbery Ring

• Synopsis: In a landmark case, a criminal crew was arrested for executing "follow-home" robberies. They would loiter at popular malls, identify targets wearing expensive jewelry or carrying luxury goods, and follow them for miles to their private residences to strike in the driveway.

• The Takeaway: The threat doesn't end when you leave the shopping district. If you've been "marked" because of your appearance, the predator may follow you until you reach a place where you feel most secure and drop your guard.

Case 4: The High-Traffic "Fishing Pond"

• Synopsis: Following a spike in strong-arm robberies, police documented the arrest of several individuals during a targeted sting operation. The investigation validated concerns that flaunting wealth in high-traffic hubs makes individuals "easy prey" for local gangs.

• The Takeaway: In crowded areas, predators look for "visual signals" of high-value payouts. Strategic invisibility is the only way to avoid being selected for a "sting" of your own.

Case 5: The Loading Zone Disorientation

• Synopsis: Two individuals were arrested after an attempted robbery in a mall parking lot. The victim was targeted during the "moment of disorientation"—specifically while loading goods into a vehicle, which is a primary window of opportunity for a snatcher.

• The Takeaway: When your hands are full and your attention is on your trunk or your car seats, you are effectively blind to your 360-degree perimeter.

Perpetrators specifically target these areas because they recognize a pattern: shoppers are often seen with expensive designer items and are perceived to be carrying significant amounts of cash. These sprees often only subside once authorities implement highly visible enforcement tactics.

It is a textbook reminder that when you advertise your wealth, you are essentially issuing an open invitation to every predator in the vicinity. By blending in and remaining uninteresting, you retain the power of the "First Move"—because the predator never even realized you were a target in the first place.

Perhaps it is just my nature as a protector to be overtly cautious, but I always take extra measures to secure our hotel rooms during family vacations. I firmly believe that once you cross the threshold, you must not mistake a locked door for a guaranteed sanctuary; in the world of Aggressive Realism, a hotel room is simply a "containment box" that can be breached by anyone with a master key or through a lack of administrative oversight.

Your first tactical step should be to verify the door's hardware, but never rely solely on the swinging security latch—these can be easily bypassed from the hallway with nothing more than a simple wire loop. Instead, I recommend carrying a heavy-duty rubber door wedge or a portable travel lock that applies tension from the inside, physically preventing the door from opening even if the deadbolt is retracted. It is also wise to keep the "Do Not Disturb" sign on the handle at all times to suggest occupancy, and to leave a light and the television on low volume when you head out for the evening. Furthermore, avoid using the hotel safe for high-value items; these are often the primary targets for "inside job" thefts. By hardening your room into a true Safe Room, you ensure your perimeter remains intact while you rest for the next day's adventures.

As I have mentioned, I am far from a seasoned world traveler, and I don't claim to possess an endless library of travel stories. What I do possess, however, is a deep-seated commitment to your protection. I encourage you to make travel safety a non-negotiable priority for yourself and your family. It is all too easy to let your guard down when you are immersed in the excitement of a foreign land, surrounded by captivating sights and new experiences. In those moments of wonder, we often forget to maintain our Aggressive Realism, inadvertently leaving ourselves vulnerable to the predators lurking just out of sight. Remember: a predator's greatest advantage is a victim who believes they are on a 'vacation' from reality."

Ultimately, travel safety is about recognizing that operating in an unfamiliar environment requires a fundamentally different playbook than your life at home. Whether you are navigating the historic plazas of Europe or a local shopping hub in San Jose, the principles of Aggressive Realism remain your most reliable defense. By conducting your own YouTube Reconnaissance to identify Dead Zones, embracing Strategic Invisibility to avoid being profiled as a high-value target, and maintaining the Guardian vs. Navigator protocol with your family, you transform from a vulnerable tourist into a hard target.

The Burden of the Protector is a heavy one; it means trading the luxury of a "relaxed" vacation for the certainty that your perimeter remains secure. It means hardening your hotel room, moving with purpose through Transition Points, and never allowing social politeness to override your survival instincts. It is far better to return from a trip feeling the exhaustion of a successful mission than the trauma of a preventable tragedy. In this modern era, the true success of a journey isn't found in the souvenirs you bring home, but in the fact that you and your loved ones arrived back at your doorstep safely, having successfully managed the risks of an unforgiving world.

Chapter 11

Domestic Safety

One of the most sobering aspects of my twenty-eight-year law enforcement career was the sheer volume of domestic violence calls I witnessed and required to investigate. When I speak of "witnessing" these incidents, I am not referring to the violent act itself, but rather the haunting aftermath: the shattered glass, the bruised faces, and the raw, clinical process of interviewing victims, perpetrators, and the most tragic witnesses of all—the children.

In my line of work, you quickly learn that children are the ultimate "victims of circumstance." They didn't choose their parents or the volatile environment they were born into. I have stood in countless living rooms where the air was still thick with the adrenaline of a fight, watching children's worlds collapse in real-time. Their tears broke my heart as they watched us lead their father away in handcuffs, a confusing mix of fear and misplaced loyalty playing out across their faces.

However, there is a specific, visceral pain in the cases where we had to arrest the mother because she was deemed the primary aggressor. While the law must be applied equally regardless of gender, the biological and emotional bond between a mother and her children often appeared significantly more profound to me on the scene. When that bond is severed by an arrest—regardless of how necessary that intervention may be for the safety of the household—the trauma reflected in a child's eyes is a haunting reminder that in the cycle of domestic violence, there are no easy wins, only different degrees of loss. I recognize that while anyone can be an aggressor, my focus on your safety stems from the statistical reality that women are disproportionately the victims of lethal domestic escalation. Dealing with these internal threats requires a level of vigilance that is often far more difficult to maintain than any street-side awareness, because the danger lives within the very walls meant to protect you.

Throughout my career, every time I responded to these calls, I couldn't help but wonder how a victim—most often the female partner—had fallen into such a dire predicament, and why she didn't simply pick up and leave at the first sign of trouble. When I began asking that question directly, the answers I received illuminated the complex, grinding mechanics of abuse. I was a law enforcement officer, trained to interpret statutes and identify probable cause; I never claimed to be a psychologist. However, through thousands of cases, I developed a street-level understanding of the "Cycle of Violence." I began to see the invisible chains—emotional, financial, and psychological—that make it incredibly difficult for victims to simply walk away.

The true devastation isn't captured in a police report; it is found in the long-term erosion of the human spirit. I saw how constant abuse functions like a psychological "slow-burn." It isn't just about the physical pain; it's about the crushing weight of hyper-vigilance. These victims spend every waking hour walking on eggshells, scanning their partner's face for the slightest shift in mood. This level of prolonged stress rewires the brain, creating a state where the victim becomes so emotionally depleted that the simple act of leaving feels as impossible as climbing a mountain. Furthermore, a primary tactic of the internal predator is to cut the victim off from their "support perimeter," leaving them alone in a vacuum of despair, convinced they are worthless.

While I don't claim to have a universal solution, my observations suggest that the ability to leave is often decided long before the first blow is struck. I believe many victims might have found the strength to walk away if they had intentionally fortified their emotional, financial, and psychological independence from the very beginning of the relationship. Establishing that foundation of self-reliance acts as a personal safety net; it ensures that if the relationship turns toxic, you have the internal resources to exit before those invisible chains lock.

Even though the names and faces have faded, the imagery remains vivid: the jagged injuries and the hollow, tear-streaked faces still haunt me today. As I watched my own daughters grow into young adults, these memories transformed into a deep, protective concern. I have spoken to them candidly, telling them that no one—regardless of their title or the depth of their supposed love—has the right to lay a hand on them against their will. I have taught them that the cycle of violence is not a static loop; it is a downward spiral that almost always escalates. There is no such thing as a "second chance" for a physical assault.

While the adage "Love is blind" is often used to romanticize courtship, I find that sentiment to be dangerously misleading. I have told my daughters that if they allow themselves to be blinded by affection during the dating phase, they are foolishly gambling with their safety and their future. The courtship stage should be the period of the most intense observation. I tell them to watch closely: How does he manage his temper when the world doesn't go his way? Does he resolve conflict through mature communication, or does he resort to intimidation, punching walls, or verbal degradation? If you witness a lack of emotional control before the commitment is sealed, you are seeing the tactical blueprint for how he will treat you for the rest of your life.

It is a dangerous delusion to believe a violent man will get better with time; the reality is that he will only get worse. These men typically begin by testing boundaries with verbal abuse and derogatory terms. When the dust settles, they offer apologies and hollow promises, but these are merely reset buttons used to keep the victim in place. Inevitably, the abuse migrates from verbal to physical. It often starts "small"—a slap on the face or a shove—accompanied by deadly threats against the victim's parents or children to ensure silence. But that first slap is a gateway. From there, the violence escalates into punching, kicking, and the use of weapons. In my career, I have seen the end of that road too many times, and it almost always begins with a red flag that was ignored during the courtship.

There's no doubt in my mind that the red flags popped up repeatedly but the victims chose to ignore them. In fact, their parents, siblings and friends also noticed some of these red flags but they either were not doing enough to help the victims or didn't bother to help them at all.

Drawing from my twenty-eight years in law enforcement, I have come to realize that the most difficult barriers for a victim to overcome aren't physical; they are the invisible constraints of financial dependency and emotional rationalization. It is a sobering reality, but financial vulnerability is often used as a tactical advantage by an abuser to maintain control. When I stood in those kitchens and living rooms, the most frequent reason given for remaining in a dangerous situation wasn't a lack of will—it was the desperate admission of having no outside resources and no immediate way to fund an escape.

This is why I strongly advocate for every woman to establish a foundation of financial independence as a core component of her personal safety before entering a marriage. Cultivating a professional identity and maintaining a dedicated financial reserve—one that is independent and secure—serves as a vital insurance policy. It ensures that the decision to remain in a relationship is always based on a healthy, mutual choice rather than a perceived necessity for survival. When you possess the means to provide for yourself and your children, you remove the most powerful leverage an aggressor can use: the fear of destitution. By prioritizing self-reliance, a woman ensures she always has the mobility and the power to protect her own future.

The second pillar of this trap is the dangerous belief that a partner is a "fixer-upper." Throughout my career, I saw many women enter relationships seeing the red flags of aggression and mistakenly believing their patience or domestic stability would eventually smooth those rough edges. In my experience, you cannot "love" a predator into becoming a protector. When a victim begins making excuses for their partner—blaming a high-stress job, a difficult childhood, or substance abuse—they are unknowingly becoming an accomplice to their own victimization. By rationalizing a "bad day," you are effectively telling the aggressor that their behavior is manageable and, therefore, repeatable. A victim should never be in the business of manufacturing excuses for the very person who is hurting them.

In the world of domestic violence, "change" is a rare commodity that I seldom saw in the field. An aggressor rarely changes because they were asked nicely; they only change when the cost of their behavior becomes higher than the benefit of their control. This usually requires the cold, hard intervention of the legal system and the total loss of their victim's presence. If you find yourself explaining away a partner's violence, you are already caught in the trap of the cycle. You must stop being a psychologist for your abuser and start being a tactician for your own life. This means maintaining a zero-tolerance policy for the first strike, trusting the authorities to handle the "bad day" through a formal police report, and recognizing that the survival of your personhood is infinitely more important than the survival of the marriage. By fortifying your independence and refusing to entertain the delusions of an abuser's potential, you shift from a position of vulnerability to a position of strength, possessing the mobility to exit the danger zone the moment the red line is crossed.

I strongly believe that while women may often be at a natural disadvantage in terms of raw physical size and strength compared to their male partners, they are by no means required to remain vulnerable. In my twenty-eight years of policing, I have seen far too many situations where a disparity in strength was used as a tool of intimidation and control. Because of this, I have relentlessly encouraged my daughters to fortify themselves—not just through general physical exercise to build a foundation of strength, but by "hardening" themselves through the religious study of self-defense.

I advocate for a long-term, disciplined commitment to martial arts such as Brazilian Jiu-Jitsu (BJJ) or Wing Chun. These disciplines are uniquely engineered for the "smaller" or "weaker" individual to overcome a larger, more powerful opponent. Rather than relying on brute force—which is a losing game when outsized—these arts utilize technical leverage, sophisticated weight distribution, and the targeting of anatomical weak points to level the playing field.

In the confined, close-quarters environment of a home, where the majority of domestic assaults occur, these skills transcend the category of "sport." They are life-saving tools. They provide a woman with the tactical ability to create space, neutralize a suffocating hold, or subdue an aggressor long enough to escape the "Dead Zone" and call for help. Mastering these arts is about moving from a state of reactive panic to one of calculated, technical response.

However, I would be remiss if I didn't address the inherent risks involved in any high-level combative training. A few years ago, a friend of mine sustained a catastrophic injury that left him paralyzed while practicing Brazilian Jiu-Jitsu. While I don’t know the specific mechanics of that incident—whether it was a freak accident, a lack of proper supervision, or a failure to "tap out" in time—it serves as a sobering reminder: The very tools designed to save your life are forged in a high-risk environment.

When you step onto the mats, you are engaging in a physical chess match that carries real-world stakes. Training must be approached with the same situational awareness you apply to the streets. You must choose a reputable school that prioritizes safety and controlled drilling over "ego-rolling." Awareness of the danger doesn't mean you should avoid the training; it means you should respect the discipline enough to train with a focused, defensive mindset. You are learning to handle a weapon—even if that weapon is your own body—and it must be treated with the gravity it deserves.

Currently, my daughters have yet to embrace such a demanding regimen, but as a father, I refuse to waver in my encouragement. I recognize that this is a significant commitment, but I view it as an indispensable layer of their personal "armor." My goal is for them to possess the quiet confidence that springs from a deep-seated knowledge: if someone attempts to lay hands on them, they have both the technical proficiency and the hardened mindset to strike back.

Ultimately, martial arts training for domestic safety isn't about "winning" a fight in the traditional sense; it is about buying time. It is about gaining those critical 30 seconds needed to break a grip, create distance, and reach a door, a phone, or a car. In a violent encounter, those 30 seconds are the thin margin between life and death. In a world where internal threats are often unpredictable, physical empowerment serves as a vital deterrent, fundamentally shifting the dynamic from victim to victor.

While there is no substitute for physical hardening—honing your cardiovascular fitness and mastering self-defense techniques—the most effective form of domestic safety is preemptive avoidance. In my twenty-eight years of policing, I have learned that physical skills are your last resort, but your primary line of defense is the rigorous, clinical screening of a partner's character before any permanent bond is sealed. You must be wary of individuals who exhibit a hair-trigger temper or a fundamental inability to resolve conflicts through civilized, verbal communication.

During the courtship phase, you must adopt the mindset of an investigator. I often use the analogy of peeling the layers of an onion: you must methodically work through the outer skins of charm to reach the core. It is a slow, deliberate process, but it is the only way to ensure the center is free of insects, dirt, or unwanted residue—those hidden character flaws and red flags that are often expertly masked in the beginning. During the initial stages of dating, most partners will naturally project a polished facade to woo you. However, you must recognize that this exterior may simply be a tactical mask. You owe it to your future self to dig deeper and see who this person becomes when that mask slips—how they handle stress, frustration, and disagreement. Only when you have reached the core can you be certain that your relationship is built on genuine integrity rather than a dangerous performance.

The adage "the apple doesn't fall far from the tree" has proven remarkably accurate throughout my decades in law enforcement. To gauge a partner's long-term trajectory, look at the family dynamic that shaped him. The childhood home is the first "classroom" for conflict resolution; the patterns of communication—or aggression—he witnessed there often become his default settings in adulthood. Observe his parents' interactions, but pay even closer attention to how he interacts with them. While he may be on his best behavior with you, the way he treats his parents is a preview of how he will treat you once the social pressure of dating fades. If he is habitually disrespectful, dismissive, or volatile toward those who raised him, you can rest assured that he will eventually direct that same energy toward you. In the field, I rarely saw a man who was a "saint" to his mother but a "devil" to his wife; a lack of respect for primary bonds is usually a symptom of a much deeper, systemic character flaw.

Furthermore, you must cast a critical eye on his inner circle, because "birds of a feather flock together." A person's choice of companions is a reflection of their own values and their definition of "normal." When you observe his friends, you are looking into a mirror of his own character. If his circle consists of individuals who are disrespectful toward women, solve problems with aggression, or lack basic accountability, you must realize he has chosen that environment for a reason. Peer groups function as a reinforcement loop; if his friends normalize toxic behaviors, they are creating a culture where those actions are validated. In my experience, an aggressor's behavior is almost always emboldened by a support system of like-minded peers. If the "flock" exhibits toxic traits, it is a dangerous gamble to assume your partner is the one outlier. His "true north" is often found in the company he keeps—pay close attention to it.

Throughout my career in law enforcement, I have observed that while they are never excuses for abuse, alcohol and financial instability are the two most common catalysts that trigger episodes of domestic violence. These elements act as accelerants to an underlying fire; they strip away inhibitions and escalate existing tensions into full-blown crises.

Because of this, you must be a disciplined observer of his relationship with substances. Pay close attention to his behavior when he is under the influence of alcoholic beverages. Does he become aggressive, irritable, or prone to emotional volatility? A man who cannot manage his temper while sober is a danger, but a man who loses all restraint when drinking is a ticking time bomb. In the field, some of the most brutal scenes I investigated involved perpetrators who used "being drunk" as a shield to deflect accountability for their actions. You must recognize that alcohol doesn't create a new personality; it simply reveals the one that was being suppressed.

Similarly, you must evaluate his financial maturity and his trajectory toward a stable career. Domestic peace is often tied to the stability of the household's foundation. Observe how he manages his money and uses his credit cards. Is he impulsive, living far beyond his means, or drowning in avoidable debt? Financial hardship creates a high-pressure environment that often becomes the "reason" an abuser uses to justify their lashing out. Furthermore, a man who is fiscally irresponsible often seeks to compensate for his lack of control in the workplace by exerting excessive control over his partner at home.

By vetting his ability to build a career and his discipline in managing resources, you are vetting his capacity for adult responsibility. You want a partner who views financial stability as a shared security goal, not someone whose fiscal chaos will eventually become a source of resentment and a trigger for violence within your four walls.

I am a firm believer that drug use and excessive gambling are not merely "poor choices"—they are self-induced behaviors that evolve into destructive, deep-seated habits that are notoriously difficult to break. In my experience, these are two of the most corrosive vices a person can bring into a marriage. You owe it to yourself and your future children to detect these patterns early, as they are often meticulously hidden behind a veneer of normalcy. If you discover these habits, you must have the courage to make a definitive plan to move on, because these addictions will eventually consume everything you are trying to build together.

During my years in the patrol division, I made it a point to go where many others wouldn't—wandering under bridges and along railroad tracks to interact with the homeless community. I wasn't there just for enforcement; I wanted to understand the "how" and the "why" behind their situation. In numerous firsthand conversations, a recurring theme emerged: the primary engine of their downfall was almost always drug use or gambling. These weren't just statistics to me; they were human stories of total systemic collapse.

I still vividly remember a conversation with a man living in a makeshift camp who possessed a striking level of eloquence and a refined manner. He told me that he once owned a successful furniture business and had millions of dollars in his accounts. He had a home, a career, and a family who loved him. Yet, piece by piece, he lost every bit of it to a gambling addiction until he was left with nothing but the clothes on his back and a spot under a bridge. I believed his story completely; his verbal communication and demeanor suggested a man who had indeed fallen from a great height.

His story serves as a haunting warning. Addiction is an insatiable creditor; it doesn't just take the money—it takes the trust, the safety, and eventually the soul of the household. While this man's story may not have a direct nexus to a specific act of domestic violence, the downward spiral of gambling is inseparable from the issue of domestic safety. Financial stress is one of the most common triggers for domestic abuse, and when a partner gambles away the family's security, the resulting desperation often leads to an explosion of violence.

In the law enforcement world, we see the end of that road, and it is a path of total devastation. You must recognize that if a partner is enslaved to these vices, they are not in a position to protect or provide for you. Do not fall into the trap of thinking you can "fix" him or that his "luck" will change. You must prioritize your own stability and walk away before his downfall becomes your own tragedy.

Domestic safety is not merely about preventing or surviving violent behavior; it is also about the proactive construction and preservation of your family's financial stability. A secure home requires more than the absence of physical conflict—it requires a solid economic foundation that provides options, mobility, and independence. In my experience, financial health is a critical component of your overall defensive perimeter.

It is imperative that when you consider entering a serious relationship, you evaluate whether the union has a legitimate chance to improve both of your lives. A partnership should be a force multiplier, where two people build a future that is more secure and prosperous than what they could achieve alone. If you find yourself attaching your future to someone who brings instability, chaos, or fiscal irresponsibility into your world, you aren't building a partnership—you are trying to catch a falling knife. In the field, I have seen that those who try to "save" someone in a freefall usually end up getting cut themselves. True domestic safety begins with the wisdom to choose a partner who adds to your strength rather than draining your survival resources.

I still vividly remember a conversation with a woman who flagged me down while I was on patrol. She was a software engineer working for a well-known, high-profile tech company—a highly intelligent, successful professional who had built an impressive career for herself. Despite her professional achievements, she was visibly upset and burdened by a situation she never anticipated: she was the one being forced to pay spousal support to her ex-husband. She asked me, almost desperately, if there was anything I could do to help her stop the payments.

Of course, as a law enforcement officer, I had no power over a civil court order, but her story stayed with me. She admitted that she knew her ex-husband was a lazy man who couldn't hold a job for more than a few month at a time, but she had entered the marriage believing she could "fix" his lack of ambition. She thought her drive would eventually motivate him. After years of struggling to carry the entire financial weight of the household on her engineer's salary, she finally gave up and filed for divorce, only to realize that the law required her to continue supporting his lifestyle long after the relationship ended. That monthly payment became a constant, painful "thorn" in her side—a permanent reminder of the high price she paid for ignoring the early red flags of his character. Her experience serves as a powerful lesson: even for a successful professional, choosing a partner who refuses to contribute can lead to a long-term loss of financial freedom and peace of mind.

This firsthand account underscores a critical truth I've observed throughout my career: work ethic and the ability to build a financially stable career are not just personal achievements—they are vital safety factors in a relationship, regardless of gender. A healthy partnership requires that both individuals contribute to the foundation of the home, but for women, maintaining individual financial independence is an absolute necessity for survival.

As mentioned earlier, throughout my years in law enforcement, I stood in the wake of countless domestic tragedies, and a hauntingly consistent theme emerged. When I asked victims why they hadn't left sooner, the answer was rarely about a lack of courage; it was a lack of cash. They felt tethered to their abusers because they didn't have a bank account in their own name, a professional skill set to lean on, or the basic financial resources required to secure a safe place to sleep. Without the means to move on, they were effectively trapped in a "Dead Zone" where the aggressor held all the economic leverage.

Financial independence is your ultimate "exit strategy." It ensures that your presence in a relationship is a daily choice based on mutual respect, rather than a forced survival tactic. By prioritizing your career and fiscal autonomy, you are not being cynical about your relationship; you are being tactical about your safety. You are ensuring that if the "atmospheric conditions" of your home ever turn toxic, you have the immediate mobility to walk away with your dignity—and your life—intact. In a world where the unexpected can happen, being your own financial provider is the most reliable armor you can wear.

When your partner begins to systematically isolate you from your inner circle—whether by alienating you from parents and relatives or distancing you from trusted friends—you are witnessing the construction of a cage. This isolation is often paired with "financial strangulation," such as confiscating bank accounts or forcing you to abandon your career. You must recognize these as urgent red flags the moment they emerge. In these critical windows, you must reach out to your support network, analyze the situation with clinical objectivity, and take immediate measures to protect yourself and your children.

Call me cynical, or call me what you will, but I am a firm believer that when a red flag appears in a marriage, you must analyze it with the precision of an investigator. In the realm of domestic safety, there is no such thing as a "coincidence"—there are only patterns of behavior that have not yet reached their final, lethal conclusion. Isolation and financial control are not signs of love; they are tactical maneuvers designed to ensure that when the "mask" eventually slips, you have neither the voice to call for help nor the resources to walk away. Protect your perimeter while you still have the means to do so.

For instance, if a partner suddenly insists on a disproportionately large life insurance policy, you must view that not as prudent financial planning, but as a potential bounty placed on your head. Similarly, if he pressures you to go on a hike up a remote mountain or boating on a secluded lake—especially when neither of you has ever expressed an interest in such rugged activities—you must recognize the tactical shift. These are not romantic gestures; they are calculated attempts to move you into a "Dead Zone." These are locations where there are no witnesses, no cell service, and where the terrain itself can be blamed for a "tragic accident."

Major news headliners frequently reveal that even the most mundane areas of a home can be weaponized; bathtubs and showers, in particular, appear as recurring crime scenes in domestic homicide cases. Because water and hard surfaces provide a convenient narrative for a "fatal slip," these areas are often used to stage a struggle as an accident. While you should not live in a state of constant paranoia, you must maintain a high level of situational awareness.

This means keeping your eyes open to shifts in your partner's baseline behavior, maintaining a viable plan of escape, and even taking small tactical precautions—like locking the bathroom door—to ensure you are never caught in a vulnerable, enclosed position. When the environment or the financial incentives change without a logical explanation, your life may be at risk. You owe it to your survival to trust your instincts over his explanations.

To understand that these warnings are not mere theories, consider the following cases which represent real-world instances. I encourage you to search the internet using keywords like "staged slip and fall forensics," "life insurance homicide motive," or "digital evidence in domestic violence cases" to see how modern investigation techniques dismantle these "accidental" narratives.

Case 1: The Cliffside "Selfie" Ambush

• Synopsis: During a birthday hike at a precarious lookout, an individual led his spouse to a cliff edge for a photograph. The spouse later testified to feeling a sudden sense of danger and attempting to pull away before being physically assaulted near the ledge.

• Adjudication: The individual was found guilty of attempted manslaughter and second-degree assault in early 2026 and was sentenced to 20 years in state prison.

Case 2: The Premeditated Anniversary Hike

• Synopsis: An individual took his spouse on a surprise anniversary hike in a remote national park. He claimed she fell while taking a photo, but investigators discovered he had scouted the exact remote cliff edge 13 times prior to the trip.

• Adjudication: He was found guilty of first-degree murder and sentenced to Life in prison without the possibility of parole.

Case 3: The Smartwatch Forensic Breakthrough

• Synopsis: A woman was found dead in her bathtub; her partner claimed she had simply slipped and drowned. However, forensic evidence and digital heart-rate data from her smartwatch proved a violent struggle occurred, showing the scene was staged to look like an accident.

• Adjudication: The partner was found guilty of second-degree murder and sentenced to Life in prison.

Case 4: The Blood Spatter Analysis

• Synopsis: A prominent professional claimed his spouse died from a fall in the shower. During a high-profile retrial, expert blood spatter analysis proved the injuries and the location of the evidence were entirely inconsistent with a simple fall.

• Adjudication: He was found guilty of second-degree murder and tampering with physical evidence, receiving a sentence of 20 years to Life.

Case 5: The "Accidental" Discharge Motive

• Synopsis: A wealthy individual killed his spouse with a firearm during a hunting trip abroad, claiming it was an accidental discharge while packing. Federal agents eventually proved the motive was tied to nearly $5 million in life insurance payouts.

• Adjudication: He was found guilty of murder and mail fraud in federal court, sentenced to Life in prison, and ordered to pay $4.8 million in restitution.

Case 6: The Financial Debt Poisoning

• Synopsis: An individual who had authored books on grief poisoned her partner with a lethal dose of a controlled substance. Investigations revealed she was facing crushing financial debt and had secretly changed the beneficiaries of his life insurance policies.

• Adjudication: In March 2026, she was found guilty of aggravated murder and sentenced to Life in prison without parole.

Case 7: The Digital Trail of Intent

• Synopsis: Following the disappearance of a tech-sector executive, prosecutors presented evidence of her partner's digital searches regarding body disposal and insurance payouts, alongside physical evidence found in the family home.

• Adjudication: The individual was found guilty of first-degree murder and misleading an investigation in late 2025, resulting in a Life sentence without parole.

Domestic safety is not merely a reaction to a crisis; it is a proactive personal protocol that benefits from clear communication long before a relationship reaches a turning point. I view this as a Shared Safety Covenant—a mutual understanding between my daughters and our family. By establishing these "rules of engagement" while life is calm and clear, we remove the paralyzing hesitation that often takes hold if a threat eventually emerges.

While the demographic data shows that the majority of spousal homicides are committed by men, women also appear in these statistics, often under starkly different and complex circumstances. Examining these cases reveals a spectrum of motivations ranging from desperate survival to calculated malice. In many instances, women who kill their partners have been chronic victims of domestic, physical, or psychological abuse. For these individuals, the act is often a desperate, final attempt at self-defense—a "turning of the tables" after years of entrapment in a cycle of violence.

Conversely, some cases involve individuals who act out of greed, a desire for control, or personal gain. In these instances, a spouse may be viewed as an obstacle to be removed rather than a threat to be escaped. The methods employed often differ from impulsive, physical confrontations; some may take a direct approach using firearms or blunt force, while others opt for clandestine methods like poisoning, which allow for a degree of separation and the potential to mask the crime as a natural illness.

Furthermore, a significant subset of these cases involves the solicitation of a third party. By attempting to hire a "hitman," the perpetrator seeks to engineer a plausible alibi and maintain distance from the physical act. These schemes are often rooted in cold, financial pragmatism, motivated by life insurance payouts or inheritance.

The following cases, representing real-world instances, illustrate these points, spanning from complex claims of self-defense to the calculated nature of poisoning and murder-for-hire. I encourage you to search the internet using keywords like "murder-for-hire solicitation arrest," "forensic toxicology poisoning cases," or "domestic violence survivor justice act" to understand the evidentiary standards used in these trials.

Case 1: The Financial Poisoning Scheme

• Synopsis: An individual who gained public attention for writing a book on coping with grief was accused of murdering her spouse. Prosecutors alleged she spiked the victim's drink with a lethal dose of fentanyl—five times the amount required to be fatal. The motive was determined to be financial, as the individual was facing significant debt and sought to claim millions in life insurance and estate assets.

• Adjudication: In March 2026, a jury found the individual guilty of aggravated murder. She faces life in prison without the possibility of parole.

Case 2: The Digital Solicitation Plot

• Synopsis: A 58-year-old individual attempted to utilize the dark web to eliminate a perceived rival. She converted over $10,000 into cryptocurrency to pay an online "assassin" to carry out the act. Unbeknownst to her, the service was a scam, and federal agents intercepted the communications.

• Adjudication: The individual pleaded guilty to one count of murder-for-hire and was sentenced in 2024 to nine years in federal prison. This case mirrors the "hitman" methodology often attempted in spousal cases to create an alibi.

Case 3: The "Imminent Danger" Legal Conflict

• Synopsis: This case highlights the complexities of the "battered person" defense. An individual shot and killed her partner, claiming the act was a necessary escape from years of documented physical and sexual abuse. Prosecutors argued the act was premeditated and occurred while the victim was not an active threat, challenging the legal definition of "imminent danger."

• Adjudication: Initially sentenced to 19 years to life, an appellate court later reduced the sentence to 7.5 years under specialized survivor justice legislation, recognizing the severe history of trauma while maintaining that the legal threshold for lethal self-defense is extremely narrow.

Case 4: The Staged Grief Reaction

• Synopsis: In a prominent caught-on-camera case, an individual was filmed by an undercover officer (posing as a hitman) confirming she wanted her spouse eliminated. She later staged a performative reaction of "grief" when police—as part of the operation—falsely informed her that her spouse had been killed.

• Adjudication: After multiple trials, the individual was sentenced to 16 years in prison. Her final appeals were exhausted recently, and she remains incarcerated.

Ultimately, ensuring domestic safety is a universal concern. It is vital to remain vigilant and adopt proactive measures to identify potential red flags early in a relationship. While it is important to maintain trust within a partnership, one should consider significant shifts in behavior or unexplained financial maneuvers as possible indicators of a threat rather than blindly dismissing them. Your safety depends on your ability to see the world as it is, not as you wish it to be.

By diligently analyzing behavioral shifts, you can distinguish between common interpersonal misunderstandings and genuine, systemic danger. Taking these observations seriously is not an act of betrayal or paranoia; rather, it is the exercise of necessary due diligence to protect your physical and emotional well-being should those red flags prove to be valid.

To ensure my daughters are prepared for the complexities of future marriages and romantic relationships, we have already begun discussing the "trigger points" that would warrant family intervention. Even though they are still in college, we recognize that safety is built on proactive communication. For this to be effective, it must be a partnership: they agree that if they, or any member of our inner circle, identify tactical signs of concern—such as deliberate isolation, unexplained withdrawal, or the loss of financial independence—we address it openly and immediately. The goal is to ensure that "making the call" for help isn't a burden they have to carry alone in a moment of fear; it is a pre-authorized plan we execute together.

When a dating relationship becomes serious, I believe in moving this conversation from theory to reality. This isn't about an interrogation; it's about transparency. I find it healthy to have an honest talk with my daughters and their partners about our family values regarding safety. The intent is not to intimidate, but to ensure total clarity: in our family, domestic peace is non-negotiable. I make it clear that our policy is to involve professional resources and authorities immediately if safety is compromised, as many states mandate an arrest when probable cause of domestic violence exists.

If a partner finds this level of family advocacy offensive, that provides my daughters with a critical piece of intelligence. They can then decide if that person is the right fit for their future. A partner who is confident in their own character and has no intention of being an aggressor generally respects a family that prioritizes the well-being of its members.

Under this covenant, if a situation ever becomes a "Dead Zone," the emotional decision to leave has already been made in advance. This removes the need for agonizing second-guessing in the heat of a crisis. My daughters know that their family—and the authorities—will be there to assist in a safe, professional extraction. This pre-determined "safety map" is designed to lead them out of a high-risk environment and back into a secure perimeter without the abuser being able to negotiate or manipulate the outcome.

I am fully aware that this protocol is easier to discuss than it is to execute. I cannot guarantee it will be a perfect shield, but in the face of such high stakes, silence is not an option. Having spent a career responding to the aftermath of domestic failures, I refuse to sit idly by. I believe in building the exit door before the room ever catches fire. I ask you to consider the same: what steps are you taking to ensure that your loved ones have a clear path to safety?

In conclusion, the reality of domestic safety is that the most dangerous threat you will ever face may not come from a stranger in a dark alley, but from the person sharing your dinner table. My twenty-eight years in law enforcement have taught me that violence is rarely an isolated event; it is the final destination of a path paved with ignored red flags, forced isolation, and financial entrapment.

To navigate this world safely, you must refuse to be a passenger in your own life. This means building your own "financial fortress" so that you are never stayed by necessity. It means hardening your physical capabilities to buy those life-saving seconds of escape. Most importantly, it means maintaining a clinical, investigative eye during the courtship phase—peeling back the layers of the "onion" to ensure the core is sound before you ever commit your future.

Do not mistake silence for safety, and do not mistake control for love. Establish your Safety Covenant now, while the air is clear, so that if the atmosphere ever turns toxic, your exit plan is already in motion. Domestic safety is not a matter of being cynical; it is a matter of being prepared. In the field, I have seen the heavy price of hesitation, and I have stood in the aftermath where the system arrived too late. I implore you to take these protocols to heart and watch for the signs with unwavering vigilance. In the end, your situational awareness is the only weapon that can stop a tragedy before it starts.

Choose strength over vulnerability, and clarity over delusion. Your life—and the lives of those you love—depends on it.

Chapter 12

Emergency Preparedness

Medical • Fire • Earthquake

Everything shared in this chapter has been gathered from publicly available resources, preparedness organizations, and general guidance found across the internet. The author is not a trained emergency professional, medical expert, firefighter, or seismologist. The responsibility for creating an emergency preparedness plan that truly works for you rests with you and your family. Use this chapter as a starting point, then dig deeper into the resources most relevant to where you live and who you're preparing for.

PART I: General Preparedness

1. Build a Personalized Emergency Plan

One of the most commonly cited pieces of advice gathered from emergency preparedness resources is that every household should have a written, personalized emergency plan — and that no single template fits every family. Various guides from organizations like FEMA, the Red Cross, and local county emergency services suggest starting with the question: what emergencies are most likely to affect your specific area? For those of us in California, that list is longer than most — wildfires, earthquakes, floods, and power outages all make the shortlist. From there, sources recommend mapping out how each person in the household will respond, where they will go, and who they will contact. A solid plan typically includes evacuation routes from the home, a designated out-of-state contact person (since local phone lines often become congested during regional disasters), and a clear designation of who is responsible for what during an emergency. Ultimately, you and your family are the only ones who can create a plan that truly fits your lives, your home layout, and your specific needs — the goal of this chapter is simply to offer a starting point collected from widely available public resources.

2. Assemble an Emergency Supply Kit

Across dozens of preparedness websites and government resources, the advice to keep an emergency supply kit is nearly universal. Most sources suggest keeping enough supplies to sustain your household for a minimum of 72 hours, though many now recommend aiming for up to two weeks given how some modern disasters — particularly wildfires and major earthquakes — can disrupt infrastructure for extended periods. Commonly suggested items include water (often cited as one gallon per person per day), non-perishable food, a battery-powered or hand-crank radio, flashlights with extra batteries, a whistle to signal for help, dust masks, plastic sheeting and duct tape, moist towelettes, garbage bags, a wrench or pliers to shut off utilities, a manual can opener, local maps, and a cell phone with chargers and a backup battery. Many sources also emphasize storing copies of critical documents — insurance policies, IDs, bank account information — in a waterproof container. The exact contents of your kit will vary depending on your household size, any medical needs, whether you have pets, and where you live. Consider your kit a living resource that you revisit and update at least twice a year.

3. Know Your Local Emergency Alert Systems

Numerous preparedness resources strongly encourage residents to familiarize themselves with the emergency alert systems available in their area before disaster strikes — not during. In California, several systems work in concert: the federal Wireless Emergency Alerts (WEA) send automatic messages to cell phones in affected areas, while systems like Cal OES, county-level alert programs (such as AlertSCC, Nixle, or Genasys depending on your county), and the Emergency Alert System (EAS) broadcast over radio and TV provide layered notification. Many sources recommend signing up for your specific county's alert system, as coverage and features vary significantly across California's 58 counties. It is also suggested to keep a battery-powered radio on hand for situations where cell service or power may be disrupted. Knowing in advance how alerts will reach you — and what the different alert tones and messages mean — can make a significant difference in how quickly and calmly you respond. Check with your local county Office of Emergency Services for the most accurate and current enrollment information.

4. Plan for Vulnerable Household Members

A recurring theme across preparedness guides is the importance of planning specifically for those in the household who may need extra assistance during an emergency — young children, elderly relatives, individuals with disabilities or chronic illnesses, and pets. Organizations like Ready.gov and the Red Cross suggest creating customized plans for each vulnerable person, including how they will be evacuated, what special supplies they need, and who will be responsible for helping them. For pets, this includes identifying pet-friendly emergency shelters or hotels in advance, since many public shelters do not accept animals. For individuals with medical equipment that requires power, sources recommend registering with your local utility company's medical baseline or life support program, and contacting your local fire department to inform them of your household's needs. Planning for these scenarios in advance — rather than in the chaos of an actual emergency — is consistently cited as one of the highest-impact steps a household can take. Every family's situation is different, and only you can identify the specific accommodations your household requires.

5. Establish Communication and Meeting Plans

Many emergency preparedness resources highlight a common and preventable problem: during disasters, family members are often separated — at work, school, or running errands — and have no pre-arranged way to reconnect. To address this, various sources recommend designating at least two meeting places: one close to home (such as a neighbor's house or a specific corner) for sudden emergencies like a house fire, and one outside the neighborhood in case evacuation is required. It is also widely recommended to identify a single out-of-state contact person that all family members can call or text to relay their status, since long-distance calls often connect more reliably than local ones during regional crises. Teaching children how to text (since texts may go through when calls cannot), memorizing key phone numbers rather than relying solely on a smartphone, and making sure caregivers and school administrators are part of the plan are all suggestions that appear regularly in preparedness literature. Your communication plan should reflect your family's real daily routines and the realistic ways you'd reach each other on any given weekday.

PART II: Medical Emergencies

6. Learn Basic First Aid and CPR

A suggestion that appears consistently across health and emergency preparedness resources is to learn at least the fundamentals of first aid and CPR before you need them. Organizations like the American Red Cross and the American Heart Association offer courses — many of them just a few hours long — that cover how to respond to cardiac arrest, choking, severe bleeding, burns, and other common emergencies. Many sources note that in the critical minutes before professional help arrives, a trained bystander can make a life-saving difference. Hands-only CPR, in particular, has been widely promoted by health organizations as something most adults can learn and perform effectively without formal medical training. Taking a certified course periodically is generally recommended, as guidelines are updated over time. Some sources also suggest keeping a basic first aid guidebook in your home supply kit as a reference. While this chapter is not a medical training guide, the near-universal consensus from preparedness resources is that basic training is one of the most valuable investments any adult can make for their household's safety.

7. Stock and Maintain a First Aid Kit

Beyond the general emergency supply kit, most medical and preparedness resources recommend keeping a well-stocked, dedicated first aid kit in both the home and in each vehicle. Pre-packaged kits are widely available, but many sources suggest customizing them to suit your family's specific needs. Commonly cited items include adhesive bandages in assorted sizes, gauze pads and rolls, medical tape, antiseptic wipes, antibiotic ointment, a digital thermometer, pain relievers such as acetaminophen or ibuprofen, antihistamines, tweezers, scissors, disposable gloves, a CPR face shield, and a first aid instruction booklet. For households with children, specific pediatric dosing guides are often recommended. It is also widely advised to check expiration dates at least annually and replace expired items promptly. A first aid kit is only as useful as its contents — and only helpful if you know where it is and how to use what's inside it. Consider your specific household's medical history when customizing what you keep stocked.

8. Manage Medications During an Emergency

One preparedness consideration that is sometimes overlooked until it becomes urgent is how to manage prescription medications during a disaster. Health and emergency management resources suggest keeping at least a week's supply of all critical medications on hand at all times, and ideally more. Many sources recommend speaking with your doctor or pharmacist about obtaining a slightly larger supply to maintain as an emergency reserve. It is also widely advised to keep an up-to-date written list of all medications — including dosage and prescribing physician information — in your emergency kit and with trusted family members. For medications requiring refrigeration, such as insulin, some sources recommend researching backup cooling options and knowing the temperature tolerance windows for those medications. In California, the state government has at times activated emergency prescription refill protocols during declared disasters — checking with your county health department or pharmacy in advance about what provisions may be available is a suggestion found in several public health emergency guides. Managing medications during a crisis requires advance planning that only you and your healthcare providers can fully assess.

9. Know When to Call 911 vs. Seek Urgent Care

Across health information resources, a recurring piece of guidance is understanding — before an emergency occurs — when a situation requires a 911 call versus a visit to an urgent care clinic or emergency room. During and immediately after large-scale disasters, 911 systems can become overwhelmed, and many sources suggest reserving emergency calls for true life-threatening situations such as cardiac events, severe trauma, stroke symptoms, respiratory distress, or loss of consciousness. For less immediately life-threatening situations, urgent care clinics can often provide faster treatment with less system strain. Resources from organizations like the CDC and various hospital networks offer guidance on recognizing the warning signs of heart attack, stroke, severe allergic reaction, and other critical emergencies worth memorizing before they happen. It is also frequently suggested to post emergency numbers — including Poison Control at 1-800-222-1222 — in a visible place at home rather than relying on memory in a high-stress moment. No written guide can replace professional medical judgment, and when in doubt, calling 911 is always a reasonable choice.

10. Mental Health and Emotional Support After a Crisis

An aspect of emergency preparedness that has received growing attention in preparedness literature is the psychological impact of surviving a disaster. Sources from organizations like SAMHSA, the Red Cross, and the CDC note that anxiety, grief, sleep disruption, irritability, and symptoms of post-traumatic stress are common responses to emergencies, and that experiencing them does not indicate weakness. Many resources suggest normalizing these reactions, particularly for children, and emphasize that recovery is rarely linear. Practical suggestions collected from mental health and disaster response literature include maintaining routines as much as possible in the aftermath, limiting excessive news consumption, staying connected with trusted friends and family, and seeking professional help when symptoms persist or become debilitating. In California, several counties operate crisis mental health hotlines that activate during declared disasters. The Disaster Distress Helpline (1-800-985-5990) is a nationally available resource. Preparing emotionally for the aftermath of an emergency — including knowing that support resources exist — is just as important as physical preparation, and every individual's mental health needs will differ.

PART III: Fire Safety

11. Install and Maintain Smoke and Carbon Monoxide Detectors

Among the most consistently repeated pieces of fire safety advice found across government agencies, fire departments, and safety organizations is the importance of properly installed and maintained smoke and carbon monoxide (CO) detectors. The National Fire Protection Association and local fire departments widely recommend installing smoke alarms on every level of the home, inside each bedroom, and outside each sleeping area. Carbon monoxide detectors are similarly recommended on every level and near sleeping areas. Many sources advise testing detectors monthly using the test button, replacing batteries at least annually (or using 10-year sealed battery models), and replacing entire units every 10 years. In California, state law has specific requirements for smoke and CO detector installation in residential properties — checking with your local fire department or the California State Fire Marshal's office for current requirements is widely recommended. Interconnected alarms, which trigger all units in the home when one detects smoke, are often cited as the safer option. This is one of the lowest-cost, highest-impact steps any household can take.

12. Create and Practice a Home Fire Escape Plan

Fire safety resources consistently emphasize that a fire escape plan is only effective if it is practiced — and that the time to learn your escape routes is not during a fire. The general framework suggested across many sources involves drawing a floor plan of your home, identifying two ways out of every room (typically a door and a window), establishing a designated meeting place outside and away from the home, and assigning responsibilities for helping children, elderly relatives, or those with mobility challenges. Many fire departments recommend practicing the escape plan at least twice a year, including nighttime drills where occupants practice navigating in low light or with eyes closed to simulate smoke conditions. Sources also note that modern home fires can become life-threatening in as little as two minutes — making practiced, automatic responses far more valuable than trying to think through options in the moment. Every home has a unique layout, and every household has unique occupants; only you can design and rehearse a plan that truly fits your space and your family.

13. Fire Prevention in the Home

A significant portion of fire safety guidance available online and from fire departments focuses not on surviving fires but on preventing them in the first place. Commonly cited prevention tips include never leaving cooking unattended on the stove, keeping flammable materials away from heat sources, having chimneys and heating systems inspected annually, not overloading electrical outlets, replacing frayed or damaged electrical cords, keeping dryer lint traps clean, and storing flammable liquids like gasoline properly away from the home. In California, where wildfire risk is an added concern, many sources also recommend creating defensible space around the home by clearing dry vegetation at least 100 feet out, using fire-resistant materials for fencing and decking near the home, and keeping gutters clear of dry leaves. Cal Fire provides detailed, California-specific guidance on defensible space and home hardening that is worth reviewing for anyone living in or near high fire-risk zones. Prevention is always preferable to response, and small habitual adjustments in your daily routines can meaningfully reduce your household's fire risk.

14. What to Do During a House Fire

Fire safety organizations broadly advise that if a fire breaks out in your home, the priority is immediate evacuation — not attempting to fight the fire or retrieve belongings. A commonly cited guideline is to check doors with the back of your hand before opening them; if a door is hot, do not open it and find an alternate route instead. Sources suggest staying low to the ground where air is cooler and less smoky while exiting. Once outside, the consistent advice is to stay out — re-entering a burning structure is one of the most dangerous decisions a person can make, and fire departments universally discourage it. If you are trapped, sources recommend closing doors between yourself and the fire to slow its spread, signaling from a window, and calling 911 if possible. Knowing the layout of your home, having practiced your escape plan, and having working smoke detectors all significantly increase the odds of a safe exit. If you have children or family members who need assistance evacuating, pre-assigning that responsibility in your escape plan is a step many fire safety resources strongly encourage.

15. After the Fire — Re-entry and Recovery

Following a house fire, preparedness and recovery resources caution against re-entering a structure until it has been cleared as safe by fire officials, even if the fire appears to be fully extinguished. Structural damage, smoldering materials, and toxic residue from burned synthetics can all pose serious hazards. Many sources roocommend contacting your homeowner's or renter's insurance company as soon as possible to begin the claims process, and documenting damage with photographs before any cleanup begins. The Red Cross and local community organizations often provide emergency shelter, clothing, and food assistance for fire-displaced families — knowing in advance where to access those services in your area can reduce stress in the aftermath. Exposure to smoke and fire debris has documented health effects, and many health resources recommend wearing N95 masks during any cleanup activities and washing all clothing and surfaces that may have been contaminated. Recovery from a fire — financial, physical, and emotional — can take time, and reaching out to local social services and mental health resources is something many organizations actively encourage survivors to do.

PART IV: Earthquake Preparedness (California Focus)

16. Understand California's Earthquake Risk

California sits atop one of the most seismically active regions in the world, and preparedness resources from USGS, Cal OES, and the California Earthquake Authority consistently emphasize that understanding your specific local risk is an important first step in preparing. The state is crisscrossed by dozens of active fault systems — most notably the San Andreas Fault, but also the Hayward, Calaveras, Puente Hills, and many others — meaning that essentially every region of the state carries some degree of earthquake risk. Resources suggest looking up your address on hazard maps available through the California Geological Survey to understand your proximity to active faults, your soil liquefaction risk, and your landslide susceptibility. Many preparedness guides also note that "the Big One" — a major rupture along the southern San Andreas Fault — is considered by seismologists to be not a matter of if but when. This is not meant to cause panic but to underscore why earthquake preparedness is treated with particular urgency in California. Familiarizing yourself with your specific risk profile is a reasonable starting point for building a plan that addresses your real circumstances.

17. The "Drop, Cover, and Hold On" Protocol

Across earthquake preparedness resources — from USGS and the Earthquake Country Alliance to FEMA and the Red Cross — the near-universal guidance for what to do during shaking is to Drop, Cover, and Hold On. The advice is to drop to your hands and knees, take cover under a sturdy desk or table if one is nearby (or against an interior wall away from windows if not), and hold on until the shaking stops. Many sources specifically caution against the outdated "triangle of life" theory or the advice to stand in a doorway, noting that modern research and engineering data do not support these as superior strategies in most situations. If you are outdoors during an earthquake, sources suggest moving away from buildings, streetlights, and utility wires and dropping to the ground. If you are driving, sources recommend pulling over away from overpasses, bridges, and buildings, stopping the car, and staying inside until shaking stops. Practicing this response — so that it becomes muscle memory — is something many resources encourage, particularly for households with children. The seconds of an actual earthquake are not the time to be thinking through what to do.

18. Seismically Retrofit and Secure Your Home

A significant thread in California-specific earthquake preparedness guidance focuses on physical modifications to the home that can reduce damage and injury risk. Two areas cited most frequently are cripple wall retrofitting (reinforcing the short wood-framed walls between a home's foundation and first floor, which are a known failure point in earthquakes) and bolting the house to its foundation. The California Earthquake Authority's Brace + Bolt program has offered financial incentives for eligible homeowners to complete these retrofits, and their website provides detailed information on qualifying criteria. Beyond structural retrofitting, many preparedness sources suggest securing tall furniture like bookshelves, water heaters, and refrigerators to walls using furniture straps, storing heavy or breakable items on lower shelves, and using museum putty or earthquake-safe fasteners for objects displayed on shelves. These modifications will not prevent all damage, but numerous resources describe them as meaningfully reducing both the risk of injury from falling objects and the severity of structural damage. Consulting with a licensed contractor who has experience in seismic retrofitting is something many sources recommend for assessing your specific home's vulnerabilities.

19. Build a 72-Hour Earthquake-Specific Kit

While the general emergency supply kit described earlier in this chapter covers many needs, earthquake preparedness resources often highlight supplies that are particularly relevant to a major seismic event in California. A major earthquake can disrupt water, power, gas, and road access simultaneously and for extended periods — and many California-specific guides suggest preparing for at least 72 hours of self-sufficiency, with some recommending up to two weeks. In addition to the standard kit contents, earthquake-specific suggestions frequently include: a wrench to shut off the gas meter (stored near the meter, not inside the house), heavy-duty work gloves for handling debris, sturdy closed-toe shoes stored near each bed (to protect feet from broken glass when getting up after nighttime shaking), a crowbar for freeing jammed doors, and a waterproof container with copies of personal documents. Water storage is particularly emphasized, given that water mains are frequently damaged in major quakes. The Earthquake Country Alliance's Seven Steps to Earthquake Safety is a frequently cited California-specific resource worth reviewing when building your kit. What you ultimately need will depend on your household's size, location, and specific circumstances.

20. What to Do Immediately After an Earthquake

Once shaking stops, earthquake preparedness resources outline a series of recommended actions in the immediate aftermath. First, many sources advise checking yourself and those around you for injuries before moving. Next, a critical and widely emphasized step is to check for gas leaks — if you smell gas, hear a hissing sound, or suspect a leak, sources recommend opening windows, leaving the building immediately, not using any electrical switches or open flames, and calling PG&E or your local utility from outside. Checking for small fires and extinguishing them if safe to do so is also commonly mentioned, since fire following earthquake is a well-documented risk. Many sources suggest putting on shoes before walking around to avoid injury from broken glass or debris. Cal OES and similar agencies recommend listening to a battery-powered radio or your phone's emergency alerts for official guidance, and avoiding using the phone for non-emergency calls to keep lines open for rescue services. It is also widely advised not to use elevators and to be cautious opening cabinets, as items may have shifted and could fall when doors are opened. Taking a methodical, calm approach in the minutes following shaking — rather than rushing outside or making panicked decisions — is consistently emphasized.

21. Aftershocks — What to Expect and How to Stay Safe

A preparedness point that earthquake resources frequently raise is that aftershocks are not just possible after a major earthquake — they are virtually certain, sometimes occurring within minutes and continuing for days, weeks, or even months afterward. USGS and other seismological resources explain that aftershocks are typically smaller than the main event but can still cause significant damage, particularly to structures already weakened by the initial quake. Many preparedness guides advise being mentally prepared for aftershocks so that they do not cause additional panic, and recommend that people continue to practice Drop, Cover, and Hold On during each aftershock. It is also commonly advised to stay out of damaged buildings until they have been inspected by structural engineers, since aftershocks can cause already-compromised structures to collapse. Some sources note that occasionally an event people experience as a moderate earthquake turns out to have been a foreshock to a larger main event — another reason why preparedness should be maintained throughout the post-earthquake period rather than treated as a one-time response. Staying informed through official channels like Cal OES, USGS ShakeAlert, and your county's emergency management office is broadly recommended during the aftershock sequence.

A Final Note to Readers

Everything shared in this chapter has been gathered from publicly available resources, preparedness organizations, and general guidance found across the internet. The author is not a trained emergency professional, medical expert, firefighter, or seismologist. The responsibility for creating an emergency preparedness plan that truly works for you rests with you and your family. No single guide can account for your specific home, your health needs, your neighborhood, or your personal circumstances. Use this chapter as a starting point, and then dig deeper into the resources most relevant to where you live and who you're preparing for. Your life — and the lives of the people you love — are worth the effort.

Chapter 13

Financial Safety

Decades ago, I stumbled upon a profound article online that fundamentally shifted my perspective on wealth, planting a seed that would eventually grow into my life's financial philosophy. If I remember correctly, the author recommended building up to seven different sources of income to achieve true success. That core message was as simple as it was powerful: to build true financial security, one must move beyond a single paycheck. While the specific tactical details of that list have faded from my memory over the years, the central philosophy took root and inspired me to strike out on my own paths. Though many of those early attempts ended in total disaster, I never lost faith in the validity of the advice. My failures were entirely my own—I simply wasn't prepared for the realities of the ventures I chose—and it ultimately took me a full decade of trial and error to finally align myself with the right path toward financial safety. It took me a long time to realize that investing in the stock market requires a great deal of research and patience, but in the long run, it became an excellent source of income for me. Whether the market is meant for you or not is something only you can find out; it can be turbulent and capable of wiping out an entire investment. No one can decide that for you; you must decide for yourself.

Through this journey, I realized there is a distinct divide in how wealth is created. Geniuses and exceptionally talented individuals with razor-sharp minds can often launch high-tech startups, securing massive backing from venture capitalists. For these individuals, a singular, obsessive focus on a visionary project is often enough to propel them into the top tier of high-net-worth earners. They don't necessarily need to worry about diversifying their income streams because their primary engine of wealth is so high-powered. However, for the rest of us—the ordinary people working to find our way—building personal safety requires a different strategy. We do not have the luxury of a multi-million dollar "exit" or a revolutionary patent. Instead, we must be industrious in a different way, piecing together multiple, sustainable sources of income to create a fortress of financial stability. It is a slower, more deliberate process, but it is the most reliable way for an average person to transform a modest beginning into a secure future.

Learning from my own experience, I instilled in my daughters since they were in junior high that the key to a stable life is to save, and that the process must start immediately. I explained the vital importance of dividing their monthly allowances into smaller pieces, ensuring one of those pieces went into their piggy banks without exception. I further emphasized that this process must be sustainable, continuing into their adulthood. Because they were young, they readily accepted my teaching; they were excited to put money into their own piggy banks, which brought me great joy. As the years passed, I provided additional funding on top of what they saved and opened a stock trading account for each of them. I am not a financial planner, nor am I offering professional advice; I am merely sharing the methods I showed my daughters so they could gain a basic understanding of filtering stocks to distinguish between overvalued assets and sound investments. My personal method is simple: I follow the philosophy of Warren Buffett and Charlie Munger, relying on Benjamin Graham's intrinsic value formula and Peter Lynch's PEGY ratio to determine a stock's worth. Today, my daughters' investments have tripled in value, and I have no doubt their accounts will hold substantial value by the time they reach retirement age.

With the advent of Artificial Intelligence and tools like Gemini, Grok, Claude, and ChatGPT, the barrier to entry for this analysis has dropped significantly. You can now use these tools to calculate a stock's intrinsic value or PEGY ratio without performing manual calculations. However, one must remain vigilant, as AI models can make mistakes. They should be used as assistants in your research rather than infallible sources of truth. Ultimately, through years of trial and error, I found that the stock market served as a vital extra source of income, but I did not stop there. I expanded my horizon by investing in real estate and was eventually able to purchase two rental properties. These assets provide a consistent stream of monthly income while allowing me to build significant equity over time. While I am nowhere near the recommended seven sources of income, the combination of the stock market, real estate, and my 401K accounts provides me with a deep sense of financial safety. This is more than enough for me, as I have lived a very modest lifestyle ever since moving past the reckless spending of my early adulthood.

I recognize that the path to financial security is diverse. A close friend of mine has seen his holdings gain nearly 500% by investing in gold since it was under a thousand dollars an ounce. Another friend has enjoyed massive returns through cryptocurrency. The fundamental lesson is that what works for one person may not fit the investment style or risk tolerance of another. I choose not to invest in crypto or gold not because I think they are poor investments, but because they simply aren't for me. At the age of 60, my total net worth is nothing to brag about; in fact, it is probably laughable to many. It's not much, but it is sufficient for me to feel comfortable leading my simple life and taking care of my family. It is plenty for me to feel a sense of financial safety as I reach my full retirement age, which is now only five years away. The main point is that if you believe in building sound financial safety for yourself and your family, you must save, invest, and build additional sustainable sources of income beyond your existing career. This disciplined approach to wealth is a far cry from my beginnings, where the very concept of a "portfolio" was unimaginable, and my life was measured not in percentages, but in the smallest possible denomination of hope.

Reflecting back, the memory of that first summer in 1980—when I was just a fourteen-year-old boy—remains etched in my mind. It was a time defined not by the grand promise of the American Dream, but by its smallest possible denomination: a single penny. Finding that coin on a sun-bleached sidewalk just days after my arrival felt like a windfall, a tiny copper omen of luck. If I had possessed the foresight, I would have kept that penny as a souvenir—a monument to the version of myself that arrived with absolutely nothing. In reality, I had just enough to clothe myself, though my "estate" consisted of a single, repetitive set of clothes that I wore with a pride born of necessity. My daily attire was a study in thrift and the residual fashion of a decade I had barely missed. I owned one old white button-down shirt, softened by age and scattered with a pattern of tiny blue flowers, which I paired with faded blue jeans that were far too long for my frame. I hadn't chosen or bought these pants myself; they were a gift from a charity, a salvaged relic likely originating from the 1970s. White cloth patches featuring a pattern of red and blue stars had been sewn onto the bottom of each seam, covering my ankles and reaching all the way to the ground. To me, those starred jeans and floral shirt were my armor, but to the world, they were a glaring signifier of my circumstances. I wore that specific outfit to school every single day for months, walking through the hallways in a bubble of linguistic innocence. I remember the kids pointing and the laughter that followed me, but because I hadn't yet mastered the language, the cruelty was lost in translation. I lived in a temporary, merciful state of ignorance until someone finally pulled me aside to explain the joke. They told me that the other students were mocking me for wearing the same clothes every day, making me realize for the first time that my humble gratitude for a charity gift was being mistaken for a lack of dignity.

Shortly after that realization, I secured a couple more shirts and pairs of jeans from the charity. This small expansion offered more than just variety; it gave me a sense of relief and a bit of breathing room as I navigated my new life. Looking back, those first donated pieces—with their floral patterns and starred seams—remain a powerful testament to the starting line of my journey. I have never forgotten those lean days or the humble place where I began. That memory has stayed with me, serving as a quiet reminder of the weight even a single donated garment can carry. In an effort to give back, I have actively participated in my workplace donation programs over the years. This commitment has grown significantly, and within just the last three years, through the generosity of my employer's matching programs, I have been able to generate approximately $38,000 in contributions. Every cent of those funds has been donated to a local charity dedicated to supporting orphans and less fortunate students in Vietnam. It is a full-circle journey for me—ensuring that other children facing their own modest beginnings have the resources and the dignity they need to forge their own paths.

I share this background not to elicit sympathy, but to offer a clear perspective on the nature of resilience. If an ordinary person like me—whose beginning was so difficult, marked not only by a lack of language skills but by starting with just a single red penny found on a sidewalk—can build a life of financial security, I am living proof that such a transformation is possible for anyone. My story is a testament to the fact that your starting point does not have to dictate your destination; however, the bridge between those two points is built with more than just hope—it requires a fundamental shift in mindset. My path was far from a straight line to success; it was a winding road marked by trial, error, and deeply humbling lessons. The truth is, I made countless financial mistakes along the way that slowed my progress. Despite working with a relentless, almost obsessive drive—often clocking 80-hour weeks on a regular basis just to stay afloat—I watched much of that hard-earned income slip through my fingers. For many years, I was my own greatest obstacle, falling into the common trap of prioritizing immediate gratification over long-term stability. I learned the hard way that true wealth is not determined by the intensity of your labor or the size of your paycheck, but by the discipline of your choices.

Ultimately, I realized that financial strategies are not "one size fits all"; what brings prosperity to one may lead another to ruin. Finding the specific path that aligned with my own temperament was perhaps the most difficult lesson of all. In my younger days, I spent recklessly, never pausing to consider the necessity of a rainy-day fund. This path reached a breaking point when I found myself drowning in debt, living out of an old Toyota Tercel while attending a local university. My credit cards were maxed out from a relentless cycle of cash advances, and my paychecks were effectively spent before I even held them in my hands.

It was then that my girlfriend—who is now my wife—stepped in and forced me to confront my financial reality. Recognizing that I lacked the discipline to navigate out of the wreckage myself, I handed her the reins; she assumed control of my paychecks and bank accounts, managing every cent with precision. In that moment of clarity, I realized that without her intervention, I wasn't just wasting my money—I was wasting my life.

With a newfound sense of purpose and a clean slate, we began to dream of entrepreneurship. Together, we opened a small sports card shop, pouring our hearts into building it from the ground up. Over time, we earned the deep-seated trust of a loyal community. Our shop evolved into more than just a place of business; it became a sanctuary where regulars stopped by not only to hunt for rare cards but to decompress, share stories, and find a sense of belonging.

It was a wonderful, fulfilling chapter of our lives, but the industry eventually shifted beneath us. The cost of maintaining a small hobby shop skyrocketed as manufacturers pivoted away from accessible, inexpensive packs toward "super-premium" products that cost ten times more. This market shift made it nearly impossible for a small-scale shop to survive. Ultimately, we faced the heartbreaking reality that the business was no longer sustainable. We made the difficult decision to sell the shop to one of our regular customers for a fraction of its value—a humble exit that allowed us to finally walk away from what had become an unbearable financial burden. A few years later, I ventured into a vending business with twenty candy machines, followed by an import-export venture, but those, too, ended poorly. I reached a point where I was so utterly broke that with the very last twenty-dollar bill I had to my name, my wife went out and bought a couple of cases of canned wieners. That became my reality: eating those canned sausages with instant noodles for breakfast, lunch, and dinner, day after day, until my next paycheck finally arrived. As the weight of my failures continued to mount, I felt I had little to offer my girlfriend; I even encouraged her to move on and find someone with a more stable future. She flatly refused to leave my side, choosing instead to believe in me when I had stopped believing in myself.

We eventually married, and we remain just as committed to each other today as we were during those lean years. Despite those early failures, we refused to give up. We pivoted our focus to real estate, starting with a modest property and eventually "trading up" to better homes in better neighborhoods several times over. Our resolve was tested most fiercely during the 2008 housing crash. We struggled dearly to keep our heads above water, but we managed to hold onto our properties because I worked countless hours of overtime and took on every side job available to save every penny possible. Fortunately, I never repeated the reckless financial mistakes of my youth. Instead of spending for the moment, we embraced a life of frugality, prioritizing our future over immediate wants. This discipline eventually provided us with a small nest egg to invest in the stock market. I have remained an active investor for the last 30 years, and it has proven to be a deeply rewarding experience. Looking back, it wasn't a stroke of genius that saved us, but the simple, hard-won lessons of persistence and the courage to live within our means.

Our daughters are growing up in a world far removed from the one I knew. They have never had to endure the anxiety of wondering where their next meal would come from, nor have they had to settle for a dinner of canned wieners just to get by. While I am profoundly grateful for their fortune, I refuse to let that comfort drift into complacency. I constantly remind them that a true financial safety net isn't woven in days, weeks, or months; it is a discipline built over decades. I want them to understand that security isn't just about what you have today—it's about what you've prepared for tomorrow. My own journey taught me this through a series of humbling lessons. While small businesses are the lifeblood of our economy, my own ventures never quite took flight, and I have only my own nature to blame. I lacked the 'killer instinct' necessary to maintain high-profit margins. Instead of maximizing gains, I was driven by a desire to give my customers the best deal possible. Whether it was my vending machine route, my import-export endeavors, or my time dealing with collectors, I consistently prioritized the other person's profit over my own bottom line.

By repeatedly placing myself on the short end of the transaction, I had to accept a difficult truth: I am not a businessman. I now see history repeating itself. Watching my daughters try to raise funds for their school clubs by selling drinks and snacks, it's clear they have inherited my generous streak. I provided the 'seed money' for their inventory, yet they always returned home short of the original amount they borrowed. Like me, they were so eager to be fair or generous that they forgot to protect their investment. Because they share my heart, I must ensure they don't share my financial mistakes. In my failures, I found the value of a different kind of wealth—one built on fair market value and the slow, steady work of long-term stability, such as real estate and the stock market. That is the foundation I am now determined to help them build, teaching them that while generosity is a virtue, financial wisdom is what allows that generosity to be sustainable. Refined by the lessons of my past, I have come to firmly believe that lasting financial security isn't found in a single paycheck, but in the cultivation of multiple, sustainable income streams that complement your primary career. For me, the path forward meant pivoting toward real estate and the stock market—"slow-burner" investments that allow wealth to accumulate quietly, without the constant friction of high-stakes sales or demanding customer service. Even in this arena, my instinct for fairness remains: I haven't raised the rent on my tenants in over a decade, knowing they have been struggling to make a living. Instead of pushing for higher rents, I prefer their stability over maximized monthly profits. While a traditional accountant might see that as a missed opportunity, the long-term appreciation of home equity has more than compensated for the difference. It taught me a vital truth: you don’t have to be a ruthless negotiator to build a fortune; you simply need the patience to let time and equity do the heavy lifting for you.

Building a robust financial safety net is not merely about accumulating a specific number in a bank account; it is about constructing a multi-layered defense system designed to outlast the most severe "rainy days." To achieve this, one must move beyond the fragile dependency on a single paycheck and embrace the dual strategy of maximizing savings and diversifying income streams. Saving serves as your immediate armor—a liquid cushion that buys you time when a crisis strikes. However, as I witnessed with those in the tech industry who lost everything, time eventually runs out if you are only drawing from a finite pool of cash. This is why maximizing your savings rate must be coupled with the industrious pursuit of additional, sustainable sources of income.

Think of multiple income streams as the pillars of a bridge; if one pillar is swept away by an economic flood or an AI-driven industry shift, the others remain to hold the structure aloft. Whether it is through rental properties that provide consistent monthly cash flow, a disciplined stock portfolio that compounds over time, or a secondary skill that can be monetized, these additional channels transform your financial life from a vulnerable line into a resilient web. The goal is to reach a point where your survival is not tied to the whims of a single employer or the health of a single industry. By aggressively narrowing the gap between what you earn and what you spend, you create the "seed money" necessary to plant these diverse sources of wealth.

Ultimately, the need for this diversification is a matter of long-term endurance. A single source of income is a point of failure; multiple sources are a strategy for survival. By maximizing your savings now, you are purchasing your future freedom and the ability to weather a storm that might last months or even years. This proactive approach ensures that if a "rainy day" turns into a prolonged season of hardship, you possess the structural integrity to remain housed, fed, and dignified. True financial safety means that even if your primary profession is upended, your family's security remains unshakeable, allowing you to navigate change from a position of strength rather than a place of desperation.

Truly recognizing your strengths and weaknesses is a process that requires radical, unflinching honesty; after all, no one possesses a more intimate knowledge of your internal landscape than you do. This self-reflection is not merely an academic exercise, but a strategic necessity for building financial safety. As I have learned through my own journey, I am a poor businessman because I lack the ruthlessness required to maximize profit at every turn. By acknowledging this, I realized that high-stakes sales or aggressive entrepreneurship were paths I should avoid. Conversely, while I don't consider myself a mathematical genius, I discovered a genuine affinity for working with numbers and the patience required for analysis, which allowed me to thrive in the stock market. It is vital that you conduct your own inventory to identify where your natural talents lie and where your temperament fails you. By building upon your strengths and either fortifying your weaknesses or strategically avoiding them, you can construct a financial fortress that is tailored to your unique identity.

The urgency of this self-reflection has never been greater, as the advent of artificial intelligence reaches a level of sophistication that threatens to displace many traditional roles. Building a strong financial safety net is not an overnight task; it takes years of disciplined effort to accomplish. If you haven't yet begun to consider your long-term security, now is the time to start, as AI is being ushered in with staggering speed. You must ask yourself the difficult question: is your profession replaceable by an algorithm? If the answer is yes, then you are standing on a precarious ledge.

I saw the reality of this vulnerability firsthand during my time in the police force. While working on several homeless encampment cleanups, I had the opportunity to speak directly with many of the residents. To my surprise, many told me they had recently been in the tech industry. They had been laid off and, once they became ineligible for unemployment checks, were unable to secure new work. Without an income, they were forced out of their homes and into their cars. From there, things began to spiral downward spiritually and physically. As their personal hygiene became increasingly compromised and they lacked a permanent mailing address, they could no longer maintain the "proper appearance" required for a professional interview. Eventually, the hope of regaining employment faded into thin air.

How you currently weigh the balance between advancing your existing career and investing time into developing those secondary "pillars" of income is a deeply personal calculation. The truth is, no one but you can determine the right equilibrium for your life; you alone possess the necessary insight into your goals, risk tolerance, and ultimate capacity for growth. This philosophy of self-reliance was driven home for me years ago while watching a friend negotiate a deal to purchase a used car. When the deal was done, he turned to me and explained his outlook: "We have to hustle to earn that extra income," he said. "When you're down and out, no one is going to be there to give you a handout. While we are still young and capable, we have to hustle as much as we can."

I couldn't have agreed with him more. Over the years, I watched him transform that mindset into a sophisticated operation. He moved from flipping individual used cars to acquiring entire auction lots before they ever reached the public block. He explained his strategy to me: by purchasing vehicles in massive bulk lots, he secured the best possible wholesale prices. He would then distribute those cars to smaller used car dealerships on credit, allowing them to pay him back as the vehicles were sold. I was incredibly impressed by his logistical brilliance and his mastery of buying and selling. Yet, even with his offer to help me enter the venture, I knew I couldn't do it. As much as I admired his success, I remained acutely aware of my own limitations; I knew that I was a horrible businessman and lacked the specific temperament required for that kind of high-stakes trade.

The diversity of these opportunities was further illustrated to me during a conversation I had with a stranger at a lounge. He simply needed someone to talk to, as his world had been turned upside down. He explained that his wine importing business—a side hustle he had built importing French wines for his small circle of elite U.S. clientele—had been hijacked by a ransomware virus. The hackers were demanding $50,000 to release his computer system. He told me the business had been thriving until recent tariffs kicked in, and now this cyber-attack threatened to end it all. I felt a deep sense of empathy for the man and wished him the best of luck, but his story was a sobering reminder: setting up a side business is one thing, but maintaining and protecting it from global economics and digital threats is a totally different story.

As you can see, the opportunities to create a side business and establish an extra sustainable source of income come with a wide array of nuances and risks. From the logistical complexity of a car lot to the high-end niche of wine importation, every venture has its own set of challenges. It is up to us to select what would work for us individually, matching our ventures to our specific skills and our ability to manage the associated risks.

Ultimately, the need for this diversification is a matter of long-term endurance. A single source of income is a point of failure; multiple sources are a strategy for survival. By maximizing your savings now, you are purchasing your future freedom and the ability to weather a storm that might last months or even years. This proactive approach ensures that if a "rainy day" turns into a prolonged season of hardship, you possess the structural integrity to remain housed, fed, and dignified. True financial safety means that even if your primary profession is upended, your family's security remains unshakeable, allowing you to navigate change from a position of strength rather than a place of desperation.

Furthermore, it is far more effective to brainstorm sustainable income streams while your primary career is still in good standing, as the absence of immediate financial pressure allows for genuine creativity and long-term planning. Conversely, developing a viable business model becomes significantly more difficult when you are between jobs; in that high-stress environment, the goal shifts from creating a "supplemental" source to a "survival" source. When an idea must immediately function as a primary lifeline, the desperation often stifles the very innovation required to make the venture successful. It is imperative to plan in advance rather than procrastinating, especially when it comes to financial planning.

In the interim, while waiting for a breakthrough idea to materialize, it is prudent to conduct a rigorous inventory of current expenses to identify unnecessary costs and maximize the savings rate. This serves a dual purpose: it builds a robust "rainy day" fund for immediate security while simultaneously accumulating the capital necessary for future investments. Refining a budget in this way ensures that when the right opportunity finally arrives, there is enough financial breathing room to pursue it without hesitation. A critical part of this refinement is adopting a ruthless stance on debt. While some prefer to leverage loans to support their lifestyle or justify interest payments as potential tax shelters, such an approach is fundamentally flawed from a practical perspective. To be clear, I am not a financial advisor, and everything I mentioned in this book should not be taken as professional financial advice; however, from a layperson's point of view, paying interest is effectively giving a bank free money for the privilege of spending wealth that has not yet been earned. It is a guaranteed negative return on one's hard work and a persistent drain on long-term potential.

Consequently, there is immense value in prioritizing the elimination of debt and paying off balances as early as humanly possible. The experience of living debt-free for the first time marks a profound shift in one's reality, offering a level of liberation that is difficult to overstate. It is a life without the weight of a mortgage or the shadow of a creditor, where every dollar earned stays in the pocket of the person who earned it. When an individual owns their life outright, their decisions are no longer dictated by the pressure of monthly obligations, but by their own goals and values.

While earning an income, diversifying revenue streams, and maximizing your savings rate are the foundational pillars of financial safety, they represent only half of the equation; the other half is the vigilant preservation of the wealth you have already built. It is equally critical to protect your hard-earned capital by insulating yourself against the predatory nature of scams, the recklessness of investing without exhaustive research, and the high-risk gamble of launching a business venture without a meticulous plan. These pitfalls are not merely minor hurdles, but catastrophic events that can pull the rug out from under you, erasing years of disciplined progress in an instant. In the worst-case scenario, such oversights do more than just deplete your savings—they can plunge you into a cycle of debt that compromises your future and forces you to start again from zero. True financial security, therefore, requires a dual-track mindset: an offensive strategy to grow your assets and a defensive strategy to ensure they are never needlessly lost.

To avoid these catastrophic pitfalls, you must cultivate a "defensive mindset" that is just as disciplined as your "offensive" strategy for growth, anchored by healthy skepticism, rigorous due diligence, and emotional control. First and foremost, you must adopt a "too good to be true" filter to guard against scammers and predatory investment schemes that rely on the lure of "guaranteed" high returns and a false sense of urgency. If an opportunity promises massive rewards with little risk or pressures you to act before you can think, it is almost certainly a trap; genuine wealth-building is a slow process, and anyone offering a shortcut is usually looking for a shortcut to your bank account. Furthermore, you should commit to the rule of absolute understanding, never putting a single dollar into an investment or business venture that you cannot explain in simple terms to a child. Exhaustive research is your greatest defense, which means reading the fine print, studying historical performance, and understanding your "exit strategy." Even when using modern AI tools for analysis, they should be treated as assistants rather than authorities, with all data verified against primary sources to ensure decisions are based on facts rather than hallucinations.

Finally, the preservation of wealth requires you to separate your emotions from your capital. Much financial ruin stems from "FOMO" (fear of missing out) or the "sunk cost fallacy"—that dangerous urge to throw good money after bad in a failing venture. Before embarking on any business, it is vital to create a "fail-safe" plan that defines exactly how much you are willing to lose and at what specific point you will walk away. By setting these boundaries while you are calm and rational, you prevent desperation from clouding your judgment when things get difficult. Ultimately, the goal of financial safety is not just to reach the finish line, but to ensure you have enough left to enjoy the life you have worked so hard to build.

Ultimately, this financial discipline mirrors a broader philosophy of self-reliance: just as the mind is trained to avoid unnecessary conflict, emotional discipline is used to de-escalate high-pressure situations before they spiral out of control. I still vividly remember the early days of this journey, when my wife—my girlfriend at the time—and I made it our mission to prioritize my credit card debt and pay it off as quickly as possible. To do so, we stripped our spending down to the absolute minimum, finding joy in simple activities that cost nothing more than a bit of gas money or a cheap lunch. We entertained ourselves by taking long walks in the park, hiking local hills, and driving out to the beach; we stayed active by playing tennis and biking on second-hand equipment we had scouted at the local flea market.

Eventually, living frugally evolved from a temporary necessity into a permanent lifestyle that we still lead today. Embracing this simplicity has been the key to staying out of debt and ensuring our hard-earned money is preserved for the future; for us, this simple lifestyle is a primary means to enhance our financial safety. While this approach works exceptionally well for us, whether it is the right path for you is certainly a personal choice that remains entirely up to you. In this framework, a debt-free foundation acts as your ultimate line of defense, providing a structural shield against the unpredictable uncertainties of the world. By integrating these habits of mental awareness, emotional control, and financial rigor, you ensure that your personal security is never a matter of luck, but the direct result of a deliberate and disciplined life.

In conclusion, the journey toward financial safety is not a sprint toward a specific number, but a marathon of disciplined, deliberate choices. My own path—from the "single penny" of my youth to the stability of a debt-free retirement—proves that while you cannot control the economic weather or the rise of AI, you can absolutely control the integrity of your own shelter. Achieving true security requires more than just a paycheck; it demands a radical commitment to living within your means, the elimination of the soul-crushing weight of debt, and the persistent cultivation of multiple income streams that align with your unique temperament. However, building these pillars is only half the battle; the other half is the vigilant preservation of the wealth you have already built. You must insulate yourself against the predatory nature of scams, the recklessness of investing without exhaustive research, and the high-risk gamble of launching a business venture without a meticulous plan. These pitfalls can pull the rug out from under you, erasing years of progress in an instant and potentially plunging you back into the cycle of debt.

To avoid these catastrophic setbacks, you must cultivate a "defensive mindset" that is just as disciplined as your "offensive" strategy for growth. This involves adopting a "too good to be true" filter to guard against shortcuts, committing to a rule of absolute understanding before investing a single dollar, and separating your emotions from your capital to avoid the traps of FOMO and the sunk cost fallacy. Do not wait for a "rainy day" to begin building your roof; start now, while you have the clarity to plan. Whether you choose the slow growth of the stock market, the tangible equity of real estate, or the simple freedom of a frugal lifestyle, the most important step is to begin. By transforming your finances into a resilient web rather than a single, vulnerable thread, you ensure that your future and your family's dignity are never left to chance, but are secured by the unwavering strength of your own self-reliance. Your goal is not just to reach the finish line, but to ensure you have the peace and resources left to enjoy the life you have worked so hard to build.

Chapter 14

Stealthy Larceny

After spending nearly three decades in law enforcement, I can tell you that identity theft is one of the most stealthy devastating crimes I've ever encountered—and I wish more people understood just how easily it happens to ordinary, careful folks. Simply put, a thief steals your personal information—your name, date of birth, Social Security number, or driver's license number—and uses it to open accounts, take out loans, or commit crimes in your name. What makes it so insidious is that you often don't find out for months, sometimes years, until a collection agency calls or a loan you never took out shows up on your credit report. I don't claim to be an expert in this area at all, as I never worked in the Financial Crimes Unit. My experience was limited to conducting preliminary investigations at the patrol level before forwarding the cases to detectives for follow-up.

However, seeing the look on a victim's face when they realize their financial identity has been hijacked is something that stays with you.

Because of what I've witnessed on the job, my humble suggestion to you is to do what I have done for myself and my family: check your credit report regularly at AnnualCreditReport.com, place a credit freeze with the three major bureaus (Equifax, Experian, and TransUnion), and never carry your Social Security card in your wallet. These small habits can make a real difference. In fact, at my age, since I don't need to apply for new credit cards or get a loan for anything, I have frozen my credit entirely so that no one can forge a loan or open cards in our names. It provides a level of peace that is worth the minor inconvenience of "thawing" the credit if we ever truly need it.

Beyond the theft of your identity lies an even more sinister threat to your most valuable physical asset. Most of us worked hard for years to save for a down payment, and it is heartbreaking to realize a home can be stolen right under your nose without you even knowing it until it is too late. In deed fraud, a criminal forges your signature on property transfer documents to "steal" the title, often taking out loans against your equity or selling the home entirely.

Retired couples and families have lost years of sleep over the resulting legal nightmares. While it sounds impossible, this happens frequently, especially with vacant land or inherited properties. A simple, vital precaution is to sign up for your county recorder's property alert service. Many counties offer free notifications whenever a document is filed using your address. It takes minutes to set up and provides a digital tripwire for your sanctuary.

Unfortunately, these heartless crimes have become a disturbing trend. The following cases from 2024 to 2026, represent information real-world instances, highlight the surge in "house stealing" schemes. I encourage you to search the internet using keywords like "property deed fraud alert," "quitclaim deed forgery prosecution," or "mortgage identity theft indictment" to understand how to safeguard your title.

Case 1: The Affluent Mortgage Sting

• Synopsis: A sophisticated crime ring targeted homeowners in high-value areas. The group used stolen personal identifying information (PII) to create fake IDs and even forged death certificates. By posing as the owners, they secured over $17.4 million in fraudulent loans from private lenders, successfully pocketing $6 million before detection.

• Adjudication: In March 2026, 11 individuals were arrested under a 15-count federal indictment. They face up to 20 years in federal prison per fraud count, highlighting the massive federal resources now being used to track these syndicates.

Case 2: The Multi-Property Identity Ghost

• Synopsis: A perpetrator used stolen identities to commit deed fraud on three separate residential homes. The deception was so thorough that even after his arrest, investigators struggled for months to verify his true legal name. He had successfully transferred the titles into his possession using counterfeit identification.

• Adjudication: In early 2025, the defendant was sentenced to four to nine years in state prison. Crucially, specialized housing bureaus were able to navigate the legal mess to return the homes to their rightful owners.

Case 3: The "Short Sale" Deception

• Synopsis: A disbarred professional targeted 15 homeowners facing foreclosure. Using false promises of legal assistance, he tricked victims into signing over their deeds to corporations he controlled. He then collected rent for years while the original owners suffered financial ruin, unaware they no longer owned their homes.

• Adjudication: In late 2025, the perpetrator was sentenced to up to seven years in prison. The court also took the rare step of nullifying the deeds to 11 properties, legally restoring the titles to the victims.

Case 4: The "Quick-Flip" Forgery

• Synopsis: Using a forged signature on a quitclaim deed, a perpetrator transferred a home into her own name. Her strategy was a "quick-flip"—attempting to sell the property to an unsuspecting third-party buyer immediately, before the legitimate owner checked public records.

• Adjudication: Following a state investigation, she was convicted of deed fraud and grand theft in 2025 and sentenced to five years in state prison.

Case 5: The Vulnerable Target Breach

• Synopsis: Scammers targeted a homeowner who was physically incapacitated and in hospice care. They forged her signature to steal the deed, hoping her condition would prevent her from noticing the change in ownership.

• Adjudication: This case became a landmark for newly expanded deed theft laws in 2024. The perpetrators were indicted for grand larceny, proving that the legal system is becoming more aggressive in protecting vulnerable homeowners.

In light of these staggering cases, it is incumbent upon you to proactively protect your home. To safeguard the sanctuary you have built, determine if your local government offers free property fraud alerts.

Many county recorders and registrars have implemented digital tripwires that allow homeowners to register their names and parcel numbers. Once enrolled, the system will send you an immediate notification via email or text the moment any document—whether a deed, mortgage, or lien—is recorded against your property. This real-time intelligence is vital; it allows you to intercept a fraudulent transaction before a scammer has the opportunity to vanish with your equity.

In addition to these automated alerts, you must maintain a disciplined habit of manual oversight. You should verify your "chain of title" at least once or twice a year by visiting your county's public records website. By searching your property's history, you can ensure that no unauthorized "quitclaim" or "grant" deeds have been filed in the shadows. You must also stay vigilant regarding your physical mail; a sudden cessation of property tax bills or utility statements is a significant red flag. Scammers often file fraudulent change-of-address forms with the post office to divert your mail, ensuring you remain completely unaware of the theft while they finalize their scheme.

A more strategic way to insulate your investment is to secure an enhanced owner's title insurance policy. While most homeowners are familiar with the lender's title insurance required by banks, that policy only protects the financial institution's interest, not yours. An enhanced owner's policy, however, often includes specific provisions for post-policy forgery, covering the substantial legal costs associated with a "quiet title" action. If a fraudster successfully records a forged deed, this insurance becomes your legal war chest, providing the professional resources necessary to fight a complex court battle and return the title to your name without draining your life savings.

Because deed theft is fundamentally an extension of identity theft, you should also treat your credit report as an early warning system for your real estate. Regularly monitoring your credit for unauthorized "hard inquiries" from mortgage companies or banks can alert you to a scammer's attempt to drain your home's equity. If you notice a sudden dip in your score or the appearance of a Home Equity Line of Credit (HELOC) that you did not initiate, it is a clear indicator that someone is posing as you to leverage your property. Staying on top of your financial profile ensures that you catch the breach at the digital level before it manifests as the physical loss of your home.

Finally, you must be particularly defensive regarding vacant or inherited properties, which are the primary targets for "title pirates." Scammers specifically look for homes where the owner is deceased or living out of state, as these properties lack the daily oversight that prevents unauthorized activity. If you inherit a home, move with speed to record the new deed and update the mailing address for all tax and utility records immediately. For properties that remain empty for any period, establishing a relationship with a trusted neighbor to watch for unauthorized "For Sale" signs or tampered locks provides a physical perimeter that no amount of digital monitoring can replace. By combining these tactical layers, you ensure that your home remains exactly what it was meant to be: a secure asset for your family's future.

In my years on the job, I responded to quite a few credit card fraud cases, and the technology criminals use has only grown more sophisticated. One of the most prevalent threats is card skimming, which involves a small device secretly attached to ATMs, gas pumps, or point-of-sale terminals. These "parasite" devices capture your card data the moment you swipe, allowing criminals to clone your physical card or sell your digital footprint on the black market. While I'm not trying to alarm you, I do want you to be more observant of your physical surroundings. Before inserting your card, give the reader a gentle tug—skimmers are often loosely attached with adhesive. Better yet, utilize tap-to-pay (contactless) technology whenever possible, as it generates a one-time transaction code and never transmits your actual card number. Above all, review your statements weekly; thieves often start with tiny "test" charges, hoping you'll overlook a few cents before they move in for the kill.

Building on these physical security measures, I know it sounds almost old-fashioned in the digital age, but mail theft remains one of the most common entry points for financial ruin. A thief who pilfers your mailbox isn't just looking for a birthday card; they are hunting for credit card offers, bank statements, or checks they can "wash" and rewrite. This often leads to a rapid account takeover. Once a criminal has enough of your data to change your contact information, they can intercept password reset messages and effectively lock you out of your own financial life. I've always encouraged people in my community to pick up their mail promptly, invest in a locking mailbox, and sign up for USPS Informed Delivery. This service provides a daily photo preview of your incoming mail, so if a new credit card or sensitive document doesn't arrive as pictured, you can report the theft immediately rather than assuming it's simply delayed.

This vigilance is particularly crucial because your Social Security number is essentially the master key to your financial fortress, and once it's in the wrong hands, the damage can take years to repair. Criminals use stolen SSNs to file for unemployment benefits, apply for high-interest loans, or even gain employment illegally under your name. I've seen hardworking people have their retirement benefits compromised and tax refunds intercepted—all due to an SSN exposure in a data breach they were never notified about. To prevent this, the Social Security Administration allows you to create a "my Social Security" account online; doing this yourself prevents a scammer from creating one in your name. Furthermore, be fiercely protective of this number. Many businesses ask for it out of habit or for their own convenience when it isn't legally required. It is perfectly okay to ask why they need it and whether an alternative identifier will suffice.

While the financial implications are obvious, some forms of stealth larceny can actually threaten your physical safety, specifically medical identity theft. This occurs when someone uses your name and insurance credentials to receive care, surgery, or prescriptions. The danger here is that their health records—their blood type, allergies, and diagnoses—get mixed into yours. Imagine being rushed into an emergency room only for a doctor to see a medical history that contradicts your actual biology. I've spoken with victims of this crime, and the combination of financial liability and potential health risk is deeply troubling. Make it a habit to review your Explanation of Benefits (EOB) statements carefully. Even if you don't owe a balance, those statements are a ledger of what was billed in your name. If you see a visit or procedure you don't recognize, contact your insurer with the same urgency you would a stolen credit card.

You must be equally prepared during tax season, as this is when refund fraud spikes sharply across the country. In this scenario, a criminal uses your Social Security number to file a fraudulent tax return early in the year, claiming a massive refund and having it routed to their own account. When you go to file your legitimate return, the IRS rejects it because their system shows you've "already filed." Sorting out this bureaucratic nightmare can take months of stress. To insulate yourself, I strongly recommend joining the IRS Identity Protection PIN (IP PIN) program. This assigns you a unique six-digit number that is required on any return filed in your name. Filing as early as possible also narrows the window of opportunity for thieves. Remember, if you receive unusual correspondence, don't ignore it—but keep in mind that the IRS will always contact you via mail first, never by phone demanding immediate payment via gift cards or wire transfers.

Transitioning from paperwork to the digital world, I'll be honest—when I started my career, "phishing" wasn't even on the radar. Today, it has become one of the most prolific tools used by modern thieves to bypass your security. Through deceptive emails, texts, or phone calls, criminals pretend to be the IRS, your bank, or even a tech support company to trick you into handing over your login credentials. These messages can look startlingly authentic, often using official logos and high-pressure language. I've seen highly educated, savvy people fall for these traps, so there is no shame in being cautious. My golden rule is simple: never click a link in an unsolicited message. If you suspect your bank is actually trying to reach you, hang up and call the number on the back of your physical card. Legitimate organizations will never pressure you to act "right now" under the threat of immediate arrest.

Beyond these digital traps, we must also be protective of our most vulnerable, as elder financial abuse is a crime that breaks my heart. Older adults are disproportionately targeted for "grandparent" scams, romance fraud, or lottery schemes. Often, the theft is committed by a trusted caregiver or family member who slowly siphons off accounts. The shame that follows often keeps victims silent, which is exactly what the predators count on. If you have an elderly parent or neighbor, check in with them gently. Encourage them to establish a "trusted contact" with their bank—a person the institution can notify if unusual or out-of-character spending is detected. No one should have to lose their life savings to someone who has deliberately weaponized their kindness and trust.

Finally, I want to mention a newer, more complex threat that is arguably the most difficult to detect: synthetic identity fraud. In this "ghost" scheme, criminals don't steal one real person's identity. Instead, they stitch together a fake persona using a mix of real and fabricated data—often pairing a real child's Social Security number with a fake name and address. Because children have "clean" credit files that go unchecked for years, criminals can build up a history of bad debt and vanish long before the victim is even old enough to apply for their first car loan. I encourage parents to check their children's credit at least once before they turn eighteen. It may sound unusual, but a child should have no credit history at all; if a file exists, it is a clear sign that a "ghost" is living off their identity.

My hope in sharing these lessons from the street is that awareness becomes your primary line of defense. You don't have to be a forensic expert to protect yourself; you just have to be a little more watchful, a little more skeptical, and a little more proactive. In an unpredictable world, that tactical mindset alone can make all the difference.

Chapter 15

Retirement Safety

This chapter, like every other in this book, is intended not as a lecture, but as a sincere, one-on-one conversation. I want to be transparent: I am not a financial advisor, a licensed investment professional, or a retirement planner. The insights and strategies shared here are not proprietary secrets; they have been distilled from widely available public resources, respected financial literacy organizations, and general guidance vetted across the professional landscape.

While the information that follows is grounded in practical reality, it is crucial that you consult with a qualified financial professional before making any significant moves with your money. My objective is simple—to encourage you, with both gentleness and urgency, to begin thinking seriously about your retirement today. No matter your current age or your starting point, the best time to secure your future is right now. With that understanding, let's sit down and discuss a vital, often overlooked aspect of personal protection: Retirement Safety.

Regardless of our current profession or where our journey began, we are all marching toward a singular, inevitable destination. Retirement is a milestone that arrives with or without our permission, governed by the biological reality that we will eventually reach an age where the physical strength to labor or the mental stamina to sustain the daily grind begins to fade. The "hustle" is not a permanent state; eventually, the engine slows down.

Ultimately, this goal is universal. No matter our background, we strive for the same thing—the ability to step away from the labor of survival and transition into a comfortable, dignified season of life. We work so that when that time comes, we have the resources to enjoy what the world has to offer and find genuine peace long before we are called to bid our final, indefinite farewell. This isn't just about money; it is about ensuring that our decades of sacrifice translate into a legacy of stability rather than a desperate struggle for survival in our later years.

Let me be the first to admit that, by modern standards of excess, I don't have much. My wife and I live in a modest, 900-square-foot bungalow built in 1942—a home we purchased over twenty years ago. It is small, it is weathered, and it certainly isn't a showpiece to impress the neighbors. However, it possesses the one feature that matters most: it is completely paid off. This humble structure is more than just a roof; it is a debt-free fortress that provides us with a level of security that a million-dollar mortgage never could.

Throughout our marriage, we have leaned into a simple, traditional life. I have spent my years in the workforce while my wife has masterfully managed our domestic affairs, turning that small house into a true home. While our retirement savings might be considered modest by some, we’ve realized that you don't need a king's ransom to find comfort if your needs are few. We have intentionally lived within our means for as long as I can remember—a discipline I fought hard to master after the reckless, spendthrift days of my early twenties. We discovered long ago that true retirement safety isn't found in how much you accumulate, but in how little you owe and how content you are with what is enough.

Furthermore, whatever assets we have managed to accumulate will eventually be passed on to my daughters. My wife and I find that we simply don’t need much to sustain ourselves in our later years. As a bit of a "square," I’ve never had a taste for international travel or the allure of luxury dining; those things just don't move the needle for me. Instead, we embrace the quiet simplicity of life and the profound, daily joy of living entirely debt-free. For us, the greatest luxury isn't a five-star hotel or a flashy car—it is the peace of mind that comes from knowing our foundation is secure and our children’s future is reinforced by the modest legacy we leave behind.

In retrospect, I believed our simple lifestyle with the strong emphasis on saving and living within our means were the key to where we are today, nearing our retirement. I certainly respect and admire those who know how to enjoy life which includes regular vacations and fine dining. Perhaps, I need to learn from them to spice up my life but then I'm too old to change my ways for anything or anyone for that matter. Whatever lifestyle you choose now, I strongly urge that you diligently and religiously save for your retirement. Failure to do so will cost you not just financially but mentally as you reach your retirement age.

Believe this or not is up to you but there is a version of your future self who is sitting in a comfortable home, free from the burden of needing to work, able to spend time with the people they love, able to rest without worry. That person exists — but only if the version of you reading these words today decides to take action. Retirement is not something that happens to lucky people. It is something that is built, slowly and intentionally, over the course of decades. The hard truth is this: the day will come when your body no longer has the strength it once did, when long hours and physical demands become genuinely out of reach. That is not a reason for despair — it is simply the natural arc of a human life. But it does mean that the time to prepare is not someday. It is now. Every year you wait is a year of growth your money will never have. Every dollar you set aside today has the potential to become many more by the time you need it. You owe it to yourself — to the tired, older version of you who has already worked so hard — to make retirement safety a priority starting today.

Being an ordinary person with no professional training in financial planning, I don't have any personal advice for you in this subject matter. Instead, I gathered the following from the World Wide Web to share with you.

PART I: Foundations — Understanding What You're Building Toward

1. Understand What "Comfortable Retirement" Actually Means for You

Before you can build toward retirement, it helps to have a picture of what you are actually building toward. Financial literacy resources across the internet suggest that "comfortable retirement" means something different for every person — for some it means traveling the world, for others it means simply not worrying about paying bills or depending on family members for financial support. A commonly cited starting point is to estimate what your monthly expenses might look like once you stop working: housing, food, healthcare, transportation, leisure, and the unexpected. Many financial planning guides suggest that retirees typically need somewhere between 70 and 90 percent of their pre-retirement income each year to maintain their lifestyle, though this varies widely depending on your health, location, and personal goals. The important thing is not to arrive at a perfect number today, but to start thinking concretely about the life you want and what it might cost. That vision becomes your target, and your target gives your savings a purpose. Without a picture of where you are going, it is very difficult to know whether you are on the right road.

2. Recognize the Power of Time and Compound Growth

Of all the concepts in personal finance, perhaps none is more important to understand — and more heartbreaking to learn too late — than compound growth. Simply put, compound growth means that the money you save earns returns, and then those returns earn returns of their own. Over time, this creates a snowball effect that can be truly extraordinary. Financial educators frequently use the example of two people: one who begins saving at age 25 and one who waits until age 40. Even if the person who starts later contributes more money each month, they may never fully catch up to the person who started earlier simply because time was working in that person's favor for fifteen additional years. This is not meant to discourage anyone who feels they have started late — starting at any age is better than not starting at all. But it is meant to underscore as urgently as possible: time is the single most powerful tool available to any retirement saver, and once time passes, it cannot be bought back. The earlier you start, the less you ultimately have to contribute to reach the same goal, because your money will do more of the work for you.

3. Face Your Current Financial Reality Honestly

One of the most challenging and most necessary steps in retirement planning is taking an honest, clear-eyed look at where you stand financially right now. Many people avoid this step because the picture feels uncomfortable or even frightening — but avoidance does not improve the situation. Personal finance resources broadly suggest starting with a simple accounting: what comes in each month, what goes out, what you owe, and what you own. This snapshot — your income, expenses, debts, and assets — is the foundation from which any retirement plan must be built. It is not about judging yourself for past decisions. It is about giving yourself the information you need to make better ones going forward. Many people are surprised to discover, once they actually write everything down, that small adjustments — reducing a few non-essential expenses, paying down a high-interest debt, redirecting a modest amount each month into savings — can make a meaningful difference over time. You cannot navigate toward a destination you haven't plotted on a map, and you cannot plot that map without first knowing where you are standing.

PART II: Saving — Building the Nest Egg

4. Start Saving for Retirement Now — Even If It's a Small Amount

One of the most consistent messages found across retirement and personal finance resources is deceptively simple: start saving something, anything, today. It is a common misconception that retirement saving is only meaningful if you can contribute large amounts. In reality, the habit of saving — and the time that habit has to grow — matters far more than the size of any individual contribution, particularly in the early years. Setting aside even a modest amount each month, consistently, over decades, can grow into a substantial sum thanks to the power of compound interest. Many financial guides suggest automating your savings so that a fixed amount moves into a retirement account before you ever have a chance to spend it. This "pay yourself first" approach removes the temptation to skip contributions during months when money feels tight. The point is not perfection. The point is consistency. A small, regular contribution that you maintain faithfully for thirty years will almost certainly outperform a larger contribution that you make sporadically or give up on after a few years of life's inevitable disruptions.

5. Take Full Advantage of Employer-Sponsored Retirement Plans

If your employer offers a retirement savings plan — such as a 401(k) or 403(b) — many financial literacy resources describe it as one of the most valuable financial tools available to working Americans, and one that too many people either underuse or ignore entirely. These plans allow you to contribute a portion of your paycheck before taxes are taken out, which reduces your taxable income today while building wealth for your future. Many employers also offer a matching contribution — meaning they will add money to your retirement account up to a certain percentage of what you contribute. Across financial resources, employer matching is consistently described as one of the closest things to "free money" available in personal finance, and not contributing enough to capture the full match is widely characterized as leaving compensation on the table. If you are not currently enrolled in your employer's retirement plan, or if you are contributing less than the amount needed to capture the full employer match, that is one of the most impactful adjustments you can make to your financial life right now. Even a small increase in your contribution percentage today can translate into tens of thousands of dollars by the time you retire.

6. Open and Contribute to an Individual Retirement Account (IRA)

For those who do not have access to an employer-sponsored retirement plan, or who want to save additional money beyond what their workplace plan allows, an Individual Retirement Account — commonly known as an IRA — is a widely discussed and accessible option. Financial education resources describe two primary types: the Traditional IRA, where contributions may be tax-deductible and withdrawals in retirement are taxed as ordinary income, and the Roth IRA, where contributions are made with after-tax dollars but qualified withdrawals in retirement are tax-free. The Roth IRA in particular receives frequent praise in personal finance literature for younger and lower-income earners, because paying taxes now at a potentially lower rate and then enjoying tax-free growth for decades can be highly advantageous. Contribution limits for IRAs are set by the IRS and change periodically, so checking current limits is always advisable. The key message is that if you are not enrolled in any retirement savings vehicle today, opening an IRA is a concrete and relatively straightforward first step that many financial resources recommend taking as soon as possible.

7. Increase Your Savings Rate Over Time

Starting to save is the most important first step — but growing your savings rate over time is what separates a modest nest egg from a truly comfortable retirement fund. Many personal finance resources suggest a simple habit: every time you receive a raise, a bonus, or any increase in income, direct a meaningful portion of that increase into your retirement savings before adjusting your lifestyle to reflect the extra income. This approach, sometimes called "lifestyle inflation prevention," allows your standard of living to improve gradually while also accelerating your retirement savings significantly. A commonly cited goal found in various financial planning resources is to work toward saving 15 percent of your gross income for retirement — including any employer match — though the right percentage for any individual depends on their age, existing savings, and retirement goals. If 15 percent feels out of reach today, the suggestion is simply to start where you are and increase by even one percentage point each year. Small, incremental increases in your savings rate, maintained consistently over a career, can produce results that feel almost remarkable in hindsight.

8. Build and Maintain an Emergency Fund Separate from Retirement Savings

A detail that financial literacy resources emphasize repeatedly is the importance of keeping your emergency fund and your retirement savings completely separate. An emergency fund — typically three to six months of living expenses held in an accessible, liquid account — exists to cover unexpected costs like medical bills, car repairs, or a period of unemployment without forcing you to raid your retirement accounts. Withdrawing money from tax-advantaged retirement accounts before the designated retirement age almost always triggers penalties and taxes, meaning that money that took years to build can be significantly diminished in a moment of financial stress. By maintaining a dedicated emergency fund, you protect your retirement savings from the unexpected disruptions that life will inevitably bring. Many financial guides suggest building your emergency fund as a parallel priority alongside starting retirement contributions, rather than as a prerequisite to one or the other. Having that financial cushion in place makes it far less likely that you will need to interrupt or reverse your retirement savings progress during difficult times.

PART III: Growing — Making Your Money Work Harder

9. Understand Basic Investment Principles

Saving money is the starting point, but growing it over decades typically requires investing it rather than simply holding it in a savings account. Many financial education resources note that while savings accounts are safe and liquid, their interest rates rarely keep pace with inflation over the long term — meaning that money sitting in a standard savings account can actually lose purchasing power over time. Investing in diversified assets, such as a mix of stocks and bonds through a retirement account, gives your savings the opportunity to grow at a rate that outpaces inflation over the long run. Many financial guides caution that investing carries risk and that markets go up and down in the short term, but also note that over long time horizons — the decades that retirement saving spans — diversified portfolios have historically recovered from downturns and grown significantly. Understanding even the basics of how investing works, including concepts like diversification, risk tolerance, and asset allocation, is something many financial literacy resources describe as empowering rather than intimidating. You do not need to become a market expert.

You simply need to understand enough to make informed choices about where your retirement contributions are invested.

10. Diversify Your Investments

A principle that appears in virtually every investment and retirement planning resource is diversification — the practice of spreading your money across different types of assets rather than concentrating it in any single investment. The reasoning is straightforward: different types of assets tend to perform differently at different times, so holding a mix helps smooth out the impact of any one investment performing poorly. Many financial education resources suggest that for most retirement savers who are not financial professionals, low-cost index funds or target-date funds offered through workplace retirement plans provide an accessible and well-diversified option without requiring deep investment knowledge. Target-date funds, in particular, are frequently mentioned as a simple choice for retirement savers because they automatically adjust their mix of stocks and bonds to become more conservative as the target retirement year approaches. The broader message from financial resources is consistent: do not put all your eggs in one basket. A diversified portfolio will not always be the best-performing option in any given year, but over the long arc of a retirement savings journey, it is one of the most reliable ways to manage risk while still participating in long-term growth.

11. Keep Investment Fees Low

A topic that receives considerable attention in financial literacy literature — and one that many people overlook entirely — is the impact of investment fees on long-term retirement savings. Every investment product charges some form of fee, often expressed as an expense ratio, and while small percentages may seem insignificant on a year-to-year basis, they compound over decades in exactly the same way that investment returns do — only in reverse. Various financial education resources have illustrated that the difference between a fund charging 0.05 percent annually and one charging 1 percent annually can, over a thirty-year retirement savings period, amount to tens of thousands of dollars in lost growth. Many resources suggest looking for low-cost index funds and being aware of any advisory fees, transaction fees, or fund expense ratios associated with your retirement accounts. This does not mean the cheapest option is always the best option, but it does mean that fees are worth understanding and worth minimizing where possible. Every dollar that goes toward fees is a dollar that is not compounding for your future.

12. Avoid Early Withdrawals from Retirement Accounts

One of the most financially costly mistakes that retirement savers can make, according to a wide range of personal finance resources, is withdrawing money from retirement accounts before the designated retirement age. In most cases, early withdrawals from accounts like a 401(k) or Traditional IRA trigger both income taxes on the amount withdrawn and an additional 10 percent penalty, meaning that a $10,000 withdrawal might net only $6,000 or $7,000 after the government takes its share. Beyond the immediate financial hit, the long-term cost is even greater: that withdrawn money loses all of its future compound growth potential. A sum that might have grown to $50,000 or more over the following twenty years is simply gone. Financial resources consistently describe early withdrawal as one of the most damaging things you can do to your retirement savings, and strongly encourage finding other solutions — such as drawing from an emergency fund, negotiating a payment plan for a debt, or exploring personal loan options — before touching retirement money. The goal is to let that account grow, untouched, for as long as possible.

PART IV: Protecting — Safeguarding What You've Built

13. Understand Social Security and When to Claim It

Social Security is a federal program that provides monthly income to eligible Americans in retirement, and understanding how it works — and when to claim it — is an important part of any retirement plan. Social Security benefits are based on your earnings history over your working life, and the age at which you begin claiming them significantly affects the monthly amount you receive.

According to information widely available from the Social Security Administration and financial planning resources, you can begin claiming as early as age 62, but doing so results in a permanently reduced benefit. Waiting until your full retirement age (which is currently 67 for most people born after 1960) results in your full benefit, and waiting even longer — up to age 70 — increases your benefit further. Many financial guides suggest that for people in good health who can afford to wait, delaying Social Security can meaningfully increase lifetime income. Social Security alone, however, is rarely sufficient to fund a comfortable retirement, and financial literacy resources consistently describe it as one piece of a larger retirement income puzzle rather than a complete solution on its own.

14. Plan for Healthcare Costs in Retirement

Healthcare is consistently cited in retirement planning literature as one of the largest and most frequently underestimated expenses that retirees face. Unlike working years when employer-sponsored health insurance covers much of the cost, retirees before age 65 must typically fund their own health coverage, and even after qualifying for Medicare at 65, premiums, deductibles, copayments, and expenses not covered by Medicare — such as dental, vision, and long-term care — can add up to substantial sums. Various financial resources suggest that a couple retiring at 65 today should anticipate spending a significant amount on healthcare throughout retirement, with estimates often running into hundreds of thousands of dollars over a retirement lifetime. Health Savings Accounts (HSAs), available to those enrolled in high-deductible health plans, are frequently recommended in financial planning literature as a powerful tool for building tax-advantaged savings specifically earmarked for healthcare costs. Planning for healthcare expenses as a specific and significant line item in your retirement budget — rather than hoping costs will be minimal — is something a wide range of financial and health resources encourage all pre-retirees to do.

15. Consider Long-Term Care Planning

Long-term care — the kind of ongoing assistance with daily living activities that many people eventually need as they age, whether in their own home, in an assisted living facility, or in a nursing home — is a topic that retirement planning resources increasingly encourage people to address well before they think they will need it. The costs of long-term care services can be substantial and can quickly deplete retirement savings that took decades to build. Financial and eldercare resources widely note that Medicare provides very limited coverage for long-term custodial care, and that many people are unprepared for the financial reality of needing extended assistance. Long-term care insurance, while not the right solution for everyone, is one option that financial planning resources suggest evaluating before health conditions make coverage difficult or impossible to obtain. Other strategies discussed in the literature include setting aside dedicated savings for this purpose, exploring hybrid life insurance and long-term care products, and having honest family conversations about expectations and preferences around caregiving. The earlier these conversations and planning steps begin, the more options remain available.

16. Protect Yourself from Financial Fraud and Scams

Retirees and pre-retirees are disproportionately targeted by financial fraud, and protecting the savings you have spent decades building is an essential component of retirement safety. Consumer protection organizations and financial resources note that common scams targeting older adults include fraudulent investment schemes, Medicare fraud, identity theft, romance scams, and imposter scams where criminals pose as government officials, grandchildren in distress, or trusted institutions. The suggestions that appear consistently across consumer safety resources include: never sharing personal financial information over the phone or online unless you initiated the contact and can verify the recipient, being deeply skeptical of any investment opportunity that promises unusually high returns with little risk, consulting a trusted family member or financial advisor before making any large financial decision, and regularly monitoring bank and investment account statements for unauthorized activity. The financial harm from fraud can be devastating and is often difficult or impossible to recover, making prevention a critical part of protecting your retirement security. Staying informed and maintaining healthy skepticism is not paranoia — it is wisdom.

PART V: Planning Ahead — The Bigger Picture

17. Eliminate Debt Before Retirement

Carrying significant debt into retirement — particularly high-interest debt like credit card balances — is something that financial planning resources broadly caution against, and for good reason. In retirement, most people are living on a fixed income from savings, Social Security, and possibly a pension. Debt payments that were manageable during working years when income was higher can become genuinely burdensome when income is reduced. Many financial guides suggest making the elimination of high-interest debt a high priority in the years leading up to retirement, and ideally entering retirement mortgage-free or with very manageable housing costs as well. The psychological and financial freedom of being debt-free in retirement is something financial educators describe as one of the most significant contributors to a genuinely comfortable retirement experience. This does not mean that all debt is equally urgent or that retirement savings should be neglected in favor of debt payoff — high-interest consumer debt is far more pressing than a low-interest mortgage, for example — but it does mean that managing and reducing debt should be a conscious and active part of your financial plan as you approach retirement.

18. Create or Update Your Estate Plan

Estate planning is a topic that many people associate exclusively with the very wealthy, but financial and legal resources broadly suggest that having basic estate planning documents in place is important for virtually every adult, regardless of the size of their assets. At its most fundamental, an estate plan ensures that your wishes are followed regarding who receives your assets after your passing, who makes medical and financial decisions on your behalf if you become incapacitated, and who cares for any dependents who rely on you. Commonly discussed estate planning documents include a will, a durable power of attorney, a healthcare proxy or medical power of attorney, and potentially a living trust. Many resources also emphasize the importance of keeping beneficiary designations on retirement accounts and life insurance policies current, since these designations override what a will says and are among the most commonly neglected aspects of estate planning. While this chapter is not a legal guide and consulting an estate planning attorney is strongly recommended, the broader message from financial and legal resources is consistent: having these documents in place protects your family and gives you peace of mind that your intentions will be honored.

19. Work with a Qualified Financial Advisor

While a great deal of valuable general guidance is available through public resources, financial literacy organizations, and online tools, many retirement planning resources suggest that working with a qualified financial advisor — particularly as retirement approaches — can provide personalized guidance that generic information simply cannot offer. A financial advisor can help you assess whether your current savings trajectory aligns with your retirement goals, optimize the tax efficiency of your savings and withdrawal strategy, navigate the complexities of Social Security timing, plan for healthcare costs, and coordinate the various pieces of your financial picture into a coherent plan. When seeking a financial advisor, many resources recommend looking for a fiduciary — a professional who is legally obligated to act in your best interest rather than simply recommending products that generate commissions. Fee-only advisors, who charge directly for their time rather than earning commissions on products they sell, are also frequently mentioned as a structure that aligns advisor incentives with client interests. The investment in professional guidance can pay dividends that far exceed its cost, particularly for those navigating more complex financial situations.

20. Stay the Course — Patience and Consistency Are Your Greatest Assets

Perhaps the most important and most human piece of advice found across retirement planning and personal finance resources is simply this: stay the course. Building a retirement fund is a decades-long endeavor, and it will inevitably pass through periods when markets fall, when life interrupts your savings plan, when the goal feels impossibly far away, or when temptation to spend the money on something more immediate feels very strong. Financial educators consistently note that some of the most damaging retirement saving mistakes are not strategic errors at all — they are emotional ones. Selling investments during a market downturn, stopping contributions during a difficult year and never restarting, or cashing out a retirement account when changing jobs are among the behaviors that most frequently derail retirement savings plans. The antidote, according to a wide range of resources, is a combination of patience, consistency, and a long-term perspective that keeps temporary setbacks in their proper context. Decades of steady, disciplined saving and investing — through the ups and the downs — is how ordinary people build extraordinary retirement security. You are capable of that. All it takes is the decision to start, and then the commitment to keep going.

Let there be no doubt that you owe it to yourself to have a comfortable retirement. Building a comfortable retirement does not require perfection, and it does not require a high income. It requires intention, consistency, and time — and the most important of those three is time. Whatever your age, wherever you are in your financial journey, the best day to begin was yesterday. The second-best day is today. You have worked hard. You have given your energy, your years, and your effort to building a life. The goal of everything shared in this chapter is simply to encourage you to direct some of that same dedication toward building a future where rest is possible, where worry is minimized, and where the years ahead belong to you. Start now. Stay consistent. Keep going. You deserve to arrive at retirement with your head held high, your bills paid, and your peace of mind intact.

Please remember: this chapter is not financial advice, and the author is not a financial professional. Every individual's financial situation is unique, and the suggestions gathered here are intended as a starting point for reflection and further research. Consult a qualified financial advisor, tax professional, or estate planning attorney for guidance tailored to your specific circumstances. Your retirement is too important to leave to chance — and too personal to leave entirely to a book.

Chapter 16

Career Safety

Naturally when most people think about going back to school or learning a new trade, they frame it as getting ahead—climbing the ladder, chasing promotions, earning more money, or impressing others. I never really saw it that way. For me, earning my two Master's degrees—one in Chinese Herbal Medicine and one in Business Administration—was never primarily about ambition. It was about protection. I viewed these academic pursuits through the lens of survival, a perspective forged during my twenty-eight years in law enforcement. Every single day I put on that uniform, I understood at a gut level that my career could end in a heartbeat—not because I chose to walk away, but because circumstances beyond my control demanded it. In the high-stakes environment of policing, a single bad call, a career-ending injury, a sudden shift in policy, or a departmental budget cut could instantly dissolve the professional identity and financial security I had spent decades building. It is a chilling realization to know that you can go from being the steady, reliable provider to facing a void of uncertainty overnight, all while the bills keep arriving with relentless indifference. For me, those degrees weren't just diplomas; they were my contingency plan—the armor I wore to ensure that if my badge was ever taken away, my future wouldn't go with it.

Career safety, as I see it, is the deliberate act of ensuring that if the floor falls out from under you, there is another solid foundation already waiting below. It is the tactical preparation for an inevitable shift in the landscape. This perspective isn't particularly glamorous or inspiring to most people, but it is honest. In this light, an advanced degree is not a trophy to be displayed—it is a vehicle. It is a high-level credential that serves as a professional insurance policy, dramatically improving your odds of landing sustainable, respectable income precisely when the world feels most unstable.

Drawing from the hard-earned lessons of a high-risk profession, I have drilled this principle into my daughters from an early age: their primary objective is to pursue their education as high as possible in their chosen fields. In our household, the conversation around "educational obligations" is frequent and firm. Surprisingly, they didn't roll their eyes or tune me out—reactions I've come to expect, as my daughters and my wife often playfully cast themselves as the "antagonists" to my persistent "nagging." But beneath the lighthearted family friction, there is a deep, unspoken understanding of why I push so hard.

They don't have to look far for the "why"; the proof hangs on the walls of our home. My own degrees serve as a silent, constant reminder of what it looks like to build a life on more than one pillar. They watched their father work full-time patrol—navigating the stresses of the street—while grinding through the rigors of graduate programs during his nights and weekends. They saw the fatigue, but they also saw the result: a man who was never trapped by his circumstances. I know they respect both the sacrifice and the outcome. Because of that, they are now determined to forge their own paths with the same academic rigor. They understand that by arming themselves with high-level credentials, they are effectively insulating their futures. They aren't just going to school to find a job; they are going to school so they never have to depend on luck, timing, or the fickle goodwill of an employer for their survival. In a world where loyalty is rare and security is an illusion, they are learning that the only person you can truly rely on to save you is the version of yourself that is over-prepared.

Being a natural observer and a patient listener, I've watched too many non-law enforcement friends and classmates over the years who were absolute masters of their craft—experienced, dedicated, decorated, and highly competent—but who had built their entire professional identity around a single role. When the market shifted, when their agency or company restructured, or when younger, cheaper talent was brought in under the banner of "innovation" or "fresh perspectives," the fall was brutal. Not just emotionally, but financially devastating. Without a diversified skill set or a high-level, portable credential, their options narrowed overnight. One day you're an indispensable veteran; the next, you're updating a résumé that suddenly looks outdated, competing for entry-level positions, or surviving on a severance package that disappears far too quickly.

The common term my friends told me was: "Brain drained." In other words, their employers believed they were spent and had become deadweight. These were their firsthand experiences they shared with me and other mutual friends at our occasional poker games.

Because of these cautionary tales, I encourage you to take a hard look at your own situation. Ask yourself: are you truly ready to take on an entirely new profession if your current one were to disappear tomorrow? This question has never been more urgent than it is today. We are living in an era where Artificial Intelligence is becoming increasingly powerful, moving beyond automation and beginning to replace complex jobs that were once the sole domain of human experience and intuition. In a world where an algorithm can be trained to do what you do for a fraction of the cost, your only real armor is a high-level, versatile education and a credential that belongs to you—not your employer. Don't wait until you are "drained" of your value to decide that you need a second floor to stand on.

In today's economy, staying stagnant is a silent gamble that almost everyone eventually loses. The modern workplace rewards adaptability and visible proof of capability far more than tenure or loyalty. Without that proof—often in the form of an advanced degree or specialized, in-demand licensure—your leverage evaporates when turbulence hits. I've consistently reminded my daughters that they must learn everything they could from their jobs and every training course that their companies offer even if the courses are beyond their classifications. I reminded them that to sustain and advance in their career, they must make themselves indispensable and extremely valuable to their companies' short term and long term operations. Failure to better yourself in your field of work is career suicide and I refused to let myself or my daughters be that vulnerable.

When it comes to career training and college degrees, I am a staunch proponent of the idea that passion comes after practicality, not before it. This is the fundamental mindset I have hammered home to my daughters, even though it flies directly in the face of the "follow your heart" platitudes that dominate modern advice. In my view, too many people waste their prime years waiting for a lightning bolt of inspiration to strike before they are willing to invest in themselves. I tell my girls plainly: while you are sitting around waiting for a "calling," time is slipping away, your competitive edge is dulling, and your window of opportunity is narrowing.

I lead by example because I've lived this transition throughout my years in law enforcement. I'll be honest—Chinese Herbal Medicine was never a childhood dream or a passionate calling that kept me up at night. I approached it with cold, calculated practicality. After years on the streets and in high-stress environments, I knew I needed a "second floor"—a backup career I could practice even if my body was no longer capable of the physical demands of policing. I meticulously researched the demand in California, the licensing pathways, and the business models. The field checked every box, so I committed. The fulfillment didn't come from a "calling"; it came from the peace of mind that I was no longer trapped by a single identity.

Being a practical person, I've always believed that you don't build a life on a feeling; you build it on a foundation. This is why I initially pushed my daughters toward the medical field. In an era where the rising tide of artificial intelligence is beginning to swallow traditional roles, the high-touch, high-stakes human element of medicine remains one of the few truly irreplaceable strongholds. However, as is often the case in our household, my two "antagonistic" daughters—with the enthusiastic backing of their mother—decided to chart their own course. They chose the battlefield, but they are using the tactics I taught them.

Sammi is currently grinding through law school, and Ally is finishing her undergraduate degree with her sights set firmly on an MBA. They might have rejected the specific industry I suggested, but they haven't rejected the logic behind it: build the fortress first. They have internalized the idea that a strong, marketable credential functions exactly like an insurance policy—and the smartest time to buy insurance is before the house catches fire. My youngest isn't hunting for a career to set her soul on fire in a romantic sense; she is building a structure solid enough to withstand economic storms, corporate downsizing, or technological upheaval.

Ultimately, they understand that a high-level credential is much more than a professional "trophy" to be hung on a wall; it is a strategic asset. By deliberately choosing fields characterized by rigorous academic standards and clear, regulated barriers to entry, they are insulating themselves against the volatility of the modern world. They are ensuring that their livelihoods won't be easily disrupted by a sudden shift in the market, a corporate restructuring, or the introduction of a new piece of software.

In my view, they are securing their "first floor"—establishing a solid, primary foundation of specialized knowledge that provides immediate stability. However, drawing from my own history of pivoting from a badge to a business degree and a medical license, I have tried to encourage them to think even further ahead toward a "second floor." I've suggested that once they master one field, they should begin building a secondary, unrelated expertise to ensure they are never dependent on a single industry. Specifically, despite their initial objections, I have pushed the idea that Sammi should pursue an MBA after earning her JD, and that Ally should look toward earning a degree in the field of Artificial Intelligence. I want them to be the ones managing the technology and the law, rather than being managed by them.

Needless to say, as is the custom in our house, they disagreed. To them, the sheer intensity of their current programs feels like enough of a fortress for now. Regardless of that debate, the core lesson has taken root: they understand that without these high-level degrees, you are left hoping for the best from an unpredictable economy or the fickle goodwill of an employer. However, now that they are in their early 20s, they have begun to exert their own power—mostly by making it very clear just how much they've come to dislike my constant nagging. They've already jokingly warned me that if I don't let up, they can't wait to give me a one-way ride to the "old people's home." Because of their objections and their growing talent for tuning me out, I feel motivated to write this book; I want these lessons to serve as a constant, permanent reminder of my perspective long after I am gone—and long after they've dropped me off at the facility.

Beyond the immediate debate, we've discovered a vital truth: once you achieve security and competence, genuine passion and fulfillment finally have the breathing room they need to grow. By securing their survival first, my daughters aren't just earning degrees—they are purchasing their future freedom. They are ensuring that their later years won't be spent in a desperate scramble for basic needs, but in the deliberate pursuit of what actually matters to them.

As you look at your own family, I would urge you to consider the same philosophy. Are you encouraging your children to gamble their future on the "fields of their dreams," or are you pushing them toward practical degrees that provide a solid floor for their lives? It's important to realize that asking them to prioritize a marketable skill isn't about crushing their spirit or stifling their creativity—it's about providing the financial and professional stability they will need to actually afford those dreams.

However, at the end of the day, that's just me being me. Every family dynamic is unique, and you have every right to lead yours as you see fit. My goal isn't to dictate your path, but to offer a perspective forged in the reality of the streets and the cold hard facts of the marketplace.

This isn't just a matter of opinion, however; I will not sugarcoat the numbers because the data speaks clearly. Over a full working lifetime, the cumulative income gap between someone with a strong advanced degree and someone without one is often measured in the high hundreds of thousands—or even millions—of dollars when factoring in salary differentials, benefits, bonuses, and retirement contributions. An advanced degree frequently translates into higher starting pay, faster promotions, greater negotiating power, and significantly better resilience during economic downturns.

I have seen both sides of this equation firsthand. I've known exceptionally intelligent, hardworking people who spent decades trapped in low-ceiling roles with little growth simply because they lacked that key credential. Meanwhile, those who made the investment in themselves—often at great personal sacrifice—unlocked doors that remained bolted shut to others. I lived this reality myself, earning both of my Master's degrees while working full-time in one of the most demanding environments imaginable. The late nights, the studying after long shifts, the missed family time—it was all real. But that payoff provided a level of stability and a range of options that continue to benefit my family today.

That being said, there is no single right path for every person. For some, a two-year vocational program in HVAC, dental hygiene, medical coding, or welding offers an excellent return with far less debt and a much faster entry into the workforce. The key is ruthless honesty about your own goals, risk tolerance, physical abilities, and local market realities. In our household, we have deliberately leaned toward advanced degrees because they offer what I call “ceiling-shattering power” and broad defensive perimeters. Law provides my eldest with a skill set that society will likely always need—advocacy, negotiation, and complex problem-solving. Business gives my youngest the versatility to pivot across industries as new opportunities and threats emerge.

I also want to emphasize that I have deep respect for the skilled trades. A licensed electrician, plumber, or welder who runs their own business can often earn an incredible living with minimal student debt and high personal autonomy. If your talents and interests lean toward the practical and hands-on, the trades are a dignified, high-earning path that deserves far more respect than our culture often gives them. Social prestige should never be allowed to outweigh pure pragmatism.

In recent years, these trade careers have surged in popularity, and for good reason: they are excellent, future-proof career choices in the face of Artificial Intelligence. While AI can draft an essay or analyze a spreadsheet in seconds, it cannot navigate a crawlspace to repair a burst pipe, rewire a historical building, or perform a complex structural weld on a job site. These roles require a combination of sensory-motor skills, spatial reasoning, and real-world problem-solving that remains far beyond the reach of current robotics. By choosing a trade, you aren't just picking a job; you are entering a high-demand field where your physical presence and human expertise are your greatest competitive advantages against the digital tide.

Regardless of the chosen path, successful navigation requires the mind of a strategist. Before I spent a single dollar on my Master's in Chinese Herbal Medicine, I treated the decision like an intelligence operation. I studied licensing requirements, market demand projections in California, reimbursement trends, and real-world practitioner earnings. I've taught my daughters to be equally disciplined. My eldest didn't simply "pick law school"—she analyzed which practice areas appear most resistant to automation and economic volatility. My youngest is mapping business concentrations against Bureau of Labor Statistics growth data. A few hours of honest research can prevent years of regret and mountains of unproductive debt.

This level of scrutiny is more vital than ever because artificial intelligence is accelerating faster than most families are willing to admit. Many white-collar tasks that once felt safe—routine accounting, basic legal research, data analysis—are already being automated. This reality makes career safety an urgent priority. While AI can process information at incredible speed, it still struggles with genuine wisdom, ethical judgment, deep human empathy, and high-stakes negotiation. It cannot replace the seasoned attorney who reads a jury, the executive who steers organizational culture, or the practitioner who adapts medical protocols to a patient's unique constitution.

We discuss this reality openly at the dinner table: aim for careers that sit above the "automation line"—roles that demand sophisticated human intelligence, physical presence, and complex interpersonal skills. AI will not snake a drain, comfort a grieving family, or successfully defend someone in court. By pursuing graduate-level education, my daughters are intentionally positioning themselves where human value remains hardest to replicate.

Of course, earning the diploma is a milestone, but it is never the finish line. Fields evolve rapidly. I continue to study developments in both herbal medicine and business strategy, and I want my daughters to view their degrees as a strong foundation, not a finished roof. In my forty-five years of working life, those who fell behind were almost always the ones who believed they knew enough the day they graduated. The people with the greatest career safety treat continuous learning as a non-negotiable habit.

Furthermore, while technical credentials get you through the door, soft skills determine how far you advance. My years in law enforcement sharpened abilities no classroom could teach: reading people accurately, communicating under extreme pressure, and staying composed when others panic. These "interrogation room" lessons have been passed directly to my daughters. Reliability, emotional regulation, and persuasive communication remain rare and highly valued. Whether my eldest stands in a courtroom or my youngest leads in a boardroom, these human skills will multiply the power of their formal credentials.

Finally, it is important to remember that a credential without financial discipline is only half the protection. As mentioned in the chapter titled Financial Safety, earning an income is one thing, but maximizing savings is another. Yet, saving alone is not enough; money sitting idle in a zero-interest account is ultimately losing value. Inflation will quietly erode the buying power of the money you worked so hard to set aside.

Instead, you must learn to make your money work for you. This means becoming competent in investing—whether in the stock market, real estate, or valuable metals. I strongly encourage taking structured training, reading reputable books, or consulting professional advisors to build a diversified portfolio. I've been a retail stock investor for over thirty years, and that discipline has been a cornerstone of my resilience. Beyond their primary careers, I emphasize the power of multiple income streams. My daughters are building strong primary "engines" in law and business, but they understand that true safety includes the freedom to walk away from toxic situations because other options—supported by both degrees and growing investments—are already in motion.

Ultimately, career safety is not about fear; it is about clarity and responsibility. It is the quiet confidence that comes from knowing you have done everything within your power to protect your future self. In an unpredictable world, that preparation—combining marketable education, continuous learning, human skills, and intelligent investing—is one of the most loving and practical gifts you can give to yourself and the next generation.

Chapter 17

Digital Safety

Personally, I have always believed that the most difficult dangers to detect and defeat are those that lack a physical form. When a threat cannot be seen, heard, smelled, or tasted, the battle feels profoundly lopsided—as if you are being forced to fight with your eyes blindfolded and your senses of hearing and touch completely suppressed. To even imagine such a predicament is suffocating; it is the ultimate tactical disadvantage to be targeted by an adversary you cannot perceive.

Unfortunately, this is the exact reality we face in the modern era. There are invisible predators lurking around us every second of the day, every day of the week. These are the digital dangers: the sophisticated viruses, the predatory scams, the relentless harvesting of our personal data, and the invisible, autonomous forces brought forth by artificial intelligence. In this digital landscape, the "walls" of your home and the "locks" on your car offer no protection. To secure your life in the twenty-first century, you must learn to defend a frontier that is as intangible as it is high-stakes.

I will be the first to confess that I am not a technical expert in the realm of digital predator prevention. I cannot claim to understand the intricate code used to detect a "zero-day exploit"—a term used to describe a secret flaw in software that the creators don't even know about yet, leaving them with "zero days" to fix it. I approach these threats from the perspective of a practical observer, focused on the fundamental habits of protection.

There is no doubt in my mind that if you use email, possess a smartphone, or carry a tablet, you are a target. Your device is an open window into your life, your finances, and your identity. The scale of this threat extends far beyond the individual; every major enterprise is hunted with a ferocity that exceeds what the average person experiences. Yet, the same "invisible forces" that can cripple a power grid are knocking at your digital door every single day. Our only defense is to adopt the same disciplined, precautionary measures that large-scale organizations use to avoid being victimized.

To simplify these complex concepts, I've broken the chapter into manageable topics with clear subtitles.

Establishing Digital Safeguards

While I am not a developer, I have learned that digital safety is less about complex programming and more about disciplined habits. These non-negotiable rituals begin with locking your digital front door. My personal favorite safeguard—one I consider absolutely vital—is dual authentication. For every digital account I own, I make it a strict rule to ensure they all have dual authentication enabled alongside a strong, complex password. This creates a redundant layer of security; even if a predator manages to crack a password, they are still met with a secondary barrier they cannot easily bypass.

I used to fall into the same trap many people do—I made my passwords something I could actually read, thinking that ease of memorization was the priority. However, I soon realized that those "readable" passwords are inherently weak and incredibly easy for digital bots to decode using simple brute-force scripts. I truly learned the value of a strong password by observing the security protocols at my workplace. I noticed that every professional system we used required an incredibly long password consisting of a completely random mix of characters. They didn't follow any recognizable pattern and didn't look like words at all. This realization shifted my entire approach; now, I embrace the complexity of long, random strings and rely on a password manager to store and generate them. You must protect your email account like a fortress; it is the master key to your entire identity.

Hardening Your Infrastructure

Beyond account access, you must focus on hardening your hardware and networks. Those frequent update notifications on your phone are critical "digital patches" for zero-day exploits. Delaying an update is the equivalent of leaving your gate unlocked after being told a prowler is in the neighborhood. Similarly, you must secure your home Wi-Fi by changing factory-preset passwords and using WPA3 encryption.

One of the most significant advantages you can give yourself is the implementation of a Virtual Private Network (VPN). A VPN acts as an encrypted tunnel for your data, masking your IP address and making your online movements invisible to hackers and data collectors. By implementing a VPN at the router level or on individual devices, you effectively wrap your digital life in a cloak of anonymity. When you are out in public, treat free Wi-Fi as an open field where predators can easily intercept your data. In these environments, a VPN is a necessity to ensure your private information doesn't become public property.

Refining Your Digital Footprint

One of the most effective ways to protect yourself is to simply become a smaller target through Social Media Sanitization. Predators often "scrape" profiles to find the answers to common security questions, such as the street you grew up on. By setting your profiles to private, you remove the ammunition a hacker needs for social engineering.

Another easy win is Disabling Auto-Fill on Browsers. While convenient, this information is often vulnerable to specific types of malware. Taking the extra thirty seconds to type that information manually adds a vital layer of friction. In the physical world, we know not to leave our wallets on a cafe table; in the digital world, we must adopt the "Screen Lock Ritual." Get into the habit of manually locking your screen every single time you stand up to prevent "opportunity crimes." Additionally, consider the "Plug-In Policy." Never plug your phone into a public USB charging station using just a standard cord, as these can be rigged for "Juice Jacking." If you must charge in public, use a USB Data Blocker to ensure that only power—not data—can flow through.

Vigilance Against Remote Control

Be extremely vigilant in detecting signs that your electronic device is being remotely controlled while you are actively using it. In the world of digital predation, this is the equivalent of noticing the door handle of your home turning while you're sitting in the living room. Remote access Trojans (RATs) can allow a predator to mirror your screen in real-time. Watch for the subtle "ghost in the machine": if your cursor begins moving independently, selecting text, or if dialogue boxes open spontaneously, your system has likely been compromised. You should also be wary of unusual battery drain or excessive heat, which suggests a hidden process—like a camera feed—is running in the background.

One of the most direct indicators is the hardware warning light on your camera or microphone. If that light flickers on while you aren't in a call, a predator may be watching or listening to you. If you suspect your device is being controlled, execute an immediate tactical response: kill the connectivity by turning off your Wi-Fi or toggling Airplane Mode, then perform a hard manual shutdown. To prevent the most invasive forms of this threat, I highly recommend using physical webcam covers; a simple sliding tab provides a 100% guarantee that no hacker can see into your private sanctuary.

Securing the Home Front

You must also exercise caution if you use indoor security cameras. While many include an LED status light, these are not foolproof. A pulsing light may signal an active stream, while a solid red light often indicates infrared night vision. However, a sophisticated predator can often disable these warning lights entirely through software. To truly secure your home, do not rely on a flickering bulb; instead, look for cameras with a mechanical privacy shutter that physically blocks the lens. If your camera lacks this, a simple piece of black electrical tape is the only "zero-day" defense no hacker can bypass.

When designing your home's perimeter, weigh the differences between wired and wireless systems. Wireless cameras are popular for their ease of installation but are vulnerable to signal jamming and battery failure. In contrast, wired systems (PoE) provide much higher reliability. These are physically tethered to a Network Video Recorder (NVR) inside your home, ensuring your footage is recorded 24/7 without Wi-Fi interference.

Most of the security cameras I have installed in and around my home are wired for this very reason. I prefer the stability of a "closed-circuit" system that keeps my data under my own roof. A local NVR provides data sovereignty, keeping your footage on a hard drive inside your house rather than a third-party cloud server. You don't lose the advantage of remote viewing, as most modern recorders allow you to connect via a secure app. Ultimately, whether you choose the plug-and-play ease of wireless or the more cumbersome installation of wired cameras for peace of mind is a personal choice you must decide for yourself.

Vigilance Against Deception

A high degree of visual skepticism is your best defense against social engineering. Predators rely on urgency, often claiming your account will be suspended to trick you into clicking a link. Adopt a "pause" rule for phishing: hover over links to see their true destination. In the era of AI-generated "Deepfakes," if you receive an urgent request for money from a loved one, implement a "Call-Back Protocol." Hang up and call them directly on a trusted number to verify. This applies to "banks" or "government agencies" as well; never provide info to someone who called you—initiate the call yourself using a verified number.

Additionally, be proactive in managing your digital "waste" by deleting old, unused accounts. Follow the 3-2-1 backup rule: keep three copies of your data, on two different types of media, with one copy stored off-site. Digital safety even extends to the physical world; never discard an old device without first wiping the drive or shredding sensitive statements. By layering these safeguards, you aren't just hoping for the best—you are actively managing your risk and ensuring that if a predator finds their way to your digital door, they find it bolted and guarded.

The Financial Toll of Digital Heartbreak

The scale of romance scams has reached a level of sophistication that should alarm every reader. These are not merely stories of "bad luck"; they are calculated, high-stakes operations that drain life savings in weeks. To understand the gravity of this threat, consider these recent reports from 2025 and early 2026. The following cases represent real-word instances. I encourage you to search the internet using keywords like "pig butchering scam statistics," "AI deepfake romance fraud," or "money laundering charges for scam victims" to see how these predatory tactics are evolving in real-time.

Case 1: The "Pig Butchering" Financial Slaughter

• Synopsis: The latest federal reports show a sharp rise in a predatory tactic where scammers "fatten up" a victim's trust over several months before "slaughtering" their finances. In 2025, losses hit record highs as predators combined deep emotional manipulation with sophisticated, fake cryptocurrency investment platforms that appeared to show the victim's "profits" growing daily.

• The Scale: Reported losses from this specific method reached nearly $1 billion in a single year, highlighting that these are not individual "hustlers," but organized criminal syndicates.

Case 2: The High-Net-Worth Target

• Synopsis: Authorities in major metropolitan areas reported that individual victims are being targeted for higher amounts than ever before. In several instances, retirees were convinced to "invest" with individuals they met on dating apps, believing they were participating in exclusive financial opportunities.

• The Result: Several individuals lost their entire nest eggs, with individual losses exceeding $2 million. These cases demonstrate that the more you have to lose, the more effort a predator will put into dismantling your defenses.

Case 3: The AI-Enhanced Professional Trap

• Synopsis: A woman in her 60s was manipulated by a scammer posing as a successful businessman working abroad. To bypass her skepticism, the predator used AI-generated voice notes and a sense of manufactured urgency to build a "safe" emotional bond.

• The Result: Over a period of six months, the predator drained $450,000 from her retirement account before disappearing. This case proves that even "gut feelings" can be manipulated by high-tech deception.

Case 4: The Real-Time Deepfake Barrier

• Synopsis: Historically, a suitor's refusal to video chat was a major "red flag." However, in 2026, scammers began using real-time AI deepfake technology to appear exactly like the stolen photos they used in their profiles during live video calls.

• The Impact: This technology allows scammers to wear a "digital mask," making it nearly impossible for a victim to realize they are speaking to a predator until the financial damage is already absolute.

Case 5: The Deployed Soldier Impersonation

• Synopsis: This scenario serves as a reminder that age is no barrier to victimization. A college student was targeted by a scammer posing as a deployed soldier who claimed he needed emergency funds for a flight home.

• The Result: The student's entire tuition savings vanished. It illustrates that predators will take the last dollar from anyone, regardless of their circumstances or the nobility of the victim's intentions.

Case 6: The Victim-to-Criminal Pipeline

• Synopsis: In a cruel twist, some victims are being tricked into "money muling." After their own funds are drained, the scammer convinces them to use their personal bank accounts to move "business funds," which are actually stolen assets from other victims.

• The Outcome: These individuals lose their savings and then face federal money-laundering charges, proving that these predators can destroy your freedom as well as your finances.

Once money is wired overseas or converted to cryptocurrency, it is effectively gone; the law enforcement recovery rate for these funds is less than 1%. Your only true defense is the skepticism and the "Call-Back Protocols" we have established in this chapter. Do not let your heart open a door that your common sense should keep bolted.

Navigating the Social Media Minefield

Although my daughters are now young adults, I continue to remind them to remain hyper-vigilant when scrolling, posting, or commenting on social media. While these platforms offer undeniable utility and entertainment, they also function as high-tech traps, hiding in plain sight. Predators are constantly watching and waiting for the slightest opening—a moment of emotional vulnerability or a lapse in judgment—to strike. This is not a matter of paranoia, but of tactical awareness in a digital landscape that is inherently predatory.

I frequently visit X (formerly Twitter) to keep pace with global news and current events. On several occasions, I have received notifications that a female user with an attractive profile picture has subscribed to my account. From the outset, my suspicion was high; I operate with a healthy dose of realism and the firm knowledge that an attractive stranger reaching out to "befriend" me online is almost certainly the first stage of a scam. However, purely out of professional curiosity and with a bit of free time on my hands, I decided to engage in a brief public chat to see how her "play" would unfold.

As the conversation progressed, I quickly recognized the telltale signs of digital grooming. When I mentioned I had to leave, she became persistent, pressuring me to chat again later—a classic move designed to establish a routine and build a false sense of intimacy. Immediately after our interaction, I conducted a reverse image search of her profile photo. As I expected, the image belonged to a famous European actress. This confirmed what my instincts had already signaled: the account was a "catfish" designed to hook a victim.

While I could not say with absolute legal certainty what her ultimate end-game was, I knew for a fact that there is no way on Earth, the Moon, or Mars that a famous international actress would randomly reach out to me in the digital or physical world. By maintaining this level of "aggressive realism," you can spot these invisible forces before they have a chance to take root in your life. If an interaction feels too good to be true, it isn't just a red flag—it is a siren.

The Discipline of Selective Interaction

Being an overtly cautious person by nature, I have developed a strict "zero-trust" policy regarding digital interactions: I never click on links sent via email or text, regardless of how legitimate they appear. This level of discipline extends even to the most mundane aspects of browsing. Recently, a pop-up dialogue box appeared on my screen, asking me to rank my experience or indicate if I liked the website I was visiting. The box was persistent, refusing to close unless I interacted with it. While most users would instinctively click "Dismiss" or provide a rating just to clear their view, I refused to touch it.

In the world of cyber-predation, a dialogue box is often a digital Trojan Horse. What appears to be a harmless "Like" button can easily be a masked link to a virus or a script designed to harvest data the moment it is triggered. Some might argue that I am being overly cautious or even paranoid, but in a landscape where a single click can compromise your entire identity, I accept that label with pride. To me, "paranoid" is just another word for "prepared."

To clear my screen without compromising my security, I refused to play the predator's game. Instead of clicking the box, I performed a full manual shutdown of my device. By restarting the system and returning to the site fresh, I effectively "killed" the persistent process without ever having to engage with the suspicious interface. It may seem like a cumbersome solution for a small pop-up, but in the digital frontier, taking the long way around is often the only way to ensure you aren't walking straight into an ambush.

The Hidden Dangers of Metadata (EXIF Data)

You must also be aware of the "invisible ink" attached to every photograph you take with a smartphone or digital camera, known as EXIF data. This metadata is automatically embedded into the image file and can contain highly sensitive information, including the exact date, time, and—most dangerously—the precise GPS coordinates of where the photo was captured. When you post an unedited photo of your pet in your living room or a new purchase in your driveway, you may be inadvertently handing a predator the digital breadcrumbs to find your front door. A motivated hacker can "scrape" this metadata to pinpoint your home address or establish a pattern of your daily routines. To neutralize this threat, you must dive into your device's privacy settings and disable "Location Services" for your camera. Before posting any image to the public domain, I recommend using a metadata-stripping tool or simply taking a screenshot of the original photo to share instead, as this creates a "clean" copy without the geographic footprint. In the digital world, what you don't see in a photo can be just as revealing as the image itself.

The "Smart Home" Vulnerability

As we move toward an increasingly connected lifestyle, we must recognize that every "smart" device in our home—from thermostats and refrigerators to lightbulbs and voice assistants—is a potential entry point for a digital predator. These devices, collectively known as the Internet of Things (IoT), are often built with convenience in mind rather than security, frequently possessing weak encryption and "lazy" default passwords. A hacker doesn't need to crack the sophisticated security on your laptop if they can move laterally through your network by first compromising a cheap smart plug. To harden your home, I recommend placing all "smart" devices on a separate "Guest" Wi-Fi network. By isolating these gadgets, you ensure that even if a predator manages to breach a minor device, they remain trapped in a digital "airlock," unable to access the primary computers where your sensitive banking and personal data reside.

The "Evil Twin" Hotspot

In the realm of public connectivity, you must be wary of the "Evil Twin" ambush. This occurs when a predator sets up a rogue Wi-Fi hotspot in a high-traffic area like an airport or cafe, giving it a legitimate-sounding name such as "Airport_Free_Wifi_Official" or "Starbucks_Guest_Connect." When your device automatically joins or you manually select this network, you aren't connecting to the establishment—you are connecting directly to the predator's hardware. From that moment on, every unencrypted packet of data you send is visible to them. Treat all public Wi-Fi as an open, hostile field where your data is at risk of interception. In these environments, a VPN is not a luxury; it is a non-negotiable shield that creates an encrypted tunnel, ensuring that even if you are connected to a rogue hotspot, your information remains invisible to the operative on the other side.

The "Check-In" Danger

One of the most common mistakes I see involves the intersection of digital habits and physical vulnerability: the "real-time check-in." Posting a photo of your meal or a "status update" while you are still physically at a restaurant or event tells the digital world exactly where you are and, more dangerously, exactly where you are not. By broadcasting your current location, you are effectively providing a "green light" to any local prowler that your home is currently unoccupied. I adhere to a strict "Post Later" rule. Never upload location-based content until you have physically left the area and returned to a secure location. By creating a time delay between your actions and your posts, you strip a predator of the real-time data they need to track your movements or target your empty residence. In this game, silence is your best security until you have safely retreated behind your own bolted doors.

Developing a Verify First Mentality

In this era of unprecedented digital deception, I have adopted a "verify-first" mentality for myself. With the advent of AI reaching a level of incredible realism, my default mindset for every video, photo, or controversial article I encounter is one of deep skepticism. I immediately ask myself: is this AI-generated, is it a sophisticated fake, or is it actually real? I refuse to accept any digital content at face value. Perhaps this is a side effect of my former law enforcement career, where I learned that I could never afford to assume anything. In the field, assumptions are dangerous; instead, I was trained to count on the evidence to lead me to the truth. I apply that same investigative rigor to the digital world today. Before I chalk anything down as fact or fiction, I conduct quick tactical research to cross-reference the data and compare sources. In essence, in a world where the line between reality and simulation has blurred, I must verify the evidence before I believe the image.

Social Media Consumption and Legacy

Like billions of others, I frequently take part in posting videos and comments on social media. Admittedly, this is a habit that requires extreme discipline and, in many cases, should be approached with caution. I have made the conscious decision to limit my activity primarily to posting videos of myself singing and playing guitar on YouTube. My intent is purely personal: I want my children—and the grandchildren I hope to have one day—to be able to hear the songs I composed and see me performing long after I have passed. For me, social media is a tool for legacy rather than a platform for mindless scrolling.

Throughout my law enforcement career, I have seen firsthand the devastating consequences of failing to respect these digital boundaries. I have unfortunately heard of officers from nearby jurisdictions who posted or texted highly inappropriate messages, operating under the false assumption that their communications were private or temporary. These lapses in judgment eventually came to light, resulting in severe public scrutiny, the tarnishing of their professional reputations, and harsh disciplinary actions. These cases serve as a sobering reminder that in our profession, your digital conduct is an extension of your character, and a single moment of indiscretion can dismantle a career built over decades.

This warning is especially critical for teenagers and young adults. In the heat of the moment, a post or a video may seem like harmless fun or a way to get a quick laugh from friends. However, what feels like a joke today may appear highly inappropriate or even offensive years into adulthood. Young people must realize that these digital breadcrumbs follow them; a reckless post from their youth can resurface during a background check or a professional review, potentially derailing their employment opportunities and future aspirations.

In many professions—particularly in law enforcement, educational environments, and the political arena—extensive background checks are a mandatory requirement for every applicant. Investigators today are trained to dive deep into an individual's digital history. Inappropriate or controversial posts on social media will very likely be discovered during these probes. Once unearthed, the status of the applicant's job prospects is immediately cast into doubt, as these posts often reflect a lack of judgment or a temperament that is incompatible with the high standards of these fields.

Beyond personal indiscretion, we must understand the gravity of our words. Posting a casual comment is one thing, but posting untruthful or defamatory statements specifically intended to inflict emotional damage on an individual, a product, or a business is a line that must never be crossed. Many people mistakenly hide behind the shield of "freedom of speech," believing it grants them immunity for anything they type. However, the claim of free speech has very real legal and civil limitations. It is often insufficient to save an individual from the legal repercussions of their posts, especially when those posts cross the threshold into libel, slander, or malicious intent.

We must all recognize the permanence of our "digital shadow." Every time we post a photo, upload a video of a performance, or leave a comment, that data is ingested and stored on a remote server, often indefinitely. This information remains in the digital ether, permanently ready to be unearthed and exposed at a moment's notice. While a post may seem harmless or even humorous today, it can be weaponized in the future—especially if you rise to public prominence as a leader, a celebrity, or a politician. In the most unfortunate circumstances, this digital trail serves as a permanent roadmap for authorities or adversaries should you ever become an individual of interest. In the digital age, you aren't just posting for the present; you are creating a record that will be scrutinized by the future.

This need for discretion is paramount when it comes to intimate or questionable photos intended for a spouse or significant other. You must exercise extreme caution here, as these images are never truly "private" once they enter the digital stream. They can be intercepted by hackers and fall into the hands of predators, or, perhaps more devastatingly, you could be betrayed by the very person you trusted with the photos in the first place. Once that "send" button is pressed, you lose control over that image forever. Whether through a security breach or a personal falling out, a single private moment can be transformed into a permanent public liability. In this frontier, your greatest defense is the foresight to know that some things are simply too high-risk to ever be digitized.

Digital Estate Planning

Securing your legacy isn't just about what you post for the future; it's about ensuring your loved ones have the access they need when you are no longer there to provide it. While I have focused heavily on the legacy I wish to leave through my music, I have also had to face the cold reality of digital access in an emergency. If you are the only person who holds the "Master Keys" to your digital life, you may inadvertently lock your family out of your legacy and finances should something happen to you. Most major platforms now offer "Legacy Contacts" or "Inactive Account Managers," which allow a trusted individual to gain access after a period of inactivity. Beyond these settings, I maintain a physical "Digital Vault"—a master list of essential passwords and recovery codes stored in a fireproof safe that only my inner circle can access. Providing your loved ones with a tactical roadmap to your digital world is not just a matter of organization; it is a final act of protection, ensuring they aren't left fighting a faceless corporation for access to your memories and assets during an already difficult time.

Closing the Digital Gate

In conclusion, defending your life in the twenty-first century requires a fundamental shift in perspective: you must treat your digital existence with the same tactical seriousness as your physical security. Throughout this chapter, we have explored how a "zero-trust" mentality—combined with disciplined habits like dual authentication, network hardening, and metadata awareness—can transform you from a target into a fortress. We have seen that the threats we face are often invisible and highly deceptive, leveraging everything from sophisticated AI deepfakes to our own emotional vulnerabilities. However, as daunting as this landscape may seem, the power remains in your hands. By layering safeguards, maintaining a healthy dose of aggressive realism, and preparing for the long-term stewardship of your digital legacy, you ensure that your "digital shadow" remains a source of connection and history rather than a roadmap for predators.

In the end, digital safety is not about living in fear; it is about building the walls and bolting the doors so that you can navigate the modern world with the confidence of a person who is truly protected.

Chapter 18

Health Safety

While we often look outward to secure our environment, true personal safety is built on a foundation of health safety—the silent baseline from which every other life activity operates. Whether it is the mental clarity needed for high-stakes decision-making, the energy required for meaningful relationships, or the stamina for peak physical performance, our ability to function depends entirely on the integrity of our biological machine. Neglecting this internal perimeter creates a dangerous compounding effect, where seemingly minor risks—like poor sleep or nutritional gaps—accumulate over time into serious, life-altering consequences. Taking a proactive stance is not just a matter of wellness; it is a strategic necessity that reduces long-term healthcare costs, prevents lost productivity, and guards against avoidable disability. Ultimately, health safety is about prioritizing prevention over reaction. Most crises are preventable through the simple discipline of regular monitoring, balanced nutrition, and consistent rest—investments that are far less costly than treating advanced illness. In the same way we scout for external threats, early intervention in health risks like hypertension or diabetes can save a life, turning what could be a life-threatening disaster into a manageable condition.

It is true that we don't all begin life on an even playing field, yet the responsibility we have toward our own wellbeing remains a paramount duty. Not everyone is fortunate enough to be granted a clean bill of health at birth; many are born into difficult battles with serious illnesses or inherited conditions that have spanned generations. For those fighting these silent, uphill wars, I have nothing but the deepest respect and a sincere wish for the strength to overcome every challenge they face.

However, for those of us fortunate enough to be born with a healthy foundation, that health is not a permanent gift—it is a loan that requires consistent repayment through discipline. We owe it to ourselves, and certainly to the loved ones who depend on us, to work relentlessly at maintaining that vitality. I am a firm believer that we are ultimately the product of our own decisions. If we choose to ignore the warning signs or neglect the maintenance of our bodies, the eventual fallout will be deeply regrettable. When poor health begins to dominate your mental and physical existence, the "perimeters" of your life shrink. In that state of decline, your career, your hobbies, and even your financial success lose their luster; without the health to enjoy them, everything else becomes secondary, if not entirely meaningless. Protecting your health is the highest form of self-respect and the ultimate insurance policy for the future.

Let me be the first to admit that I fell victim to the "illusion of invincibility." I was one of those individuals born with a robust constitution; for as far back as I can remember, I was incredibly lucky—I didn't suffer from chronic issues, and I couldn't even recall the last time I'd had a common cold. Throughout my life, I stayed in shape, keeping my height and weight proportional while remaining active in sports. Because my body seemed to be functioning perfectly on the surface, I became reckless. I treated my health like a machine that didn't require maintenance, rarely stepping foot in a doctor's office for a check-up.

That complacency came to a sudden halt in 2017. As I began preparing for retirement, I finally decided to undergo a long-overdue physical. When the blood work came back, the results were a staggering wake-up call. My family doctor informed me that my blood glucose levels were dangerously high. She immediately referred me to a series of specialists, including an endocrinologist, who delivered a verdict I never expected: I had diabetes, and likely had been living with it for years.

Needless to say, I was in total shock. The "forensic evidence" of my own blood work proved that while I was busy watching the street for external threats, a silent predator had been compromising my internal security for years. I had become a full-blown diabetic, not because of a lack of luck, but because of a lack of vigilance. The revelation was a lesson I learned the hard way and I hope you won't make the same mistake.

Despite this diagnosis, I continue to feel remarkably strong and healthy. I attribute this resilience to the physical exercise regimen I've maintained throughout my adulthood—a varied mix of weightlifting, biking, walking, heavy-bag work, tennis, and basketball. Even during my busiest workdays, I make it a point to stay active, aiming for 50 to 100 push-ups and using simple resistance bands whenever I can find a spare moment. These small bursts of effort keep my blood flowing and ensure my body stays primed, regardless of my schedule. These activities built a layer of physical armor that continues to serve me well. However, I have come to realize that feeling "strong" is not the same as being "secure." I now understand that internal threats can be silent and invisible. Consequently, I am taking my health safety more seriously now than ever before.

Important Note: I want to be clear that I am not a physician or a trained medical professional. The following points are based on my personal experiences and observations. Before making any significant changes to your lifestyle or medical routine, you must check with your own physician to seek professional medical advice tailored to your specific needs.

Health safety serves as the fundamental baseline from which every other life activity operates, forming the bedrock upon which our careers, relationships, and decision-making capabilities are built. When this baseline is neglected, it creates a dangerous compounding effect where seemingly small, manageable risks—such as erratic sleep or poor dietary choices—accumulate into life-altering consequences that can dismantle our entire personal security apparatus. Conversely, a proactive approach to wellbeing drastically reduces long-term healthcare costs and guards against the risk of preventable disability that could sideline you for years. The core of this discipline lies in choosing prevention over reaction, acknowledging that regular monitoring, proper nutrition, and consistent rest are far less costly—and far less painful—than treating an advanced illness that was allowed to go unchecked. Ultimately, health safety is the glue that holds all other forms of personal protection together; it is the force multiplier of personal protection, and when it deteriorates, every other area of your safety weakens simultaneously and often invisibly.

Building upon this foundation, physical health and injury prevention are directly linked to our daily survival and response capacity. Maintaining physical fitness is not about aesthetics; it is about improving reaction time, balance, and strength, which directly reduces the risk of accidents and allows for faster, more effective responses to environmental hazards. Regular medical check-ups are vital for catching underlying conditions in vision, hearing, or cardiovascular health that act as the sensory inputs for our safety systems. Furthermore, unmanaged chronic conditions such as diabetes, epilepsy, or heart disease can cause sudden incapacitation in high-risk environments, making consistent medication adherence and monitoring an essential safety protocol rather than a mere medical suggestion. This physical resilience extends to immune health and infection control, where a robust immune system reduces absenteeism and keeps you capable of responding to emergencies, while vaccinations and hygiene practices protect both you and the people who depend on your strength.

Crucially, what you put into your body serves as the literal fuel for these safety systems, and your nutritional intake directly determines your ability to react, recover, and remain alert. To support sustained energy and prevent dangerous crashes in alertness, you should prioritize complex carbohydrates like oats and whole grains, while incorporating Omega-3 rich foods like salmon and walnuts to bolster brain function and emotional regulation. Leafy greens further support this cognitive perimeter by ensuring steady oxygen flow to the brain. For physical resilience, lean proteins are essential for repairing the muscle tissue needed for safe movement, while calcium and magnesium-rich foods build the bone density and muscle function required to prevent fractures or cramping during a crisis. Even your immune defense is built in the kitchen; Vitamin C, zinc, and probiotic foods like yogurt create an internal shield that accelerates wound healing and maintains the gut health so closely tied to your mood and resilience.

In contrast, poor nutrition acts as a slow, invisible safety hazard whose effects compound over time until they become acute, life-altering risks. I learned this the hard way. For years, I operated under the reckless assumption that because I looked fit and felt strong, I could get away with a diet that ignored the long-term consequences of what I was putting into my body. That lack of discipline eventually caught up with me, resulting in a diagnosis of Type 2 diabetes—a condition I likely could have avoided had I treated my nutritional intake with the same tactical seriousness I applied to other areas of my life.

You must be wary of refined sugars and ultra-processed snacks that cause energy spikes followed by debilitating brain fog, or excessive caffeine that disrupts the sleep patterns necessary for sound judgment. Skipping meals is equally dangerous, as the resulting hypoglycemia can lead to dizziness and a higher risk of fainting during critical tasks. On a physical level, trans fats and excessive sodium cause inflammation and cardiovascular strain, which is particularly hazardous in high-stress roles where your blood pressure is already under pressure. My personal experience with Type 2 diabetes has taught me that chronic overconsumption of sugar and processed meats doesn't just change a lab result; it places immense strain on your entire system and can lead to sudden incapacitation. Alcohol, even in moderate amounts, remains a primary threat to vehicle and personal safety by slowing reaction times and distorting your perception of risk. I share this not as a lecturer, but as someone who allowed his own internal perimeter to be breached through dietary neglect.

Transitioning from the physical to the mental, cognitive safety is equally critical for navigating a high-pressure world. Poor mental health—marked by chronic stress, anxiety, or depression—impairs judgment and increases risk-taking behavior, while fatigue and sleep deprivation remain leading causes of workplace accidents and traffic incidents. Physical health and mental clarity are deeply interconnected, as the brain depends entirely on proper nutrition, hydration, and circulation to maintain logical reasoning. Dehydration is a particularly subtle threat; even mild fluid loss impairs concentration and coordination, making regular water intake and electrolyte balance essential for safe functioning. Without this baseline, we suffer from "brain fog" that erodes our thinking capacity long before we realize our judgment has been compromised, making it nearly impossible to advocate for ourselves or call for help in an emergency.

This internal stability directly influences our domestic and financial safety as well. Within the home, physical strength prevents common accidents like falls, while mental alertness ensures that safety routines, like checking the stove or locking doors, are followed consistently. In relationships, strong mental health provides the emotional clarity needed to recognize warning signs of toxic dynamics. Financially, your health is your single greatest asset; chronic illness reduces your ability to work and earn, leading to career stagnation and medical debt. Mentally sharp individuals are far better equipped to protect themselves from financial exploitation and scams. Even in the driver's seat, health safety is a requirement; vision, reflexes, and emotional regulation are the primary tools of a safe driver, yet these are the first to fail when someone is plagued by unmanaged illness or the drowsiness caused by poor health habits.

While these principles are technically sound, I must admit that I am the last person to tell anyone exactly how to manage their personal health safety. I am not a physician, a nutritionist, or a medical professional; I am simply an ordinary guy who is still learning and trying to improve after falling victim to the "illusion of invincibility" myself. I am merely sharing the hard lessons I've learned alongside unconfirmed information I've gathered from the internet and various AI tools like Gemini, ChatGPT, Grok, and Claude. It is essential to take this information with a grain of salt, as it is totally up to you to decide what works for your body, and you must seek advice from your own physician before making any changes.

In my own journey toward better health, I have begun exploring several strategic shifts, such as establishing a biological baseline through annual blood work and diversifying my physical portfolio with functional strength training. I've added "movement snacks" into my workday—like 50 to 100 push-ups and resistance band work—to keep my blood flowing and prevent metabolic stagnation. I strive to implement intake discipline by following an 80/20 rule with whole foods, auditing my stress levels through tactical breathing, and owning my personal data by using wearable technology. Whether these measures will ultimately reverse my diagnosis or simply hold the line is a verdict I am still waiting for, but I am no longer waiting idly. By adopting these habits, we shift from a passive state of hoping for the best to an active state of managing our most valuable asset. In the end, health safety is the thread woven through every other form of security; you cannot effectively ensure the safety of yourself or others if your own health is compromised, for health is the foundation upon which all safety stands.

Ultimately, the lesson I hope you take away from these pages is that health safety is not a separate category of life to be addressed only when something goes wrong; it is the very thread woven through every other form of security you possess. It determines whether you can effectively protect your home, sustain your financial future, operate a vehicle with precision, and maintain the mental clarity needed to navigate a complex world. As I have learned through my own journey with Type 2 diabetes, you can be vigilant against every external threat on the horizon and still suffer a catastrophic breach if you neglect the maintenance of the machine itself.

Don't make the same mistake I did. I spent years assuming my physical fitness was a permanent shield, only to discover that my internal security had been compromised by my own recklessness. I don't share my mistakes to discourage you, but to remind you that your health is your most versatile and valuable asset. It is the force multiplier that makes your skills, your weapons, and your strategies effective. When your health is compromised, your world inevitably shrinks, and the perimeters you've worked so hard to establish begin to crumble from the inside out.

Conversely, when you invest in your physical and mental wellbeing, you are essentially buying insurance for your future self—ensuring that you remain the pilot of your own life rather than a passenger in a declining vessel. As you move forward, remember that protecting your vitality is the highest form of self-respect. It is a continuous, daily commitment to preserving the physical and mental capacity that underpins your survival and the safety of those who depend on you. Take the data from your doctors seriously, listen to the warning signs your body sends, and never trade long-term security for short-term convenience.

You are your own first line of defense — and that defense is only as strong as the health that supports it.

This brings us to the end of our journey together. From the moment you learned to read a room in Situational Awareness, to guarding your finances, your home, your career, your mind, and now your body — every chapter in this book has been pointing to the same truth: personal safety is not a destination. It is a practice. It is the sum of thousands of small, deliberate decisions made every single day, in every area of your life.

You now have the awareness. You have the tools. What you do with them is entirely up to you. Stay vigilant, stay disciplined, and above all — stay alive.

Epilogue

If you've made it this far, you've essentially completed a full patrol of your life. We have walked the fences of your bank accounts, inspected the locks on your digital identity, examined the structural integrity of your career, and looked deep into the mirror to address the internal state of your sanity. It is a lot to take in. For some, it might even feel overwhelming—like a never-ending checklist of things that could go wrong. But as we reach the end of this conversation, I want to show you that these layers of protection are not separate, exhausting tasks. They are a single, unified ecosystem. In law enforcement, we know that a defensive line is only as strong as its weakest point. If your financial house is in order but your health is neglected, the shield fails. If your career is secure but your trust is blind, the shield fails. The integrated foundation is the point where these layers overlap to create something more powerful than the sum of their parts: total resilience.

When I was a fourteen-year-old boy on that boat in 1979, I had zero defenses. I was at the mercy of the ocean, the pirates, and the winds. I survived by grace and luck. But I spent the next forty-five years ensuring that I would never be that vulnerable again. What I discovered is that safety is a force multiplier. When you secure your financial life, you reduce the stress on your sanity. When you invest in your professional stability, you provide the resources for your medical well-being. Each layer of protection you build makes the other layers easier to maintain. You aren't just checking boxes; you are building a fortress where the walls support one another. Preparation is not about living in fear of the storm; it's about knowing your roof is bolted down so tightly that you can actually sleep while the storm rages.

To my daughters, Sammi and Ally: I know there were times during the writing of these chapters—and during the two decades of our lives together—where my nagging felt like a burden. I know that my insistence on verifying everything and expecting the unexpected earned me the label of the family cynic. But I want you to understand the reason why one last time. I don't watch the door because I am afraid of what is outside. I watch the door because I am in awe of what is inside. You, your mother, and the life we have built are the most precious assets I have ever been tasked to protect. Vigilance is not a sign of a small, scared life. It is the price of a free, secure one. Being paranoid is a passive state of worry; being formidable is an active state of readiness. My goal was never to make you afraid of the world, but to make the world respect your boundaries. I want you to move through life with the quiet confidence of someone who has already run the drills, checked the locks, and secured the second floor.

As you close this book, I have one final patrol briefing for you. Safety is not a destination. You don't arrive at being safe and then stop. It is a lifestyle of continuous, small adjustments. You don't need to fix everything today. You just need to start. Pick one area—perhaps it's freezing your credit, or finally booking that medical screening, or starting that backup educational course—and secure it. The version of your future self—the one sitting in that quiet, debt-free home twenty years from now—is depending on the choices you make this afternoon. Twenty-eight years in a uniform taught me that the world is unpredictable, sometimes harsh, and often indifferent to our plans. But it also taught me that the prepared person is rarely the victim. Whether you are on a boat in the middle of the Pacific or sitting at a desk in a high-rise, the rules are the same: believe half of what you see and none of what you hear, trust but verify, and build your fortress before the house catches fire. Thank you for walking this beat with me. The watch is now yours to hold. Stay safe, stay watchful, and above all, stay formidable.

One final thought: if you ever feel inspired to write, I strongly encourage you to dive in without hesitation. Having written books for over twenty years, I can say with certainty that writing is more accessible now than ever before. I use Google Docs because it catches spelling and grammatical errors in real time. Whenever I hit a clunky paragraph or a complex sentence, I lean on free AI tools like Google Gemini to suggest rewrites, making it incredibly easy to fine-tune the prose. Modern technology handles the mechanics; the real magic—and the real challenge—lies in crafting compelling storylines, intricate plots, and the perfect narrative tone to deliver your message.

Thank you.

www.ingramcontent.com/pod-product-compliance
Lightning Source LLC
LaVergne TN
LVHW010634110826
845149LV00014B/2841

* 9 7 8 1 9 6 6 1 8 2 0 5 4 *